The Letters of Katherine Mansfield

VOLUME TWO

*The Works of
Katherine Mansfield*

BLISS

THE GARDEN PARTY

THE DOVE'S NEST

THE LITTLE GIRL

POEMS

IN A GERMAN PENSION

Edited by
J. Middleton Murry

JOURNAL
OF KATHERINE MANSFIELD

THE LETTERS
OF KATHERINE MANSFIELD

THE
Letters of Katherine Mansfield

Edited by
J. Middleton Murry

VOLUME II

Alfred · A · Knopf
New York · 1929

Copyright 1929 by Alfred A. Knopf, Inc.
ALL RIGHTS RESERVED INCLUDING THE RIGHT TO REPRODUCE
THIS BOOK OR PARTS THEREOF IN ANY FORM

Published February, 1929
Second Printing July, 1929

MANUFACTURED IN THE UNITED STATES OF AMERICA

THE LETTERS
OF KATHERINE MANSFIELD

To Richard Murry   *January 1920*

I owe you letters, thanks — I'm in your debt all round and you must be thinking I am an ungrateful creature — to say the very least of it. But I feel as though I've been on a voyage lately — on the high seas — out of sight of land, and though some albatross post has brought *your* news under it's wing I've never been able to detain the bird long enough to send an answer back. Forgive me.

The little book is a rare find. I've not only read every word and stared the pictures (especially the crocodile and the little lamb who doth skip and play, always merry, always gay) out of countenance. I've begun a queer story on the strength of it about a child who learnt reading from this little primer[1] — Merciful Heavens! think of all the little heads bowed over these tiny pages, all the little hands tracing the letters — and think of the rooms in which they sat — and the leaping light they read by, half candle light, half fire — and how terribly frightened they must have been as they read about this Awful God waiting to pop them into Eternal Flames — to consume them utterly and wither them like grass. . . . Did you read the poems? And did your eye fasten upon Mr. John Rogers, the first martyr in Queen Mary's Reign, laughing, really rather callously, as he burned away in sight of his wife and Nine Small Children? They certainly were peculiarly hideous children and his wife looks as though she had wasted his substance upon buying hats, but all the same it's a bit steep to show your feelings as he is doing.

I am working very hard just now — I can't walk about or go out. Nearly all my days are spent in bed or if not in bed on a little sofa that always feels like lying in a railway carriage — a horrid

[1] A little seventeenth century book with woodcuts, of which I forget the title.

little sofa. I have seen hardly any people at all since I've been here — *nobody* to talk to — The one great talker is the sea. It never is quiet; one feels sometimes as if one were a shell filled with a hollow sound. God forbid that another should ever live the life I have known here and yet there are *moments* you know, old Boy, when after a dark day there comes a sunset — such a glowing gorgeous marvellous sky that one forgets all in the beauty of it — these are the moments when I am *really writing* — Whatever happens I have had these blissful, perfect moments and they are worth living for. I thought, when I left England, I could not love writing more than I did, but now I feel I've never known what it is to be a writer until I came here —

To J. M. Murry   *January 1920*

. . . Ever since you left you have carried the sun in your pocket. It's bitter cold, raining fast, *sleeting,* and an east wind. D. says he has never known the glass so low. The cold is intense. One's fingers ache. You could not believe this was the same place. And the sky seems to have great inkstains upon it. . . .

The post office has struck — no one knows for how long. It just announces a strike. The country is in a queer state. Yesterday on his way here D. met the men from the railway below who shouted " You'd better pack up your traps and go. We don't want any more of you English here. We're going to clear you out." But 10–1 that is an exaggeration. He is an alarmist of the very first water and sat here yesterday suggesting that even at 3 o'clock in the afternoon no one could hear my screams if I were attacked, and that a revolver for a person like me was ridiculous. *They'd* knock it away in no time. I have come to the conclusion that he's not only a *real insane lunatic* but a *homicidal maniac.* I thought the first time he was here he was a trifle insane, but then you liked him so and I felt that you would laugh at me for always " suspecting " people. . . . But I know I'm right. His glance, without any barriers, cruel, cruel like a man raving with delight at the sight of a torture; his *flat-sounding* voice, somehow so repressed and held back; his physical great stiffness and the shape of his flat head — real criminal shape. See him in profile, his eyes glittering. He's a *terrible* object. He is attracted to me because he realises my sensitiveness. I'm weak for him to terrify. It relieves him to sit in that small room and suggest that navvies will break in and "slit your throat" while L. M. is in San Remo. Well ... Well. ...

The new maid is here. If to be a maid is to drop the stove-rings on to the tiled floor, she's an excellent one, and very cheap at 5 francs a day. ...

If only this black weather would lift. The wind *howls*. All goes well here. I *work* and *work* and *work* and stay in bed until the sun returns.

To Miss Fullerton   *Wednesday*
January 14, 1920

Your letter has made me spring so high that 30 francs a day is mountain peaks below! I do not know how I am to thank Cousin Connie and you for this letter. Will you please believe that large warm beams of gratitude are coming out of this letter and that the inkpot is flashing and stars are dropping off the pen.

But *seriously* — thank you from my heart! The Hermitage sounds the very place for me and Ida is quite content to go to the Pension Anglaise. I know I shall be able to earn the extra money to keep us both quite easily in such surroundings. Besides, I shall get well at such a rate that they will turn me out for a fraud by the time April is over.

Could they take us soon? Ida is going in to San Remo to-day to see about our passports and so on and I wondered whether, if we can get a car, they would be ready for us to-day week (next Wednesday). Or is that too soon? We shall prepare ourselves for Wednesday, and then if we must wait a few days it will not matter. I should like if possible to take the rooms for a month to begin with, tho' I am sure I shall stay longer.

I keep re-reading your letter as I write. My dear, what trouble you have taken — and how soon you have answered. I had marked Friday in my diary as the day I could " perhaps " hear.

I told the doctor man that I wanted very much to leave here and he said that I must — there were no two opinions. My lungs are much better and my heart is only temporary caused, he says, by the fever and "acute nervous strain." But that will vanish away as soon as the solitary confinement is over.

To J. M. Murry *Wednesday*
L'Hermitage, Mentone
January 21, 1920

... I have escaped. Do you know what that means? There has been a postal strike in Italy. No letters, no wires. Nothing comes through. A strike of the railways, and now from to-day a strike of automobiles. We just got through by taking a roundabout route and escaping the police. ...

I have got away from that hell of isolation, from the awful singing at night, from the loneliness and fright. To tell you the truth, I think I have been *mad,* but really, medically mad. A great awful cloud has been on me. . . . It's nearly killed me. Yes. When J. took me in her arms to-day she cried as well as I. I felt as though I'd been through some awful deathly strain, and just survived — been rescued from drowning or something like that. You can't understand, it's not possible you should, what that isolation was when you left again and I again was ill. ...

If I don't get well here, I'll never get well. Here — after the journey — was this room waiting for me — exquisite, large, with four windows, overlooking great gardens and mountains, wonderful flowers — tea with *toast* and honey and butter — a charming maid — and these two dear sweet women to welcome me with papers, books, etc. This is really a superb place in every way. Two doctors live here. . . . The cleanliness is almost supernatural. One feels like a butterfly. One only wants to fan one's wings, on the couch, the chairs. I have a big writing table with a cut-glass inkstand, a waste-paper basket, a great bowl of violets and *your* own anemones and wall-flowers in it. The directress is a very nice Frenchwoman only too anxious to look after me and see that there is no change in anything. . . . There is also a sort of Swiss nurse in white who has just been in and says she answers the bell at night. She is so good to look at that I shall have to ring.

I've got away from under that ghastly cloud. All is absolutely changed. I'm here with people, with care. I feel a different creature *really* — different eyes, different hair. The garden is gorgeous. There is a big shelter, chauffé. What do you think of that?

8.30 A.M.
January 22, 1920

... I have had such a gorgeous night in this huge room, with stars coming through the west and south windows and little airs. At eight arrived the breakfast. I really hope this place is showing off a little and this present behaviour is abnormal. If it isn't, pray see that our new house has folding doors, wide staircases. Nothing else will contain me. Oh, blankets and sheets of such rare quality — blankets that feel like lambs — sheets *glacés*. Electric lamp by the bedside under a small gold shade — great pot of hot water muffled in a real soft thick bath-towel. All these things are acting with such effect upon the infant mind of your girl, and a west view of mountains covered with little pines and a south view of distant sea and olive groves (as seen from 2 marble balconies) that she feels almost intoxicated.

Getting away yesterday was really pretty awful. Ma'am Littardi arrived asking 50 lire for the *hire* of the stove; the youth who has been sleeping arrived asking for 5 lire a night (8 nights) and the laundry arrived with a bill for 57 lire. ... The taxi fare was £6, and he demanded 25 *francs* for having seen us through the police at Vintimille. I don't care. I'm still alive and I'm away. But the *comble* was that the day before yesterday when I was gone upstairs to fetch the revolver two beggars came and rang. The door was open. So I came down as quick as I could. But they'd gone and were at the foot of the steps — an old man and an old woman *with a bundle*. I saw them get into a small mule cart and drive away. At 11 P.M. that night I asked L. M. to fetch my overcoat as I wanted to sew on a button. It was gone, with the green scarf — the woolly. What do you think of that? Italy, my Italy!

Sunday
January 25, 1920

... C. came in yesterday to see me, carrying a baby Pekinese. Have you even seen a really baby one about the size of a fur glove, covered with pale gold down, with paws like minute seal flappers, very large impudent eyes and ears like fried potatoes? Good God! What creatures they are. This one is a perfect complement to Wing. We MUST have one. They are not in the least fussy or pampered or spoilt. They are like fairy animals. This one sat on my lap, cleaned both my hands really very carefully, polished the nails, then bit off carefully each finger and thumb, and then exhausted and blown with 8 fingers and two thumbs inside him, gave a great sigh and crossed his front paws and listened to the conversation. He lives on beef-steaks and loaf-sugar. His partner in life, when he is at home, is a pale blue satin bedroom slipper. Please let us have one at The Heron. ...

I went down yesterday for lunch and dinner. I am here on false pretences. I am the only healthy creature here. When I entered the *salle à manger* I felt that all the heads were raised and all the noses sniffed a frampold rampant lion entering. It's not that these people are *ill*. They look exactly as though they were risen from the dead, stepped out of coffins and eating again *pour la première fois*. Their hair is thin and weak and poor; their eyes are cold and startled, their hands are still waxen and THIN! They are walking-sticks. All the little arts and allurements they have shed and not yet picked up again. They are still sexless, and blow their noses in a neuter fashion — neither male nor female blows. At the tables there are the signs and tokens of their illnesses — bottles, boxes. *One* woman gave me a nasty knock. She had a réchaud beside her — a lamp and a stand — and she re-heated everything, even the plates. There, but for the grace of God, went Wig. The waitresses of course thrive in this atmosphere. They are two pretty full-bosomed girls, with spider-web stockings, shoes laced up their legs, little delicate wispy aprons, powered necks, red lips, scent — and they move like ballet-dancers, sliding and gliding in the fullness of their youth and strength over the polished floors. All this amuses me very much. ...

Never again shall I cut myself off from Life again. I haven't any illusions, darling. I know all about it and am not really a baby saying " a-gooh-a-gah! " but, in spite of everything, I know *il y a quelquechose* . . . that I feed on, exult in, and adore. One must be, if one is a Wig, eternally giving and receiving and shedding and renewing and examining and trying to place. According to you, I suppose, my thinking is an infant affair with bead frames and coloured blocks — well, it's not important. What is important is that I shall go up in flame if I do not show you these cornflowers and jonquils. [There is a little drawing of a pot of them.]

The day is cloudy, but it doesn't matter. Landscape is lovely in this light; it's not like the sea. The mimosa — great puffs of mimosa and great trees of red roses and oranges bright and flashing. Some boys are being drilled outside. The sergeant-major keeps on saying: " T'ois cinquante, n'est-ce pas? " and there is a most *forlorn* bugle.

Here is a story my little *femme de chambre* told me. Please read it.

"Do you know, Madame, *que les fleurs sont trop fortes* to be left dans la chambre pendant la nuit et surtout les joncs. If I put them sur le balcon — n'est-ce pas? — and bring them in early in the morning? Vous sa — vez quand ma petite mère était très juene, elle était las maîtresse d'une petite école pour les tout petits enfants. Et sur son jour de fête les bébés lui ont apporté un bouquet énorme, grand comme un chou, rond comme ça, Madame — de ces joncs. Elle les a mis dans sa chambre à coucher. C'était un vendredi. Le soir elle s'est endormie — et puis, tout le samedi, le dimanche, jusqu'au lundi matin, elle dort pro*fonde*ment. Quand les petits élèves sont arrivés le lundi, la porte était fermée. Ils ont frappé. Pas de résponse. Enfin, mon père, qui n'était mon père à ce temps-là, alors est venu du village et il a forcé la porte — et voilà ma mère, qui n'était pas ma mère ni même mariée à ce temps-là; — toujours dans un sommeil *profond,* el l'air était chargé de la parfum de ces joncs qu'elle a mis sur une petite table près du lit. . . ."

Don't you like that story? Do you see the infants looking in with their fingers in their mouths, and the young man finding her blanche comme une bougie, and the room and the flowers? It's a bit sentimental, p'raps, but I love it. I see such funny little worms with satchels and socks and large tam o'shanters.

To Mrs. Sylvia Lynd   *January 31, 1920*

I can't tell you how pleased I was to get your letter — how sorry to know that you've been so ill. You're better now? It's a cursed thing to have. I had an attack once — ten years ago — above a grocer's shop in Rottingdean; no more than ten years ago or less, the year our great Edward the Peace Maker died. He died when I was in the very thick of it. But it's an absolute mistake that you should be ill. You're not at all the person to be ill. I always see you in my mind's eye sitting up and laughing, but sitting up in a way that few people have any idea of — delightfully.

Look here! I'm coming back to England in May for a few months at least. Let us meet. Let us arrange it now. Will you come and spend the whole day? That is not half big enough, but my plans are so vague. I don't know where we shall be living. J. seems to be either camping in a waste-paper basket at Adelphi Terrace, or walking the country looking for a real country house far from station, church and post-office. But I don't want to miss you, so spare a day for me. I'll look for the review of ——. I did it badly — very badly. The trouble with the book is it's over-ripe. It's hung in the warm library too long; it's gone soft. But that's the trouble with that whole set of people and with all their ideas, I think. One gets rather *savage* living in a little isolated villa on a wild hillside and thinking about those things. All this self-examination, this fastidious probing, this hovering on the brink — it's all wrong! I don't believe a writer can ever do anything *worth* doing until he has — in the profoundest sense of the word — *accepted* life. Then he can face the problem and begin to question, but not before. But these people won't accept life; they'll only accept a point of view or something like that. I wish one could let them go, but they go on writing novels and Life goes on — big, expensive; so poor little K. M. goes on lifting up her voice and weeping — but she doesn't want to!

I've left Italy (Italy is a thoroughly bad place at present), and as you see, I'm in France. It's lovely weather — warm, mild. The air smells of faint, far-off tangerines with just a touch of nutmeg. On my table there are cornflowers and jonquils and rosemary sprigs. Here they are for you. The flowers are wonderful. How lovely the earth is. Do you know that I had fifteen cinerarias in

Italy, and they grew against the sea? I hope one will be able to call these things up on one's Death-bed.

This is not a letter. It's only to say I have yours which arrived *to-day*. It's only to greet you and to send my love and to beg you to get better quickly. All those things! Good-night.

To *Richard Murry*   *February 1920*

Here is a letter with an Ominous drawing of yourself in Aids to Eyesight. I hope you won't have to wear them, You have as you doubtless know, beautiful eyes, very rare, expressive, original and seldom seen eyes, the kind of eyes you might imagine a person having if he'd been born at sea while his wise parents cruised about among the Pacific islands and had spent the first days of his natural little life wondering what all that blue was. However, if you *do* have to have 'em glassed and framed — so do I. Mine — or rather one of mine is not at all the orb it used to be. I'm going to wear horn specs " those of the largest kind " for working in. What a trio we shall present at the Heron. Pray make a drawing of us — surprised at our labours and suddenly all at various windows looking out to see who that is coming up the flagged walk — three faces at three windows — six prodigious eyes! Whoever it was faints among the pink peonies. . . .

Yesterday, no the day before, I received a copy of *Je ne Parle pas*. I want to thank you for having printed it so beautifully. It makes me very happy to see your name on the back page. *My* share doesn't satisfy me at all, but yours fills me with pride. I hope a little handful of people buys it, for the sake of covering the expense. The page you send me of Cinnamon and Angelica looks very well. Are you going to make a *map* for the frontispiece with the arms of C. and A. very fairly drawn? Or a tiny, tiny Durer-like drawing of Apricia, with a great flowery branch in the foreground — you know the kind of things I mean? It is somehow *most right* that you should draw. When I come back you'll shew me your sketches? Another quite small insignificant little half-hour job for *you* is a stone carving for the garden of the Heron, something that will abide for ever with somewhere about it our names in beautiful lettering saying we lived and worked here.

I am out of Italy, as you see, and in France. I shall stay here until the end of April if I can manage it. That Italian villa got pretty dreadful and yet, now the time there is over, I wouldn't have it otherwise. I found out more about " writing." " Here " is a room with the window opening on to a balcony and below the balcony there is a small tree full of tangerines and beyond the tree a palm and beyond the palm a long garden with a great tangled — it looks like — a wood at the bottom of it. *Palms,* Richard, are superb things. Their colour is amazing. Sometimes they are bronze, sometimes gold and green, warm deep tiger-gold — and last night, under the moon in a little window, they were bright silver. And plus that, the creatures are full of drawing. How marvellous life is, if only one gives oneself up to it! It seems to me that the *secret* of life is to *accept* life. Question it as much as you like after, but first accept it. People to-day stand on the outskirts of the city wondering if they are for or against Life — is Life worth living — dare they risk it — what is Life — do they hate or love it — but these cursed questions keep them on the outskirts of the city for ever. It's only by risking losing yourself, giving yourself up to Life, that you can ever find out the answer. Don't think I'm sentimental. You know and I know how much evil there is, but all the same *let's live* to the very uttermost — let's live all our lives. People to-day are simply cursed by what I call the *personal.* . . . What is happening to ME. Look at ME. This is what has been done to ME. It's just as though you tried to run and all the while an enormous black serpent fastened on to you. You are the only young artist I know. I long for you to be rich — really rich. Am I a dull little dog? Forgive me. I am working awfully hard and that always makes me realise again what a terrific thing it is — our job.

To J. M. Murry   *February 1920*

. . . You've sold my book.[1] Do you mind asking them to send the cheque to me? Pure childishness. But I want to see it with my own eyes and send it with my own hands to Kay. I feel the Bank will *close.* . . . Re the matter of the book — I Suppose I shall have final say. I couldn't have *The Woman at the Store* reprinted,

[1] *Bliss and other Stories.*

par example. If it's left to C. or if C. has a say, it would be bad.
. . . I do want the story called *Second Helping* that I'm at now to be included. . . .

Another change in the near future. I have not mentioned it, but this place is *intolerably* noisy. I am so sensitive to noise, oh, so sensitive. It *hurts* me, really. They bang my door, other doors, shout, shriek, crash. I can't endure it and really can't work or sleep. The doctor suggested *une forte dose de véronal.* Merci. But really it's *bad.* I just mentioned this to J. She came one day when I was feeling it a bit badly. To-day she arrived with a carriage and fur rugs and silk cushions. Took me to their villa. It is really superb, *exquisite* outside and in. They had a *chaise longue* in the garden — a tiny tray with black coffee out of a silver pot, Grand Marnier, cigarettes, little bunch of violets, all ready. Then we went in to tea. Their villa is really — it's a dream. I mean even the furnishing is *perfect* — Spanish silk bed coverlets, Italian china, the tea appointments perfect, stillness, maids in tiny muslin aprons flitting over *carpets* . . . and so on. Then they showed me into a room, grey and silver, facing south, with a balcony — the only touch of colour a little rose brocade couch with gilt legs — and J. said, " Now, my dear, we want you to come here, and live here. It's *dead* quiet. You can be alone all day if you like. There is the garden. We are here . . . We want you here until May. You're going to get well. You can't afford to fight or see ugly people or have ugly trays." And then she laughed and said, " The Lord has delivered you into our hands, and please God we'll cure you." What do you think of that? . . . *Why* should they do that? *Why* should J. say, " Then I'll be at rest about you, darling. I shall know you're safe "? It's as though my Mother were here again. I miss her so. I often long to lean against Mother and know she understands things . . . that can't be told . . . that would fade at a breath . . . *delicate needs* . . . a feeling of fineness and gentleness. But what Mother hadn't is an understanding of WORK.

The villa is very large — a huge hall lighted from above. It has delicate balconies, and a tower. I want you to see it. I can't make you see it. I want you to see the garden and the potting-shed where I can walk and look at the little plants. Huge springing palms — great branches of orange against the sky. [A drawing of one.] No, I can't draw them. . . .

... I cannot have the *German Pension* reprinted under any circumstances. It is far too *immature,* and I don't even acknowledge it to-day. I mean I don't "hold" by it. I can't go foisting that kind of stuff on the public. *It's not good enough.* But if you'll send me the note that refers to it I will reply and offer a new book by May 1st. But I could not for a moment entertain republishing the *Pension.* It's positively *juvenile;* and besides that, it's not what I mean; it's a lie. Oh no, never.

February 1920

Very well, Isabel, about the *Pension.* But I must write an introduction saying it is early, early work, or just that it was written between certain years, because you know, Betsy, it's nothing to be proud of. If you didn't advise me I should drop it overboard. But, of course, I'll do the other thing, and certainly it airs one's name. But why isn't it better? It makes me simply hang my head. I'll have to forge ahead and get another decent one written; that's all. . . .

I've told the people here I'm leaving. It was *awful.* How I hate having to do this, especially as they have been so immoderately kind. They make such a dreadful fuss of me — everybody, down to the servants. Even the masseuse says: "It was so wonderful just to come into the room, and then we all say we know Mrs. Murry's room by the good smell outside the door — cigarettes and flowers." As to Armand — oh, it's been *dreadful.* These people are so queer. Just because the room is arranged as we arrange a room, and gay, and I wear my little coats and caps in bed, it seems to them *amazing.* It's not in the least.

Villa Flora, Mentone
Wednesday
February 25, 1920

... It is raining here, but such lovely rain! The drops hang on the rose bushes and on every tip of the palm fronds. Little birds sing; the sea sounds solemn and full and silver gulls fly over. I can smell the earth and I can feel how the violets are growing and all the small things down there under my window. It is exquisite.

Talking about flowers, you know Gentlemen's Buttonholes? (A double daisy, small.) They grow here in every conceivable colour, and massed together they really are a superb sight. I am sure Sutton would have them. We *must* remember to grow them so in our garden, in a round bed. *Country Life,* of course, makes it almost impossible to wait for a garden. When one reads the collection of flowery shrubs, *par exemple* — mock orange (you remember that? It was at Mylor), four kinds of flowering quinces, Mexican fuchsia. . . . Oh *dear* me! And then the annuals that, sown in January and February, are flowering in Avrilo — there are at least 24 kinds and if you are clever you can grow them so that one kind marches up with banners after the other until the chrysanthemum is there. I think I shall become a very violent gardener. I shall have shelves of tomes and walk about the house whispering the names of flowers. We must have a tiny potting shed, too, just big enough for you and me. I see as I write little small forked sticks with labels on them. Daphne grows in England: Eden Phillpotts has a great bush. I shall write for a cutting. I read in *Country Life* of a most excellent apple called "Tom Putts" — silly name, but it seems to be a very fine fruit and the trees bear in their second year. *Country Life* intoxicates me — the advertisements and the pictures and the way they *harp* on hardy annuals. We must have a boy for heavy work, but I want to do a fearful lot myself — large gloves again and very short corduroy velveteen skirt — Buff Orpington colour. Now I must lay down my trowel. . . .

To Richard Murry — February 1920

Yes I *did* get your letter written to a place called Hermitage, *very much* called Hermitage, where Russian children stamped overhead and Roumanians roared below and French infants rushed at you in the lift. After Italy it seemed all right at first but then they began feeding us on haricot beans and I hate haricot beans. They have no imagination. What with that and the noise I turned against it and my Cousin who has taken this villa for le saison asked me here. *Here* is about as perfect as it could be. A great garden, lemon and orange groves, palms, violets in blue carpets, mimosa trees — and inside a very beautiful "exquisite" house with a spirit in it which makes you feel that nothing evil or ugly could ever come near. It's *full* of life and gaiety but the people are at peace — you know what I mean? They've got a real background to their lives, and they realise that other people have too. I am basking here until I come back, some time in May.

Mentone is a lovely little town, small and unreal like all these places are, but even here there are real spots. The colour and movement everywhere make you continually happy. It's all ruled by the sun; the sun is King and Queen and Prime Minister, and people wear hats like this: [A drawing] I mustn't bring one back for J. *or* you, but they are very tempting!

I'm not ill any more. Really I'm not. Please think of me as a comfortable cross between a lion and a lamb.

I wish you had a quiet spot where you could draw in peace. But your room at the Heron will be your *studio*. It's such a waste of life to bark and bite like people do: I think we ought just to ignore them and go our way.

It's no good getting mixed up in " sets " or cliques or quarrels. That is not our job. *By their works ye shall know them* is our motto. And life is so short and there is such a tremendous lot to do and see: we shall never have time for all. I wish we could find the house, don't you? I don't think J. will find it before I'm back (that's in 9 weeks time) but there will be a lot to do when it is found. It's just going to be the perfect place for us all — our real home. You must be down in all your spare time and when you're in London you must always have the feeling it's *there,* with the smoke going out of its chimneys and the hens laying eggs and the bees burrowing in the flowers. I feel we must keep bees, a cow, fowls, 2 turkeys, some Indian runner ducks, a *goat,* and perhaps one thoroughly striking beast like a unicorn or a dragon. I am always learning odd things such as how to light a scientific bonfire — but now you're laughing at me. However, just come and see my bonfire one of these days, and you will turn up your eyes in admiration.

In the Hermitage letter you asked me what were my views about Adam in this great swinging garden. Now that's awfully difficult to answer. For this reason. I can't help seeing all the evil and pain in the world: it must be faced and recognised, and I can't bear your sentimentalist or silly optimist. I know it all:

I feel it all. And there is *cruelty* for instance — cruelty to children — how are you going to explain that? and, as you say, the beauty — yes, the beauty that lurks in ugliness, that is even outside the pub in the gesture of the drinking woman. I can't explain it. I wish I could believe in a God. I can't. Science seems to make it *im*possible. And if you are to believe in a God it must be a good God and no good God could allow his children to suffer so. No, Life is a mystery to me. It is made up of Love and pains. One loves and one suffers, one suffers and one has to love. I feel (for myself individually) that I want to live by the spirit of Love — love *all* things. See into things so deeply and truly that one loves. That does not rule out hate, far from it. I mean it doesn't rule out anger. But I confess I only feel that I am doing right when I am living by love. I don't mean a personal love — you know — but — the big thing. Why should one love? No reason; it's just a mystery. But it is like light. I can only truly see things in its rays. That is vague enough, isn't it? I do think one must (we must) have some big thing to live by, and one reason for the great poverty of Art to-day is that artists have got no religion and they are, in the words of the Bible, sheep without a shepherd. . . . We are priests after all. I fail and waver and faint by the way, but my faith is this queer *Love*. One can't drift, and everybody nearly is drifting nowadays — don't you feel that?

To J. M. Murry   *February 1920*

It's the most divine spring — summer weather — very hot. This is the kind of thing that happens at 1.30. A big car arrives. We go in from our coffee and liqueurs on the balcony. May is waiting to dress me — I wear " somebody's " coat — " anybody's " — we get in, there are rugs, cushions, hassocks, and yesterday the tea basket, and away we go. Yesterday we went to La Turbie (I can't spell it and am ashamed to ask). It's up, up high, high on the tops of mountains. It's a tiny, ancient Roman town, incredibly ancient! with old bits with pillars and capitals — Oh, dear — it is so lovely. The road winds and winds to get there round and round the mountains. I kept seeing it all, for you — wishing for you — longing for you. The rosemary is in flower (our plant it is). The almond trees, pink and white; there are wild cherry trees and the prickly pear white among the olives. Apple trees are just in their first rose and white — white hyacinths and violets are tumbled out of Flora's wicker ark and are *everywhere*. And over everything, like a light, are the lemon and orange trees growing. If I saw the house which was *ours,* I saw twenty. I know we never shall live in such houses, but still they are ours — little houses with terraces and a verandah — with bean fields in bloom with a bright scatter of anemones all over the gardens. When we reached the mountain tops we got out and lay on the grass, looking down, down — into the valleys and over Monaco which is, if anything in this world is, Cinnamon's capital. The palace, seen from so high — with its tufts of plumy trees — the harbour basin with his yacht and a sail-boat and a minute pinnace. Angelica's chemises were hanging out to dry in a royal courtyard. I saw them through the glasses. The hedge sparrow and cushions and rugs for her — the American whose name is D. lay flat on her back smoking — J., never still for a moment, roamed about and one heard her singing. She couldn't keep still and C. (of course) unpacked the tea basket and fed us all and poured cream down us and then gave away the cakes to two funny little mountain children who watched us from behind a rock. We stayed there about 2 hours and then dropped down by another road to Monte — the light and the shadow was divided on the hills, but the sun was still in the air, all the time — the sea very rosy with a pale big moon over by Bordighera. We got home by 6.30 and there was my fire, the bed turned down — hot milk — May waiting to take off all my things. "Did you enjoy it, Madam?" Can you imagine such a coming back to Life?

February 1920

Yesterday — it being mid-summer — Mrs. D. drove me in a kerridge and pair to Monte Carlo. I take back my words about the Riviera *not* being what it is made out to be. *It is* and more. It was the most marvellous afternoon. We drove towards the sun up hill down dale, through mountain roads, through lemon and orange groves — little children throwing bouquets of violets and hyacinths into the carriage — past the sea, under huge mountains —

and the FLOWERS. Of course, it is all quite artificial: there's no imagination in it anywhere. *Monte* is *real Hell.* To begin with it's the cleanest, most polished place I've ever seen. The villas are huge and they have strange malignant towers. Immense poppies sprout out of the halls and roses and geraniums hang down like carpets. All the shops are magasins de luxe, lingerie, perfumes, fat unguents and pawnbrokers and pâtisserie. The Rooms are the devil's headquarters. The blinds are down, there's a whitish glare from the electric light inside — carpet on the outside steps — up and down which pass a continual procession of *whores,* pimps, governesses in thread gloves — Jews — old, old hags, ancient men stiff and greyish, panting as they climb, rich great fat capitalists, little girls tricked out to look like babies — and below the Room a huge outside café — the famous Café de Paris with *real* devils with tails under their aprons cursing each other as they hand the drinks. There at those tables, sit the damned. The gardens — if you could see them — the gardens in Hell. Light, bright delicate grass grown in half a night, trembling little pansies, grown in tiny beds, that are nourished on the flesh of babies — little fountains that spray up into the air all diamonds — Oh, I could write about it *for ever.* We came back through pine forests, past Cap Martin and then at the edge of the brimming sea. I've never heard of Monte before — never dreamed there was such a place. Now I want to go to the Rooms and see it all. It's *dreadful,* but it's *fascinating* to me. We stopped the carriage outside the café and waited for about five minutes. I thought of the Heron and *Our* life — and I thought how strange it was that at the Heron I should no doubt write a story about that woman over there, that ancient long-nosed whore with a bag made of ostrich feathers. . . . I wonder if you'd like to see such a thing, would you? I don't in the least know. Cruelty is there — and vultures hover — and the devil-waiters wear queer peaked caps to hide their horns.

There is a book which we must positively not be another week without. It is Forster's *Life of Dickens.* How is it that people refer to this and have many a time and oft talked of it to me and yet — as though it was of course a very good Life, a very good Life indeed, about as good as you could get and immensely well worth reading. But so dispassionately — so as a matter of course. Merciful Heavens! It's one of the most absolutely fascinating books

I have ever set eyes on. I found to-day Vol. III. in the book shelves. Whether the other two are here or not I don't know, but I do most solemnly assure you it is so great that it were worth while building a house in the country and putting in fireplaces, chairs and a table, curtains, hot wine and you and me and Richard and whoever else we "fancy" exprès for reading this. It's *ravishing*. What will you do when you come to the description of how his little boy aged four plays the part of hero in a helmet and sword at their theatricals and having previously made the dragon drunk on sherry stabs him dead, which he does in such a manner that Thackeray falls off his chair, laughing, and rolls on the floor. No, that's nothing. Read of his landlord *M. Beaufort,* read of his home in Boulogne. —

Now I am exaggerating. Since I wrote all that I finished the book. It's not GREAT, of course, it's not; it's fascinating and it's a bit terrible as a lesson. I never knew what killed Dickens. It was money. He couldn't, as he grew older, resist money; he became a miser and disguised it under a laughing exterior. Money and applause — he died for both. How fearful that is! But still we must have the book. We must have his complete works. . . .

Yesterday I had a wonderful afternoon. Mrs. D. took a carriage and we (she) stopped. I bought for the house, Oh dear! the most ravishing perfect — surprises you ever did see. You'll *never* recover from them. She bought some too and a dress for me, a girl's dress, blue chiffon with a pinky fringe — a summer dress. No, I can't draw it. But I really think what I bought for the house will bouleverse you. I paid 77 francs of the £10 you gave me, and mean as I say to get more. This is a *frightful* town for shopping — glass, china, inlaid work, bits of brocade, trays. We had champagne for dinner, and J. seeing my softened mood gave me her Missal to read. But that's no good. Who made God?

To the Hon. Dorothy Brett   March 26, 1920

If I write letters which convey my feelings so ill I ought to be stopped. God in his infinite wisdom ought to touch my pen with wings and make it to fly hence from me for Ever. He ought with his Awful Breath to breathe upon the ink so that it catches on fire and is consumed utterly.

I've a review to write. We shall keep our big talk until the end of Avrilo when you must come (will you?) and spend the day and bring your slippers in a satin bag as one used to when an infant and "invited out.". . . But why can't I give you — send you for a present — this day like a pearl? There's no sun; the sky is folded, the sea moves and that is all. It is so still, the air is so gentle that every tiny flower seems to be a world unto itself. I am sitting at the window and below a silent, silver coloured cat is moving through a jungle of freezias. "There by the grace of God, goes K. M." you know.

Don't feel bitter! We must not. Do let us ignore the people who aren't real and live deeply, the little time we have here. It really does seem that the world has reached a pitch of *degradation* that never could have been imagined — but we know it — we are not deceived. And the fact of knowing it and having suffered, each in our own way, *cannot* make life — the life of the universe — what we mean when we stand looking up at the stars — or lie watching the ladybird in the grass — or feel — talking to one we love — less marvellous. I think that we — our generation — ought to live in the consciousness of this huge, solemn, exciting, mysterious background. It's our religion, our *faith*. Little creatures that we are, we have our gesture to make which has its place in the scheme of things. We must find what it is and make it — offer up ourselves as a sacrifice. You as a painter and me as a writer. What is it that urges us? Why do you feel that you *must* make *your* discovery and that I *must* make *mine*? That first because we are artists and the only free people we are obedient to some law? There's the mystery! And we shall never solve it — we only know a little more about it by the time we die and that's all — and it's enough.

But just because we *do* feel this we can't afford to be bitter and, oh, we mustn't let the wrong people into our Holy of Holies.

Don't think I am become an elderly fogey, I believe like anything in happiness and being gay and laughing but I am sure one can't afford to be less than one's *deepest self* always. That's all I mean by renewing oneself — renewing one's vows in the contemplation of all this burning beauty. We belong to the Order of Artists and it's a strict order but if we keep together and live together in love and harmony we'll help each other. Oh, I worship life. I fall on my knees before Love and Beauty. If I can only make myself worthy. . . .

To Anne Estelle Rice   March 1920

I'm leaving here April 27th and coming to England until the fin d'octobre when I return here. I'll be in Hampstead for the summer. . . . We must meet soon. I'm *ever* so much better and can walk and talk but part of my left lung is gone and that means my heart is not a boxer's heart and I'll never be able to climb trees or run or swim again. Isn't that a bit steep of Almighty God? I'm always praising him, too, but there you are. I'm terribly happy all the same and I don't *think* the world has lost an athlete, darling, do you?

The weather here is simply supreme. It's summer, hot enough for cold chicken, un peu de salade, champagne and ice-cream, all of which are very much here. The flowers are marvellous, Anne. We go for picnics up among the mountains and long day excursions by motor. We fly into Monte and buy hats for some reason. "C'est l'heure des chapeaux" at present and hats seem to be flying in the air. A whiff of the Rooms gives one civilization encore, and the bands, the gay frocks, the children pelting the car with tiny bouquets — all seem part of the spring picture. All the flowers I share with you and the lemon groves and orange trees. I see little houses perched up on the high hills and dream we are there sur la terrasse. I shall always love you like that. When the light is lovely I think, Anne would see it, and when a funny old man stands in the middle of the road cursing his goats it's a drawing by Anne.

I am living here with "relations" — the dearest people *only* they are not artists. You know what that means? I love them and they've just been too good and dear to me, but they are not in the same world we are and I pine *for my own people,* my own wandering tribe.

To J. M. Murry   March 1920

I am longing to be home. It is a great strain to live away from one's own tribe, with people who, however dear they are, are not ARTISTS. These people's minds are about 1894 — not a day later. They still talk of such-a-pretty-book and whether one can or can't (*Oh ye Gods!*) have a platonic friendship with a man and (Oh ye Gods!) agree that you can't while the male is male and the female female!!!! I "shock" them, but if they knew how they shock me. They make me inclined to roll up my sleeves, pin back my hair, lock the door and take myself and my knife off to the dissecting room — where all such idlers are shut out for ever.

Oh, how PURE artists art — how clean and faithful. Think of Tchekhov and even J.'s talk and Anne's laughing, generous way — so remote from all this corruption. Let us remain chaste and youthful with our work and our life and our poetry. Even —— won't do, you know. One can't afford to mix with people. One must keep clear of all the worldly world. And we can do it. I feel our happiness will simply be without end when we are together again.

March 1920

I am all for Broomies.[1] I, too, have this idea we may retire there and live on love when we are old. I love the little place. It's the right size and it's remote and very simple. William and Dorothy might have lived there or any of our *own kind*. If we do have money we can always make it better and better but I am greatly desirous of our owning it (bad English). I think it's *us*. We can leave it to Richard. It seems to me nicer than anything else. I see it under the stars — so quiet — its thorn hedges spangled with moonlight — our pony cropping — my dear love at the window telling me how fine the night is. Please let us decide on it if you agree. I want it with all my heart.

April 1, 1920

An awful thing happened here yesterday. Just a week ago a young woman was seen wandering about under the trees at Cap Martin and crying — all day. *Nobody spoke to her.* At dusk a little boy heard her crying for help. She was in the sea about fifteen feet from land. By the time he had told somebody it was dark

[1] A cottage on a Sussex common, which we bought but never entered.

and she had disappeared. Her purse and jacket were on the beach. She had a *return* ticket to Nice — five francs and a handkerchief in it — that was all. Yesterday the sea washed her up just opposite the Villa. She came rolling, rolling in with each wave and they waited till she was tumbled on the beach. All her clothes were gone except her corset. Her arms and feet were gone and her hair was bound round and round her head and face — dark brown hair. She doesn't belong to a soul. No one claims her. I expect they'll shovel her under to-day. Poor soul —

*Good Friday
April 2, 1920*

I am very thankful you liked the reviews. The B —— book was *awful* — dead as a tack. These people have no life at all. They never seem to renew themselves or to GROW. . . . The species is now adult and undergoes no other change, until its head-feathers turn white and fall out. . . . Awful!! Even if one does not acquire any " fresh meat " — one's vision of what one possesses is constantly changing into something rich and strange, isn't it? I feel mine is. 47 Fitzherbert Terrace, p.e., is colouring beautifully with the years and I polish it and examine it and only now is it ready to come out of the store room and into the uncommon light of day.

Oh my stars! How I love to think of us as *workers,* writers — two creatures given over to Art. Not that I place Art higher than Love or Life. I cannot see them as things separate — they minister unto each other. And how I long for us to be *established* in our home with just a few precious friends with whom we can talk and be gay and rejoice. . . . *Ecce quam bonum et quam jucundum habitare fratres in unum! Sicut unguentum in capite, quod descendit in barbam, barbam Aaron.* (Now that surprised you, didn't it?) I'm a cultivated little thing, really.

It's a cold and windy day and makes me cough. I still cough, still walk with a stick, still have to rest nearly all the time. They still talk about me as tho' I were the size of a thimble. So you mustn't expect a very fierce girl and you mustn't be disappointed if I have to go slow.

Easter Sunday
April 4, 1920

I think it would be a famous idea to have sketches and stories.[1] I wrote one on the spot, called *Daphne* — about a plant. I'll try and bring a whole lot home, and you could stick them in under noms de plume — if you wanted to.

Yes, it's true about Catholics: their world is not our world — my *duty* is to *mankind* — theirs is to a personal deity — a really-living KING with a flashing face who gives you rewards. I read a panegyric by a Jesuit t'other day which did astonish me.

"God shall be our most passionate love. He shall kiss us with the kisses of his mouth" and so on. It disgusted me. They horribly confuse sexuality and the state of beatitude. I know really a good deal about Catholics now. Of course, there's no doubt J. is a saint. But she has given herself up to the whole thing. She works like mad for the glory of God — lives for his glory — refers everything to God or his saints, and in fact it is to her what Art is to us. But it has *warped* her — even her. I try to pretend she can see our point of view, but when she says of *Je ne parle pas*, "How *could* you say her big belly? I feel Our Lady would have disliked it so much." *Well* — what are you to say to that?

April 1920

I've just got your note about *Je ne parle pas*. No, I certainly won't agree to those excisions if there were 500,000,000 copies in existence. They can keep their old £40 and be hanged to them. Shall I pick the eyes out of a story for £40? I am furious with S. No, I'll never agree. I'll supply another story but that is all. The *outline* would be all blurred. It must have those sharp lines. *The Times* didn't object. As to *The Wind Blows,* I put that in because so many people had admired it (Yes, it's *Autumn II.,* but a little different) and queer people spoke so strongly about it I felt I must put it in. But this had better be held over till I get back. I'll never consent. I'll take the book away first. Don't worry about it. Just tell S. he's a fool. As to *The Little Governess* it *was* on my list and I asked you to include it!! (Caught out!) But don't you worry. It will have to wait. Of course I won't consent!

[1] In *The Athenæum*.

Letters 1920

April 7, 1920

I feel I was too undisciplined about my story and Constable. I leave it to you. You're my cricket. If you agree to what they say — why then, all's well (and I *DO* want the money).

Our queer correspondences again. I have been steeped in Shakespeare these last days with a note book — looking up every word, finding what are inkles and caddises. . . . I nearly know the sheep shearing scene from *A Winter's Tale* by heart. It's the more *bewitching* scene — but that's one of my favourite plays. If I am strictly truthful I know nearly all of it *almost* by heart. And I began reading the songs in *Twelfth Night* in bed this morning early —

> Mark it Cesario, it is old and plain;
> The spinsters and the knitters in the sun
> And the free maids that weave their thread with bones
> Do use to chant it: it is silly sooth,
> And dallies with the innocence of love,
> Like the old age. . . .
> *Clo:* Are you ready, sir?
> *Duke:* Ay, prithee, sing.   (*Music*)
> *Clo:* Come away, come away, death, etc.

Oh, how that does all ravish me. I think I could listen to that for a small eternity.

To Sydney and Violet Schiff   *April 7, 1920*

I feel that I deceived you to-day about my health and I succumbed to the awfully great temptation of deceiving myself. Really and truly, thinking it over, I am afraid I am not well enough to live in that darling little flat. You see there are days when I am completely hors de combat; I can't walk a step further than I walked to-day and I have to take horrid and extravagant care of myself always. Sometimes I get a week when I can't move and I am always under a doctor's care and if I do go out I'm supposed not to breathe the dust. This sounds ridiculous; I wish I didn't have to say it. I feel there is *plenty* of room to be well in une petite appartement but there is not enough room to be ill and

I have to provide for it. When I said I had to write for pennies I didn't mean for the essential pennies but for all the luxuries which are, alas! my necessities. Yes, forgive me, I was carried away to-day and I forgot I must behave like an invalid. But when I came in and lay down and rested I thought: you know these things aren't for you, and you were deceiving those two dear people. You must let them know at once.

Will you forgive me? And thank you for a lovely day. I'm lying here living it over and seeing in my mind's eye your garden and hearing the torrent. And much more important than those things — delighting in the fact of having met you.

To Richard Murry   *April 1920*

Talking about English flowers

>Bring hither the pink and purple columbines
>And gillyflowers,
>Bring coronations and sops-in-wine,
>Beloved of paramours:
>Strew me the ground with the daffadowndilly
>With cowslips and kingcups and lovèd lilies;
>The pretty paunce and the chevisaunce
>Shall match with the faire flower delice —

I quote from memory — but that's hard to beat, don't you think? But I am all for feathery-topped carrots — don't you love pulling up carrots, shaking them clean and tossing them on to a heap! And feeling the cauliflowers to see which one is ready to cut. Then OUT comes your knife. When I was about the height of a garden spade I spent weeks — months — watching a man do all these things and wandering through canes of yellow butter beans and smelling the spotted speckled broad bean flowers and helping to plant Giant Edwards and White Elephants. Oh, dear, I do love gardens! Think of little lettuces and washing radishes under the garden tap. I'd better stop. I just saw you climb into a cherry tree, and leaning against the trunk of the tree I saw and smelt the sweet sticky gum. But we'll have all these things.

I bought you one of the most exquisite little boxes yesterday I've ever seen. You know how some things *belong* to people. It stood on a shelf in the shop and said R. M. so I carried it off and I'll bring it home.

April 1920

Please note: Seats are booked in the train, *if* the train goes, for April 27th and I do hope, time and tide permitting, you will meet me at the station — will you? Isn't it gorgeous to think we have 6 months in front of us and what's to prevent you and me from flitting over the heath and, while He draws and paints enchanted landscapes, She lies on the grass and tells him about the lions and tigers and crocodiles and boa constrictors that she used to feed under the palm trees at Mentone. Do you know the heron has got beautiful blue legs? I read that the other day.

Your little drawings are most awfully nice. I'll draw you some palms, there are so many different kinds. My favourite tree I really think, tho', is the lemon tree, it's far more beautiful than the orange — And then the prickly pear has a lot of drawing: it's a very queer affair and then there's the pepper tree hung of course with pepper pots — but I wish you were here to sneeze at it with me. J. seems so very busy that he never has time to write me a real letter. I miss them so! For the Tig you know is an animal which removed from its native soil, however golden the cage and however kind and charming the people who hand it things through the bars or even pat it — *longs* for fat envelopes to eat and when left without them she finds it an awful effort not to just creep into a corner and pine. But it can't be helped — I have asked J. for them so often that I'm sure he'd send them if he had them — he just hasn't — that's all.

Will you be quite changed when I come back? Please carry something that I can recognize you by such as — an emerald green handkerchief printed with a design of pink shrimps *or* a walking stick tied with a large bow of pale blue ribbon. No, Heaven bless you, I shall know you anywhere and you'll know me.

Of course I *don't* know how to light a fire with damp wood, damp paper and 1 match. BUT please reply telling me how to as who knows how soon I may have to do it. (Do you see the hint conveyed in these words?)

Letters 1920

To J. M. Murry   *April 20, 1920*

I am staying in bed until lunch as I had a heavy day yesterday buying small presents to bring back and so on. Exhausting work because one gets so frightfully excited as well. C. went with me in the morning and bought *me* an antique brooch, very lovely; three stones set in silver. Then she bought me a pastel blue muslin frock with frills like panniers at the side. Ida, who was by, said she thought C. had a very bad influence on me because she spoiled me so. And the poor old dear got pink just like Granma used to and said, " Well, the child has had no fun, no life, no chance to wear pretty things for two years. I'm *sure* J. would want to do what I'm doing. . . ." You remember in Italy how I longed to return to Life with all kinds of lovely possessions. Funny it should have all come true. I also bought the most exquisite fruit plates with small white grapes and gold leaves on them pour la famille Murry, and a dish, high, to match, to take the breath. I've no money. I think I must be a little bit mad. Oh, could I bring the flowers, the *air,* the whole heavenly climate as well: this darling little town, these mountains — It is simply a small jewel — Mentone . . . and its band in the jardins publique with the ruffled pansy beds — the white donkeys standing meek, tied to a pole, the donkey women in black pleated dresses with flat funny hats. All, all is so terribly attractive. I'd live years here with you. I'm immensely attached to it all and in the summer we'd go up to the Alpes Maritimes and live in the small spotless inns with milk hot from the cow and eggwegs from the hen — we'd live in those steep villages of pink and white houses with the pine forests round them — where your host serves your dinner wearing a clean white blouse and sabots. Yes, I'm in love with the Alpes Maritimes. I don't want to go any further. I'd like to live my life between Broomies and them.

April 26, 1920

Oh, how I agree about Shylock! I think *The Taming of The Shrew* is so deadly too. I am certain Bill never wrote it: he bolstered up certain speeches but that is all. It's a hateful, silly play, so barely constructed and arranged. I'd never go to see it. I think we shall have a Shakespeare festival one year at Broomies — get actors there to study their parts — act out of doors — a small Festa — a real one. I'll be stage director. *I am dead serious about this.* Your Stratford makes me feel it. Really it's grilling hot to-day! I feel inclined to make a noise like a cicada.

To Sydney and Violet Schiff
Sunday
2 Portland Villas, Hampstead
May 2, 1920

At last the writing table is in perfect order and I have put a notice round the neck of the small angelic creature who is " knock man " to my door: " Engaged." At last I'm free to sit down and think of last Sunday and wish it were this. This is cold, reluctant, uneasy. Now and again a handful of rain is dashed against the window. The church bells have stopped ringing and I know that there is a leg of something with " nice " spring greens, rhubarb tart and custard in every house in Hampstead but mine. It's very cold, very grey; the smoke spins out of the chimney. But thank God there *is* a far-away piano, rocking, plunging, broken into long quivering phrases — it sounds as though it were being played under the sea.

How glad I am — how deeply glad — that we stopped the car on the other side of the tunnel and got out and leaned against the wall — with one broken village behind and then the falling terraces of green. Will you ever forget how those mountains were heaped and folded together? And the fat comfortable man taking a cigarette at his ease in the lap of the world and the small impudent children watching us while we enjoyed our timeless moment? I shall go on reliving that day down to the very last drop. But so I shall with all the time we spent together.

I have been thinking about your new work. Have you done any more? It's *very* good. Delicate perception is not enough; one must find the exact way in which to convey the delicate perception. One must inhabit the other mind and know more of the other mind and your secret knowledge is the light in which all is steeped. I think you have done this. Do *more.*

M. is desperately pessimistic about — everything — more especially — he feels that the wicked writers are triumphing to such an extent that it's nearly impossible ever to beat them. Things have gone too far. I don't feel that at all. I think our duty lies in ignoring them — all except those whose faults are important — and in working ourselves, with all our might and main. It is waste of time to discuss them — and waste of energy. It's a kind of treachery to all that we intend to do. I am sure the " day will come."

It is joy to have one's room again. Everything is in its place. The black and gold scarf lies across a little couch.

Good-bye, this is not the letter I wanted to write — it's only the fringe of it.

To the Hon. Dorothy Brett *May 20, 1920*

The STOVE is come, installed, burning, giving out the most blessed beneficent heat imaginable! I *cannot* tell you how good it is to be in this room — in a whole warm room with no smoke, no making up fires, just a silent, discreet, never-failing heat. If I were a savage I should pray to it and offer it the bodies of infants. Thank you a billion times for your dear thought. And now a belated thank you for the yellow roses — which are perfection. Now stop being generous, or I'll have to lead a baby elephant washed in rose soap, hung with lily buds and marigolds, carrying a flamingo in a cage made of mutton-fat jade on its back, to your doorstep as a return for past favours.

To Violet Schiff *August 1920*

I'm much better. The "trouble" has been I've had an overdose of vaccine and it laid me low. Ten million — or twenty million — hosts of streptococci attacked and fought one another. I have done with vaccine.

My Catholic cousins (the Villa Flora ones) have bought a new large villa in Garavan — the other bay. It has, at its gates, a doll's house with a verandah, garden, everything complete. And this I have taken from them. I shall be in touch with them, still, and they are getting me a maid and so on, but at the same time I'm *free* — can you imagine the delight of writing to the Villa Violet, of telephoning to them (my Isola Bella has a telephone [1]) and asking them if they will come over? Don't you envy me?

By the time you come my garden will be full of flowers. Heavens! what a joy that will be. And we shall ignore time — trick the wretch just for a little.

To Sydney and Violet Schiff Friday
August 1920

We both enjoyed immensely our evening. The play began so splendidly and — even though it did not keep it up — I for my part was so happy to be there. . . . We discussed all the way home, a new *Athenæum* — the idea of throwing overboard all the learned societies and ancient men and reviews of Dull old Tomes, and opening the windows to the hurrying sounds outside, and throwing all the old gang into the river. . . . After all — is it good enough to be *halfway* between what we really want to do and what we don't care a pin for.

What will the Bishops and the Antiquarians say to the short stories? And just supposing we really told the truth about everything — *confidently*. The car rushed through St John's Wood and we decided to do it, but not to use violence — I wonder if it is possible. . . .

I wish you could see my roses. They are so exquisite that yesterday I made Jones photograph them so that I should be able to show you how they looked.

Oh, the *devastating* cold. I cannot keep warm and all day long people walk up and down the stairs and just don't knock at my door. Do you ever want to *hide,* Violet, to be completely hidden so that nobody knows where you are?

Sometimes one has a dreadful feeling of *exposure* — it's intolerable. I mustn't say these things.

To Violet Schiff August 1920

Forgive me for not answering before.

I had asked some people for next Sunday; I was hoping they would refuse. But no, this morning they will be " so pleased to

[1] It hadn't.

come." So M. and I regretfully cannot. I do want to see you both soon and really *talk*. It seems, I suppose it isn't really, so long since we have had time to talk.

What I always want to do with you both is to share the event and then to share the impressions of it — the " afterwards." If only there were more time but it seems to go faster and faster. One is so conscious of it sometimes.

I feel as though we were trying to talk against the noise and the speed of the train — trying to hear each other — trying to convey by a look, a gesture, what we long to talk about for hours — days — What a story one could write about a train journey across strange country — A party of people with the carriage to themselves, travelling together, and two of them who have something they must say to each other. Can you imagine it? the impatience, the excitement, the extraordinary nearness of them all to one another — the meals in the restaurant car, " the new warm plates seemed to come flying through the air " — and the preparing for the night — those who *do* sleep — those who don't — My God! there's such a novel to be written there; will there be time to write it?

Monday
August 1920

Please don't think about my health. Folkestone or Margate (dread places) wouldn't give it me back again. No, I shall go away in September — somewhere, I don't know where — preferably — and here one wants to throw down one's pen (no, to lay it down, *carefully* and *gently*) and to dream of some place where nobody says: " But one moment, if you have fish for lunch you won't have it for dinner, will you, and I *had* thought of it for breakfast to-morrow. . . . I'm not interrupting seriously. You've not really started work yet, have you? "

Violet: " You know I think K. M. is rather ungrateful and exasperating."

Ah, don't think that. It's only impatience. There is so much to write and there is so little time.

August 1920

It was a joy to hear from you and you are too generous in your criticism of my work for the paper. Nevertheless, it's immensely stimulating to know that I gave you pleasure — I often say things *expressly* for you both. I am sure you know I do. This week I had happened to read a really typical article in an imbecile " woman's paper " and I threw my three silly novels away and wrote about it instead. I am afraid the greater number of readers will think I have gone mad. But Oh, they are such *dull* dogs sometimes and I am ill — I *must* be gay — my heart and my cough, my dear woman, won't let me walk up and down stairs, even, at present. I am afraid I cannot come to you. You know how much I would like to. And I'm not sure when I can get away to France; I'm not " up " to the journey — as they say, at present. It is very cursed; I try not to mind; I mind *terribly*.

But forgive me. You have a right to be disgusted with me for being ill — I know — if I ever am well and strong again I'll try and make up for this unsatisfactory K. M.

To J. M. Murry
Tuesday
Villa Isola Bella, Menton-Garavan
September 14, 1920

What shall I tell you first? I have thought of you often and wondered if the beau temps is chez vous aussi, now that I've gone away.

We had a good journey but a slight contretemps in Paris. Ida disappeared with the porter to find a taxi, and she forgot the door she'd gone out — rushed off to another and lost me. After about half an hour I appealed to the police but they were helpless. The poor creature had lost her head and when we did meet finally it was only because I saw her in the distance and simply *shouted*. This tired me and made my nose bleed and I had a very bad night and had to do my review in bed next day, being fanned and bathed with eau de cologne. It's of no importance *to me* but I felt all the time I was betraying you and the paper. Forgive me once again.

We arrived here yesterday at 4.50 after a day of terrible heat. Mentone felt like home. It was really bliss to sit in the voiture and drive through those familiar streets and then up a queer little leafy "way" and then another at right angles to a gate all hidden by green where la bonne Annette stood waving her apron and the peke leapt at her heels. This villa is — so far — perfect. It has been prepared inside and out to such an extent that I don't think it will ever need a hand's turn again. The path from the gate to the two doors has a big silver mimosa showering across it. The garden is twice as big as I imagined. One can live in it all day. The hall is black and white marble. The salon is on your right as you enter — a real little salon with velvet covered furniture and an immense dead clock and a gilt mirror and two *very* handsome crimson vases which remind me of fountains filled with blood. It has two windows: one looks over the garden gate, the others open on to the terrace and look over the sea. I mustn't forget to mention the carpet with a design of small beetles which covers the whole floor. The dining room is equally charming in its way — and has French windows, too. It abounds in cupboards full of wessels and has a vrai buffet with silver teapot, coffee and milk jug which catch the flashing eye, all is delightful. There are even very lovely blue glass finger bowls. . . . On the other side of the passage is the garde-linge big enough for all our boxes as well. The linen is overwhelming. It is all in dozens — even to maid's aprons. . . . The kitchen premises are quite shut off with a heavy pair of doors. The kitchen gleams with copper. It's a charming room and there's a big larder and a scullery big enough for a workshop and outside there's a garden and three large caves and the lapinière. Upstairs are four bedrooms — the maids on the entresol. The others have balconies and again are carpeted all over and sumptuous in a doll's house way.

Annette had prepared everything possible. The copper kettle boiled. Tea was laid. In the larder were eggs in a bowl and a cut of cheese on a leaf and butter swimming and milk, and on the table coffee, a long bread, jam, and so on. On the buffet a dish heaped with grapes and figs lying in the lap of fig leaves. She had thought of everything and moreover everything had a kind of chic — and she in her blue check dress and white apron sitting down telling the news was a most delightful spectacle.

The heat is almost as great as when we arrived last year. One can wear nothing but a wisp of silk, two bows of pink ribbon and a robe de mousseline. Moustiques and moucherons are in full blast; we are both bitten to death already. They are frightful. But so far I can accept them without a reproach, the compensations are so great.

I must tell you a very big date palm grows outside my bedroom balcony window. At the end of the garden wall — (a yellow crumbling wall) there is a vast magnolia full of rich buds. There is a tap in the garden. In the vegetable garden the French artichokes are ready to eat and minute yellow and green marrows. A tangerine tree is covered in green balls.

The view is *surpassingly* beautiful. Late last night on the balcony I stood listening to the tiny cicadas and to the frogs and to someone playing a little chain of notes on a flute.

September 1920

Your letter and card this morning were so perfect that (only you will understand this) I felt you'd brought up a little kitten *by* Wingley and put it on our bed and we were looking at it together. But it was a very kitten of very kittens . . . with wings. I must answer it this once and risk breaking the agreement *not* to write.

Yes, that suddenness of parting — that last moment — But this last time I had a deep, strange *confidence*, a feeling so different to that other desperate parting when I went to France. We are both so much stronger and we *do* see our way and we do know what the future is to be. That doesn't make me miss you less, though. . . .

I'm in bed — not very O.K. The moustiques have bitten me and I've had pains and fever and dysentery. Poisoned, I suppose. It was almost bound to happen. But don't worry. Annette is in the kitchen and her soups and rice climb up the stairs.

I think I've got a maid, too, Mme. Reveilly, 5bis. Rue des Poilus. She's a police inspector's *sister* and she looks indeed as though she had sprung out of a nest of comic policemen. Fat, dark, sitting on the sofa edge, grasping, *strangling* indeed a small black bead bag. " Si vous cherchez *une personne de confiance* Madame et *pas une imbecile* . . ." she began. I feel that was a poor compliment to my appearance. Did I look like a person who wantonly cherished imbeciles to do the house work? But of course all the time she recounted her virtues I saw the most charming imbecile with woolly shoes like rabbits and a great broad beaming smile ... whom I couldn't help dismissing rather regretfully.

The villa is even lovelier than it was. Once I am up again and out again, I feel it will be almost *too* fair. I do miss you, tho'. I have (I have told you a thousand times) always such a longing to share all that is good with you and you alone. *Remember that.* Events move so awfully strangely. We live and talk and tear our *Daily News* up together and all the while there is a growth going on — a gorgeous deep-down glories like bougainvilleas twine from your window to mine. ...

I've begun my journal book. I want to offer it to Methuen — to be ready this Xmas. Do you think that's too long to wait? It ought to be rather special. *Dead* true — and by dead true I mean like one takes a sounding — (yet gay withal). Oh, it's hard to describe. What do you advise?

September 18, 1920

I'm longing to see your "Wilde-Harris." I am *sure* O. W. was negligible but he *is* an astonishing figure. His letters, his mockeries and thefts — he's a Judas who betrays himself.

... Which is the more tragic figure — the master without a disciple or one disciple without a master? ... That's by the way. Can I have the *Times Lit. Sup.?* I freeze, I burn for the printed word.

Saturday. I sent my review last night. I do hope it arrives in time. Dearest, I'm better. Temperature normal — pain gone — up and lying in the salon. I am eating again too and now really *will* mend. But I have *never* been so thin — not even in Paris. I simply melted like a candle with that fever. I rock when I stand. But Hurrah! it's over.

Sunday afternoon
September 19, 1920

It is true — isn't it — that we are going to walk out together every single Sunday? All through the week we are hard at work — you, in that horrible black town that I hate, me, on my beautiful island; but when Sunday comes (it was my first thought this morning) we adorn ourselves, and soon after midi I hear that longed for but rather peculiar, rather funny whistle. I run to the window, I kiss my hand, spin down the stairs, and away we go. But for this week at least we'll not go far — only out of sight of the world — that's far enough. For your Wig is still so weak that she can't walk straight — sometimes I fling myself at the doors or take a great high step in the air. But I *am* really on the mend, and as to my cough — fancy, I've been here five days and I cough hardly at all. This morning in fact I didn't cough *at all* and can't remember if I have until now, 6 P.M. I only have to get my strength back after this " attack." That is all about me.

(There is so much to tell you. I tell you in my mind and then the effort of writing is too much.)

Later

My feeling for this little house is that somehow it ought to be ours. It is, I think, a perfect house in its way and just our size. The position — up a side road *off* a side road standing high — all alone — the chief rooms facing South and West — the garden, the terrace all South — is ideal. You could do all the garden. There's a small vegetable plot outside the kitchen and scullery — there is a largish piece in the front — *full* of plants and trees — with a garden tap and at the side another bed — a walk — a stone terrace overlooking the sea — a great magnolia tree — a palm that looks as though the dates must ripen. You shall have photographs of all this. And then it's so solid inside and so, somehow, spacious. And all on two floors and as well all the kitchen premises away, shut away and again perfectly equipped. I shall, of course, keep the strictest accounts and see exactly what it would cost us to live here.

Marie, the maid, is an excellent cook — as good as Annette was. She does all the marketing, and as far as I can discover she's a very good manager. A *marvel* really. Of course she cooks with butter but then one doesn't eat butter with one's meals so it comes to the same thing. The food is far better than any possible house we go to in England. I don't know to whose to compare it — and all her simple dishes like vegetables or salads are so good. It's a great pleasure to go into the kitchen for my morning milk and see this blithe soul back from market in the spotless kitchen with a bunch of lemon leaves drying for tisane and a bunch of camomile hanging for the same.

All is in exquisite order. There are pots on the stove, cooking away — mysterious pots — the vegetables are in a great crock — in bundles — and she tells me of her marvellous bargains as I sip the milk. She is the kind of cook Anatole France might have.

As to the weather it is really heavenly weather. It is too hot for any exertion, but a breeze lifts at night, and I can't tell you what scents it brings, the smell of a full summer sea and the bay tree in the garden and the smell of lemons. After lunch to-day we had a sudden tremendous thunderstorm, the drops of rain were as big as marguerite daisies — the whole sky was violet. I went out the very moment it was over — the sky was all glittering with broken light — the sun a huge splash of silver. The drops were like silver *fishes* hanging from the trees. I drank the rain from the peach leaves and then pulled a shower-bath over my head. Every violet leaf was full. I thought of you — these are the things I want you to have. Already one is conscious of the whole sky again and the light on the water. Already one listens for the grasshopper's fiddle, one looks for the tiny frogs on the path — one watches the lizards. . . . I feel so strangely as though I were the one who is home and you are away.

Tuesday, September 21: I dropped this letter and only to-day I pick it up again. . . . And I still haven't told you about this house or the life or the view or what your room is like. It all waits. Will you just take me and it for granted for about a week? In a week I'll be a giant refreshed — but I've simply got to get back my strength after the last blow.

But you know how soon I come to the surface. It did pull me down. It's only a few days. It's over. I'm on the *up grade,* but there you are — just for the moment. Each day the house finds its order more fixed and just (that's not English). Marie does every single thing. I am having an awning made so that I can lie out all day. The weather is absolute exquisite radiance, day after day, just variegated by these vivid storms. It's *very* hot and the insects are a trouble, but it's perfect weather.

I'll just have to ask you to take a wave of a lily white hand to mean *all* for the moment. I *wish* I were stronger. I'm so *much* better. My cough is nearly gone. It's nothing but de la faiblesse and I know it will pass. But not to be able to give you all this when I want to — that's hard to bear.

To Richard Murry   *September 1920*

I was very glad to hear from you. The drawing of the Flight into Mentone was really superb — Athy was the spit of himself. Yes, I think you'd find the South of France was good country. I could be content to stay here for years. In fact I love it as I've never loved any place but my home. The life, too, is so easy. There is no division between one's work and one's external existence — both are of a piece. And you know what that means. My small, pale yellow house with a mimosa tree growing in front of it — just a bit deeper yellow — the garden full of plants, the terrace with crumbling yellow pillars covered with green (lurking-place for lizards) all belong to a picture or a story. I mean they are not remote from one's ideal — one's dream. The house faces the sea, but to the right there is the Old Town with a small harbour — a little quai planted with pepper and plane trees. This Old Town, which is built flat against a hill — a solid wall, as it were, of shapes and colours — is the finest thing I've seen. Every time I drive towards it it is different.

And then, there's no doubt that the people here — I mean the working people — make no end of a difference. My servant Marie is a masterpiece in her way. She's the widow of a coachman — just a woman of the people, as we say, but her feeling for life is a constant surprise to me. The kitchen is a series of Still Lives; the copper pans wink on the walls. When she produces a fish for lunch it lies in a whole, tufted green seascape with a large tragic mouthful of "persil" still in its jaws. And last night, talking of her desire to buy bananas she explained it wasn't so much that they should be eaten but they gave "effect" to the fruit dish. " A fine bunch of grapes, deux poires rouges, une ou deux belles pommes avec des bananas et des feuilles" she thought worth looking at.

You know to live with such people is an awful help. Yesterday, *par example,* I had a sack of charcoal and some pine cones delivered. And passing the kitchen I saw the woodman, in a blue overall and yellow trousers, sitting at the table with Marie taking a glass of wine. The wine bottle was one of those wicker affairs. One doesn't (God forbid) want to make a song about these things, but I didn't realise they *went on* naturally and simply until I came here. In England one gets the feeling that *all is over*. Do you know what I mean? And there's never time for more than a rough sketch of what one wants to do, and what one feels. I hope you don't think I'm running down your country. It's not that. It's life in any city.

To J. M. Murry   *September 25, 1920*

I am beginning my Sunday letter. I can't resist the hour. It's 6.30, just on sunset — the sea a deep hyacinth blue, silver clouds floating by like sails and the air smells of the pine and the bay and of charcoal fires. Divine evening! Heavenly fair place! The great RAIN has brought a thousand green spears up in every corner of the garden. Oh, you'll be met by such Flowers on Parade at Christmas time. There's a winey smell at the corner of the terrace where a huge fig tree drops its great purple fruits. At the other the magnolia flashes leaves; it has great buds brushed over with pink. Marie has just brought in my chaise longue and the green chair which is yours to escape l'humidité du soir. . . . Do these details bore you in London? Oh, I could go on for ever. But I do think this place, villa, climate, maid, all are as perfect as can be. Marie's cooking infuriates me. Why don't I help you to her escaloppe aux tomates — with *real* purée de p. de terre — deux feuilles de salade and des œufs en neige. And her Black Coffee!!

Sharing her return from market tho' is my delight. I go into the kitchen and am given my glass of milk and then she suddenly rushes into the scullery, comes back with the *laden* basket (privately exulting over her purchases). "Ah cet-te vie, cet-te vie. Comme tout ça est chère, Madame! Avant la guerre notre jolie France, c'était un jardin de Paradis et maintenant c'est que le Président même n'a pas la tête sur les épaules. Allez! allez! Douze sous pour les haricots! C'est vrai qu'ils sont frais — qu'ils sont jolis, qu'ils sont enfin — enfin — des haricots pour un petit Prince — maiz douze sous, douze sous! . . ." etc., etc. This at a great pace of course. Does it come over? Does it seem to you the way a cook ought to talk? There's a mouse in the cupboard. When she brought my bregchick this morning . . . " le p'tit Monsieur nous a visité pendant la nuit, Madame. Il a mangé presque toute une serviette. Mais pensez-vous — quelles dents. Allez-allez! c'est un maître!!" I don't know. I won't bore you with any more of her — but it seems to me that this is the way that people like her *ought* to talk.

I heard again from Methuen to-day. They now say they'd like 2 books for next spring. I think there must have been some trunk work, some back stair work in this on your part. But I'll see what I can do without promising in my fatal way what I can't perform. I wish I could begin real creative work. I haven't yet. It's the atmosphere, the . . . tone which is hard to get. And without it nothing is worth doing. I have such a horror of triviality . . . a great part of my Constable book is *trivial*. It's not good enough. You see it's too late to beat about the bush any longer. They are cutting down the cherry trees; the orchard is sold — that is really the atmosphere I want. Yes, the dancing and the dawn and the Englishman in the train who said "jump!" — all these, with the background.

Speaking of something else, which is nevertheless connected — it is an awful temptation, in face of all these novels to cry "woe — woe!" I cannot conceive how writers who have lived through our times can *drop* these last ten years and revert to why Edward didn't understand, Vi's reluctance to be seduced or why a dinner of twelve courses needs remodelling. If I did not review novels I'd never read them. The writers (practically all of them) seem to have no idea of what one means by continuity. It is a difficult thing to explain. Take the old Tartar waiter in *Anna* who serves Levin and Stepan — Now, Tolstoy only has to touch him and he gives out a note and this note is somehow important, persists, is a part of the whole book. But all these other men — they introduce their cooks, aunts, strange gentlemen, and so on, and once the pen is off them they are *gone* — dropped down a hole. Can one explain this by what you might call — a *covering* atmosphere — Isn't that a bit too vague? Come down O Youth from yonder

Mountain height and give your Worm a staff of reason to assist her. What it *boils down to* is . . . " either the man can make his people live and keep 'em alive or he can't." But criticks better that. . . .

September 27, 1920

I wish and I wish and I wish. Why aren't you here? Even though I am as poor as a mouse, don't publish *Sun and Moon*. I'll send you a story this week. *Do* publish it if you can. Of course, don't if you're full up. But alas for my £25 a month — it's gone. This, however, is sheer wailing. . . .

The lizards here *abound*. There is one big fellow, a perfect miniature crocodile, who lurks under the leaves over a corner of the terrace. I watched him come forth to-day — *very* slithy — and eat an ant. You should have seen the little jaws, the flick flick of the tongue, the great rippling pulse just below the shoulder. His eyes, too. He listened with them — and when he couldn't find another ant, he stamped his front paw — and then, seeing that I was watching, *deliberately* winked, and slithered away.

There is also a wasps' nest in the garden. Two infant wasps came out this morning and each caught hold of a side of a *leaf* and began to tug. It was a brown leaf about the size of three tea leaves. They became furious. They whimpered, whiney-pined — snatched at each other — wouldn't give way and finally one *rolled* over and couldn't roll back again — just lay there kicking. I never saw such a thing. His twin then couldn't move the leaf at all. I pointed out the hideous moral to my invisible playmate.

October 1, 1920

Suppose you didn't glance at a novel by a man called Prowse, *A Gift of the Dusk*. A simply terrible book — awful — ghastly! and about as good as it could be. It's just a kind of . . . journal the man kept while he was at a sanatorium in Switzerland. It *is* the goods if you like! But he must be a wonderful man. I wish I knew if he is dead. Will you PLEASE ask Beresford if you see him (Collins is the publisher)? I wish very much I could hear of him — One's heart goes out to anyone who has faced an experience as he has done. " One must tell everything — everything." That is more and more real to me each day. It is, after all, the only treasure, the only heirloom we have to leave — our own little grain of truth.

October 4, 1920

Walpole's novel which I mean to do for next week ought to be a very good prop to hang those very ideas on that I tried to communicate to you. I want to take it seriously and really say why it fails — for, of course, it does fail. But his " intention " was serious. I hope I'll be able to say what I do mean. I am no critic of the homely kind. " If you would only explain quietly in simple language," as L. M. said to me yesterday. Good Heavens, that is out of my power.

The garden menagerie includes snakes — a big chap as thick as my wrist, as long as my arm, slithered along the path this morning and melted into the bushes. It wasn't horrid or fearful, however. As to the mice — Marie's piège seems to snap in the most revolting way. A fat one was offered to a marauding cat at the back door yesterday, but it refused it. " Polisson! Tu veux un morceau de sucre avec? " I heard Marie scold. She is very down on the cats here; she says they are malgracieux. Yes, she is a most *remarkable* type. Yesterday afternoon, it was terribly gloomy and triste outside and she came in for the coffee tray, and said how she *hated* Mentone. She had lived here 8 years with her pauvre mari and then they lived 2 years in Nice where he died and was buried. She said she could *bear* Nice because " il se repose là-bas mais ici — Madame — il se promenait avec moi — partout partout — " and then she beat her little black crêpe bodice and cried " trop de souvenirs, Madame — trop de souvenirs." Oh, how I love people who feel deeply. How restful it *is* to live with them even in their " excitement." I think for writers, it is right to be with them — but the feeling must be true — not a hair's breadth assumed — or I hate it as much as I love the other. As I write that I don't believe it any more. I could live with you and not care two pins if people " felt " anything at all — in fact, I could draw away and be very aloof and cold if they did — *I* don't know. It's too difficult. . . .

I feel this letter is cold and poor; the fruit is not good to eat. It's rather like that withered fig tree. Do you know there is a kind of fig-tree which is supposed to be of the family of that unfortunate one — it is dark stemmed and its leaves are black, they flap on the blackened boughs, they are like leaves that a flame has passed over. *Terrible.* I saw one once in a valley, a beautiful valley with a river flowing through it. There was linen drying on the banks and the women were beating the water and calling to one another — gaily — and there was this *sad* tree. L. M. who was with me said " of course the *explanation* is that one must never cease from giving." The fig tree had no figs — so Christ cursed it. *Did you ever!* There's such a story buried under the whole thing — isn't there? — if only one could dig it out.

Thursday
October 7, 1920

As for me I am in the open day and night. I never am in a room with the windows shut. By great good fortune I've got Marie who every day looks after me better. And she is so sympathetic that all she cooks tastes especially good. She looks after me and anxiously asks if " la viande était assez saignante " — but *sanely* — in the way one not only can stand, but one loves, and when I go into the kitchen and say, " Marie, je tremble de faim " her " tant mieux " as she butters you a tartine is just absolutely right. So you see I *do* count my blessings; this house, this climate, and this good soul. . . .

It's blowing guns to-day — a choppy sea — my favourite sea, brilliant blue with the white lifting — lifting as far as one can see, rather big unbroken waves near the shore. Butterflies love a day like this. They love to fling themselves up in the air and then be caught by the wind and rocked and flung and lightly *fluttered.* They pretend to be frightened. They cling as long as they can to a leaf and then — take a butterfly long breath — up they go — away they sail, quivering with joy, and delight. It must be a kind of surf bathing for them — flinging themselves down the wind.

You know how when one woman carries the new born baby

the other woman approaches and lifts the handkerchief from the tiny face and bends over and says " Bless it." But I am always wanting to lift the handkerchief off lizards' faces and pansies' faces and the house by moonlight. I'm always waiting to *put a blessing* on what I see. It's a queer feeling.

October 8, 1920

I am not in the least settled down to anything yet. The journal — I have absolutely given up. I dare not keep a journal. I should always be longing to tell the truth. As a matter of fact, I dare not tell the truth — I feel I *must* not. The only way to exist is to go on — and try and lose oneself — to get as far as possible away from *this* moment. Once I can do that all will be well. So it's stories or nothing. I expect I shall kick off soon — perhaps to-day, who knows? In the meantime I peg away too, in my fashion.

October 1920

Oh, if you knew what a joy your Shakespeare was. I straightway dipped in *The Tempest* and discovered Ariel riding on *curlèd clouds*. Isn't that adjective perfect? I'd missed it before. I do think *The Tempest* is the most radiant, delicate, exquisite play. The atmosphere is exactly the atmosphere of an island after a storm — an island re-born out of the sea with Caliban tossed up for sea wrack and Ariel blowing in a shell. Oh, my divine Shakespeare!! Oh, most blessed genius. Again I read of the love of Ferdinand and Miranda, how they met and *recognised* each other and their hearts spake. Everything — everything is new born and golden. God knows there are desert islands enough to go round — the difficulty is to sail *away* from them — but dream islands ... they are rare, rare.

Just as I folded that I had *callers*. A M. et Madame showed on to the Terrace very gracious but OH DEAR! What a ghastly idea it is. What can one say? I can't play " ladies " unless I know the children I'm playing with.

Now there's an asp come out of a hole — a slender creature, red, about twelve inches long. It lies moving its quick head. It is very evil looking but how much nicer than a caller. I was warned yesterday against attempting to kill them. (Do you see me trying to kill them?) But they *spring* at you — if you do. However, I'll catch this one for you at the risk of my life and put it in your Shakespeare for a marker at the scene where the old man carries in the basket of figs. You will have to hold your Shakespeare *very firmly* to prevent it wriggling, Anthony darling.

Lovingly yours,
EGYPT.

October 1920

I send the story.[1] As usual I am in a foolish panic about it. But I know I can trust you. You know how I *choose* my words; they can't be changed. And if you don't like it or think it is wrong *just as it is* I'd rather you didn't print it. I'll try to do another.

Will you tell me — if you've time — what you think of it? Again (as usual) I burn to know and you see there is NO ONE here.

It was one of my queer hallucinations; I wrote it straight off. And I've no copy.

I hope you like my little boy. His name is HENNIE.

October 1920

It is such a Heavenly Day that I hardly know how to celebrate it — or rather I keep on celebrating it — having a kind of glorified Mass with full Choir. (But à bas the Roman Catholics!) It's just blue and gold. In the valley two workmen are singing — their voices come *pressing* up, *expanding,* scattering in the light — you know those Italian voices! I think from the sound they are building a house: I am sure the walls will hold this singing for ever, and on every fine day, put your hand there on that curve or that arch, and there'll be a warmth, a faint vibration. . . . The sun woke me at 7 o'clock — sitting sur mes pieds comme un chat d'or mais c'etait moi qui a fait ron-ron. And at 7.15 Marie brought déjeuner — petits pains with miel des Alpes and hot coffee on a fringèd tray. Her old bones were fairly singing, too. I said, "Vous

[1] *The Young Girl.*

allez au marché, Marie?" She said, rather aggrieved — "Mais comme vous voyez, Madame, je suis en train d'y aller" — and then I noticed she was "dressed" for the occasion, *i.e.,* she had flung on her shoulders a most minute black shawl with a tiny bobble fringe. This she always holds over her mouth to guard against le frais du matin when she scuttles off with her panier and filet. She really *is* a superb type.

Good God! There are two lizards rushing up the palm tree! Lizards *glisten,* Heaven bless them. In the trunk of the palm high up some tiny sweet peas are growing and some frail dandelions. I love to see them. As I wrote that, *one* lizard fell — simply fell with a *crash* (about 5000 feet) on to the terrace — and the other *looked* over one of those palm chunks — really it did. I've never seen such an affair. It was Wig that fell — of course. Now she's picked herself up and is flying back. She seems as good as new — but it's a mad thing to do.

October 13, 1920

I am amazed at the sudden "mushroom growth" of cheap psycho-analysis everywhere. *Five* novels one after the other are based on it: it's in everything. And I want to prove it won't do — it's turning Life into a *case.* And yet, of course, I do believe one ought to be able to — not ought — one's novel if it's a good one will be capable of being *proved* scientifically correct. Here — the thing that's happening now is —*the impulse to write is a different impulse.* With an artist — one has to allow — Oh tremendously — for the sub-conscious element in his work. He writes he knows not what — he's *possessed.* I don't mean, of course, always, but when he's *inspired* — as a sort of divine flower to all his terrific hard gardening there comes this sub-conscious . . . wisdom. Now these people who are nuts on analysis seem to me to have *no* sub-conscious at all. They write to *prove* — not to tell the truth. Oh, I am so dull aren't I? I'll stop. I wish they'd stop, tho'! It's such gross impertinence.

Later. I've just been to the Villa Louise, stolen three whopping lemons and had a talk to their jardinier who comes here le vendredi to plant flowers autour du palmier. This man drew a design of the flower bed on the gravel and then, after telling me the names of the flowers, he described them. You know, it was *terrific* to hear him. In trying to describe the scent. . . . " C'est — un — parrr-fum — " and then he threw back his head, put his thumb and finger to his nose — took a *long* breath and suddenly exploded it in a kind of AAAhhh! almost staggering backwards — overcome, almost fainting; and then, in telling me of des paquerettes, " ce sont de tout petite fleurs qui se regardent comme s'ils disent: c'est moi qui est plus jolie que toi! " Oh dear me — I wonder if it *is* so wonderful. I sat down on a bench and felt as though waves of health went flowing through me. To think the man *cares* like that — *responds* — laughs like he does and snips off a rosebud for you while he talks. Then I think of poor busmen and tube men and the ugliness of wet, dark London. It's wrong. People who are at all sensitive ought not to live there. I'll tell you (as it's my birthday to-morrow) a tale about this man. He came to see me. I had to engage him. First he passed me in the garden and went to Marie to ask for Madame Murry. Marie said — " But you've seen her already — " He said: " No — there's only une petite personne — une fillette se quinze ans — enfin — sur la terrasse." Marie thought this a very great joke. Bit steep — wasn't it? I expect I'll be about five by Xmas time — just old enough for a Christmas tree. . . .

Doctor Mee — who was Mother's doctor, too — can't get over my improvement in the last fortnight. He's *staggered*. But he says he does wish you would go to Gamage and buy her a pair of *shoulder straps* — you know the things, I mean. They're to keep me from stooping. I stoop mainly from habit. I feel so much better that I almost have to tie myself to my chaise longue. But I know now is the moment to go slow. Alas, I'm so infernally wise in these things. Oh Heavenly day. I wish you'd shared my boisson — that fresh lemon with a lump of sugar and Saint-Galmier.

Every morning I have a sea-water bath in a saucer and to-day after it, still wet, I stood in the full sun to dry — both windows wide open. One can't help walking about naked in the mornings — one almost *wades* in the air. I'm writing, facing Italy — great mountains, grey-gold with tufts of dark green against a sheer blue sky. Yes, I confess it's hard work to wait for you. Can we hope for more than — how many? — springs and summers. I don't want to miss one.

October 17, 1920

I've just got back from Dr. B. I expect you'd like to know what he's like. He seems to me a very decent, intelligent soul — quite as good as any other doctor. He approved absolutely of my life and conditions of life here and is going to keep an eye on me. The result of his examination was the eternal same. Of course, one can see that the disease is of long standing but there is no reason why — provided — subject to — if — and so on and so on. Not in the least depressing. Yet the foolish creature always does expect the doctor to put down his stethoscope to turn to her and say — with quiet confidence: " I can cure you, Mrs. Murry."

He has the same disease himself. I *recognised* his smile — just the least shade too bright and his strange joyousness as he came to meet one — just the least shade too pronounced his air of being a touch more alive than other people — the gleam — the faint glitter on the plant that the frost has laid a finger on. . . . He is only about 33, and I feel that his experience at the war had changed him. In fact, he seemed to me fully like what a young Duhamel might be. I'm to go on just as I'm going until he sees me again, *i.e.*, half an hour's walk — the rest of the time in my chaise longue. There's really nothing to tell. He had such a charming little old-fashioned photograph in a round frame on his mantelpiece — faded — but so delightful — a girl with her curls pinned back and a velvet ribbon round her throat. . . . His mother, I suppose. This seemed to me more important than all else.

It's 3.30, Sunday afternoon. Marie is out and L. M. has gone off to tea with some cronies and a French poodle. So I have the house to myself. It's a cloudy, windless day. There is such a great stretch of sky to be seen from my terrasse that one's always conscious of the clouds. One forgets that clouds *are* in London and here they are — how shall I put it — they are a changing background to the *silence*. Extraordinary how many planes one can see — one cloud and behind it another and then a lake and on the far side of the lake a mountain. I wonder if you would feed on this visible world as I do. I was looking at some leaves only yesterday — idly looking and suddenly I became conscious of them — of the amazing " freedom " with which they were " drawn " — of the life in each curve — but not as something *outside oneself*, but as part of one — as though like a magician I could put forth my hand and shake a green branch into my fingers from . . . ? And I feel as though one received — accepted — absorbed the beauty of the leaves even into one's physical being. Do you feel like that about things?

Ah, but you would have loved the golden moth that flew in here last night. It had a head like a tiny owl, a body covered with down — wings divided into minute feathers and powdered with gold. I felt it belonged to a poem.

Tomlinson's story was *very* good.[1] It just missed it, though at the end. I mean judging from the Tchekhov standpoint. The thing I prize, admire, and respect in his stories is his knowledge. They are true. I trust him. This is becoming most awfully important to me — a writer *must* have knowledge — he must make one feel the ground is firm beneath his feet. The vapourings I read, the gush, wind — give one a perfect Sehnsucht for something hard to bite on.

I don't know whether it's I that have "fallen behind" in this procession but truly the books I read nowadays astound me. Female writers discovering a freedom, a frankness, a license, to speak their hearts, reveal themselves as . . . sex maniacs. There's not a relationship between a man and woman that isn't the one sexual relationship — at its lowest. *Intimacy* is the sexual act. I am terribly ashamed to tell the truth; it's a very horrible exposure.

October 1920

I return de la Mare's letter. I long to hear of your time with him. It's very queer; he haunts me here — not a persistent or substantial ghost but as one who shares my joy in the *silent world* — joy is not the word, I only used it because it conveys a stillness, a remoteness, because there is a far away sound in it.

You know, I have felt very often lately as though the silence had some meaning beyond these signs, these intimations. Isn't it possible that if one yielded there is a whole world into which one is received? It is so near and yet I am conscious that I hold back from giving myself up to it. What is this something mysterious that waits — that beckons?

[1] *In a Coffee Shop.*

And then suffering, bodily suffering such as I've known for three years. It has changed for ever everything — even the *appearance* of the world is not the same — there is something added. *Everything has its shadow.* Is it right to resist such suffering? Do you know I feel it has been an immense privilege. Yes, in spite of all. How blind we little creatures are! It's only the fairy tales we *really* live by. If we set out upon a journey, the more wonderful the treasure, the greater the temptations and perils to be overcome. And if someone rebels and says, Life isn't good enough on those terms, one can only say: " It *is!* " Don't misunderstand me. I don't mean a " thorn in the flesh " — it's a million times more mysterious. It has taken me three years to understand this — to come to see this. We resist, we are terribly frightened. The little boat enters the dark fearful gulf and our only cry is to escape — " put me on land again." But it's useless. Nobody listens. The shadowy figure rows on. One ought to sit still and uncover one's eyes.

I believe the greatest failing of all is *to be frightened*. Perfect Love casteth our Fear. When I look back on my life all my mistakes have been because I was afraid. . . . Was that why I had to look on death? Would nothing less cure me? You know, one can't help wondering, sometimes. . . . No, not a personal God or any such nonsense. Much more likely — the soul's desperate choice. . . .

P.S. — Can you bring Ribni at Xmas? There is a shop in Nice which cures Poupées cassées. When I read of it I almost telegraphed for Ribni. I want him to be made good as new again. He haunts me — Ah, I can see a story in this idea. . . .

To Sydney and Violet Schiff
Sunday
October 24, 1920

I did not answer your letter at the time because I was ill, and I become utterly weary of confessing it.

Especially as it's the kind of thing one does so hate to hear — one can't really sympathise with. People who are continually crying out are exasperating. And they (or at any rate I) are dreadfully conscious of it.

But now that I have been let out on ticket of leave at least —

I long to write to you. You are never far from my thoughts. Some afternoons I feel positive that the voiture down below there is come from Roquebrune and that in another moment or two you will be here on the terrace. But there is too much to talk about. In London there never seems time. One is always just beginning when one is whirled away again. Here, one is so uninterrupted, it is like one immensely long night and one immensely long day.

But it takes long before the tunes cease revolving in one's head, before the sound of the clapping and the sensation of the crowd ceases to possess one. One cannot hail solitude as one can hail a dark cab. To disentangle oneself completely takes long. . . . Nevertheless, I believe one must do it — and no less — if one wants to work.

To J. M. Murry   *October 1920*

To be free — to be free! That's all I ask. There's nine o'clock striking gently, beautifully from a steeple in the old town. The sound floats across the water. I wish you were here and we were alone. . . . Did I tell you I have a little bookcase made by a carpenter *wot* lives on the hill? He made it most rarely: dovetailed the corners — isn't that right — and cut a little ornament on the top shelves and then painted it pale yellow. 24 francs. His wife sent with it a bouquet of Zinnias, the like of which I've never seen. These people with their only child, a lovely little boy of about five, live in their *own* house with their *own* garden. He seems to work for his own pleasure. Where do they get the money? The little boy who's like an infant St. John wears little white overalls, pink socks and sandals. " Dis bon jour à Madame! Où est ton chapeau! Vite! Ote-le!" and this hissed in a *terrible* voice with rolling eyes by the father. The little boy slowly looks up at his father and gives a very slow ravishing smile.

It's really queer about these people. Marie was saying the mimosa tree *leans* — it's got a list on it — and, of course, prophesying that ("esperons toujours que *non*, Madame, *mais* . . .") it will fall and crush us all. When she described how the tree leant she took the posture — she became a mimosa tree — little black dress trimmed with crepe, white apron, grey hair — changed into a tree.

And this was so *intensely* beautiful that it made me almost weep. It was Art, you know. I *must* get up. The day is still unbroken. One can hear a soft roaring from the sea and that's all.

I've just got the milk book to pay. It's a minute pink *carnet de* ... *appartenant à* ... *commencé le* ... you know the kind, with *broad* lines inside, and on the back the Table de Multiplication — but only up to 6 fois 1 font 6. Doesn't that make you see its real owner?

October 1920

It's very cold here. I have a fire and a rug and a screen. But, of course, the cold is not London cold — it's pure and it's somehow *exciting*. The leaves shake in the garden — the rose buds are very tight shut — there's a kind of whiteness in the sky over the sea. I loved such days when I was a child. I love them here. In fact, I think Mentone must be awfully like N.Z. — but ever so much better. The little milk-girl comes in at a run, letting the gate swing; she has a red stocking tied round her neck. Marie predicts a strike, snow, no food, no fuel and only la volonté de Dieu will save us. But while she drees her weird she begins to laugh and then forgets. A *poor* little cat, terrified, with pink eyes, looked in and begged — and then slunk away. To my joy I hear it dashed into the dining room, seized a poisson on the console and made off with it. Hooray!

What silly little things to tell you — but they make a kind of Life — they are part of a Life that I LOVE. If you were here you'd know what I mean. It's a kind of freedom — a sense of *living* — not enduring — not existing — but being alive. I feel I could have children here for about a farthing each, and dress them in little bits cut off one's own clothes. It wouldn't matter as long as they had feathers in their hats. It's all so EASY.

October 1920

If a thing is important I *have* to put a ☞ hand pointing to it because I know how sleepy you are in the morning and I *imagine* these devilish devices wake you or terrify you (*pleasantly*). Yes, really the papers are disgusting. —— gave Jane Burr a whole column with *Sorel* and *Syndicalism* and any-fresh-fish-to-gut-on-the-problem-of-marriage-is-to-be-welcomed, etc. She makes me feel a very old-fashioned creature. I feel if I met her I should have to say: " And are you one of these *New Women?* "

Did you see that Connie Ediss has had the thyroid gland treatment (she's 50) and is now become 19 and climbs trees. I should just think *she did* climb trees. That seemed to me terribly significant. I remember her singing: " It seemed a bit of all right " years ago. Poor old S. will become a *great climber,* I expect!

I seem a bit silly to-day. It's the wind. I feel inclined to sing,

> "When I was young and had no sense
> I bought a Fiddle for eighteen pence."

Perhaps it was Marie's lunch. A good cook is an amazing thing. And we have *never* had one. I'm interrupted by the electrician who comes to mend a wire. He is a boy of certainly not more than 14 in a blue overall. Just a child standing on the table and fixing wires and turning over tools (rattling them!) in a box. I don't know — The world is changing. He's a *very* nice little boy. He asked Marie pour une échelle. We haven't one. " Donnez-moi une chaise." She brought one, " C'est trop bas. Vous avez une table *solide*" (as tho' none of your fandangles here). But *she* scorns him and made him stand on a newspaper — nearly tied a bib round him.

To Hugh Walpole   *October 27, 1920*

I must answer your letter immediately. It has dropped into the most heavenly fair morning. I wish instead of writing you were here on the terrace and you'd let me talk of your book which I *far* from detested. What an impression to convey! My trouble is I never have enough space to get going — to say what I mean to say — fully. That's no excuse, really. But to be called very unfair — that hurts, awfully, and I feel that by saying so you mean I'm not as honest as I might be. I'm prejudiced. Well, I think we're all of us more or less prejudiced, but cross my heart I don't take reviewing lightly and if I appear to it's the fault of my unfortunate manner.

Now I shall be *dead frank*. And please don't answer. As one writer to another (tho' I'm only a little beginner, and *fully realise* it).

The Captives impressed me as more like a first novel than any genuine first novel I've come across. Of course, there were signs enough that it wasn't one — but the movement of it was the movement of one trying his wings, finding out how they would bear him, how far he could afford to trust them, that you were continually risking yourself, that you had, for the first time, really committed yourself in a book. I wonder if this will seem to you extravagant impertinence. I honoured you for it. You seemed to me determined to shirk nothing. You know that strange sense of insecurity *at the last,* the feeling " I know all this. I know more. I know down to the minutest detail and *perhaps more still,* but shall I dare to trust myself to tell all? " It is really why we write, as I see it, that we may arrive at this moment and yet — it is stepping into the air to yield to it — a kind of anguish and rapture. I felt that you appreciated this, and that, seen in this light, your *Captives* was almost a spiritual exercise in this kind of courage. But in fact your peculiar persistent consciousness of what you wanted to do was what seemed to me to prevent your book from being a creation. That is what I meant when I used the clumsy word " task "; perhaps " experiment " was nearer my meaning. You seemed to lose in passion what you gained in sincerity and therefore " the miracle " didn't happen. I mean the moment when the act of creation takes place — the mysterious change — when you are no longer writing the book, *it* is writing, *it* possesses you. Does that sound hopelessly vague?

But there it is. After reading *The Captives* I laid it down thinking: Having " broken with his past " as he has in this book, having " declared himself," I feel that Hugh Walpole's next novel will be the one to look for. Yes, curse me. I should have said it!

I sympathise more than I can say with your desire to escape from autobiography. Don't you feel that what English writers lack to-day is experience of Life. I don't mean that superficially. But they are self-imprisoned. I think there is a very profound distinction between any kind of *confession* and creative work — not that that rules out the first by any means.

About the parson and his sister. Yes, they *are* truly observed, but they wouldn't come into my review because I didn't think they really came into the book! What was Maggie to them — or they to Maggie? What did they *matter* to Maggie — what was their true relation? I can't see it. I can't see the reason for those two. I can imagine Maggie forgetting them utterly the moment she set foot in London. That their religion was more foreign to her than the other one doesn't need to be told. The point is Maggie never was in Skeaton; she was somewhere else. As to her holiday in that place where everything was green — I never knew what happened on that holiday? The parson's sister — what a story you might have made of her and Paul! (I don't think that Paul's passion for Maggie would have lasted, either. He would have become frightened of her, physically — and terribly ashamed.) Yes, I feel Skeaton could have had a book to itself with Paul's sister — getting old you know, her descent into old age, her fears increasing, and then something like the Uncle Matthew affair breaking into her life. . . .

And I stick to what I said about Caroline. Yes, you might have trusted Caroline, but a young female wouldn't. If Caroline had come to her father's door Maggie would have *stiffened,* have been on her guard immediately. As to trusting her with a letter to Martin — never!

Some of their love making was very beautiful — it had that tragic, youthful quality.

But enough. Forgive this long letter. I'll try to see more round the books. I've no doubt at all I'm a bad reviewer. Your letter made me want to shake hands with you across the vast.

I hope this isn't too illegible. But I'm rather a feeble creature in a chaise longue.

To J. M. Murry   *October 1920*

I am exceedingly glad you joined hands with the Oxford Professori. *The Daily Mail* FOAMED to-day on the subject. It almost went so far as to say the library at Liège and such acts of burning were by Professors only. It — but let it pass! In the *Times* I noted a book by a Doctor Schinz — not a good book, but the *Times* noticed it as though Schinz were kneeling on Podsnap's doormat. Faugh!

How long *can* it go on! You know whenever I go away I realise that it has happened. The change has *come*. Nothing *is* the same. I positively feel one has no right to run a paper without preaching a gospel. (I know you do, but I mean with all the force of one's soul.) I get an evangelist feeling, when I read Fashion News in the *D.M.* and then Strike News and Irish News and so many thousands out of work. But above and beyond that I realise the " spiritual temper " of the world. I feel as though the step *has* been taken — we *are* over the edge. Is it fantastic? Who is going to *pull us up?* I certainly had no end of an admiration for L. G. but then he's capable of that speech on reprisals — which really was a vile speech from a " statesman." It was perfectly obvious he had no intention of saying what he did when he got up to speak — he was carried away. It *is* all over really. That's why I shall be so thankful when you pack your rucksack and come over here. The only sort of paper for the time is an out and out *personal, dead true, dead sincere* paper in which we spoke our HEARTS and MINDS.

You know there are moments when I want to make an appeal to all our generation who do believe that the war has changed everything to come forward and let's start a crusade. But I know, darling, I am not a crusader and it's my job to dwell apart and write my best for those that come after.

Does your *soul* trouble you? Mine does. I feel that only now (October 1920) do I desire to be saved. I realise what salvation means and I long for it. Of course, I am not speaking as a Christian or about a personal God, But the feeling is . . . I believe (and VERY MUCH); help thou my unbelief. But it's to myself I cry — to the spirit, the essence of me — that which lives in Beauty. Oh, these *words*. And yet I should be able to explain. But I'm impatient with you. I always " know you understand and take it for granted." But just very lately I seem to have seen my whole past — to have gone through it — to have emerged, very weak and very new. The soil (which wasn't at all fragrant) has at last produced something which isn't a weed but which I do believe (after Heaven knows how many false alarms) is from the seed which was sown. But it's taken 32 years in the dark. . . .

And I *long* for goodness — to live by what is permanent in the soul.

It all sounds vague. You may wonder what induces me to write this. But as I walked up and down outside the house this evening the clouds heaped on the horizon — noble, shining clouds, the deep blue waves — they set me thinking again.

October 1920

I would have enjoyed Goodyear pa-man. I remember giving F. G. my photo and he telling me his father had said it was a *fine head*. I remember how he laughed and so did I — and I said " I shall have to grow a pair of horns and have it stuffed to hang on Murry's door." When I recall Goodyear I can't believe he is — nowhere — just as when I recall Chummie he comes before me, *warm,* laughing, saying " Oh, abso*lu*tely." What a darling boy he was!

I love this place more and more. One is conscious of it as I used to be conscious of New Zealand. I mean if I went for a walk there and lay down under a pine tree and looked up at the wispy clouds through the branches I came home plus the pine tree — don't you know? Here it's just the same. I go for a walk and I watch the butterflies in the heliotrope and the young bees and some old bumble ones and all these things are added unto me. Why I don't feel like this in England Heaven knows. But my light goes out in England, or it's a very small and miserable shiner.

This isn't a letter. It's just a note. Yes. I shall provide small pink carnets for our accounts at Xmas. Slates, too, with holes burnt in them for the sponge string. Did you ever burn a hole in the frame? Thrilling deed. It was Barry Waters' speciality, with his initials burnt, too — and a trimming. I can see it now.

Saturday
October 30, 1920

Your Tuesday letter came, telling me that you were reading Mrs. Asquith. I read certain parts of her book and felt — just that — there *was* something decent. At the same time the whole book seems to me *in*-decent. Perhaps I feel more than anything that she's one of those people who have no past and no future. She's capable of her girlish pranks and follies to-day — in fact, she's at the mercy of herself now and for ever as she was then. *And that's bad*. We only live by somehow absorbing the past — changing it. I mean really examining it and dividing what is important from what is not (for there IS waste) and transforming it so that it becomes part of the life of the spirit and we are *free of it*. It's no longer our personal past, it's just in the highest possible sense, our servant. I mean that it is no longer our master.[1] With Mrs. A. this process (by which the artist and the "living being" lives) never takes place. She is for ever driven.

"I am the Cup that thirsteth for the Wine" —

These half-people are very queer — very tragic, really. They are neither simple — nor are they artists. They are between the two and yet they have the desires (no, appetites) of both. I believe their *secret whisper* is: 'If only I had found THE MAN I might have been anything . . ." But the man isn't born and so they turn to life and parade and preen and confess and dare — and lavish themselves on what they call *Life* "Come woo me — woo me." How often I've *seen* that in —— as her restless distracted glance swept the whole green country-side. . . .

(By the way, I do love Sir Toby's saying to Viola, " Come *taste your legs,* Sir. Put them in motion," when he wanted her to leap and fly. I wish I had a little tiny boy to say that to.)

There's a violent N.W. wind to-day — a howling one — I had to go into town. The great immense waves were sweeping right up to the road and over. I wish you'd seen them. Three brigs are in — the sailors' pants hanging on lines and dancing hornpipes. Leaves are falling; it's like autumn. But the shops are full of flowers and everywhere little girls, wrapped up to the eyes, go by at a run carrying a bouquet of chrysanthemums in a paper — For to-morrow is Le Toussaint.

October 1920

You say you would " dearly love to know exactly what I feel " — I thought I had told you. But my writing is so bad, my expression so vague that I expect I didn't make myself clear. I'll try to —

---

[1] That is the wrong image. I used to think this process was fairly *unconscious*. Now I feel just the contrary. (K. M.'s note.)

What a book is hidden here!

> "Between the acting of a dreadful thing
> And the first motion, all the interim is
> Like a phantasma or a dreadful dream;
> The genius and the mortal instruments
> Are then in council; and the state of man
> Like to a little Kingdom suffers then
> The nature of an insurrection."

The "thing" was not always "dreadful" neither was the "dream," and you must substitute "spirit" for genius — otherwise there you have my life as I see it up till now — complete with all the alarms, enthusiasms, terrors, excitements — in fact the nature of an insurrection.

I've been dimly aware of it many times — I've had moments when it has seemed to me that this wasn't what my little Kingdom ought to be like — yes, and longings and regrets. But only since I came away this time have I *fully realised* it — confronted myself as it were, looked squarely at the extraordinary "conditions" of my existence.

... It wasn't flattering or pleasant or easy. I expect your sins are of the subconscious; they are easier to forgive than mine. I've *acted* my sins, and then excused them or put them away with "it doesn't do to think about these things" or (more often) "it was all experience." But it hasn't ALL been experience. There IS waste — destruction, too. So I confronted myself. As I write I falsify slightly. I can't help it; it's all so difficult. The whole thing was so much *deeper* and more *difficult* than I've described it — *subtler* — less conscious and more conscious if you know what I mean. I didn't walk up and down the room and groan, you know. As I am talking to you I'll dare say it all took place on another plane, because then we can smile at the description and yet mean something by it.

And I don't want to imply that the Battle is over and here I am victorious. I've escaped from my enemies — emerged — that is as far as I've got. But it is a different state of being to any I've known before and if I were to sin now — it would be mortal.

There. Forgive this rambling involved statement.

Monday. Midi: waiting for lunch. "En tirant la langue comme un chien" as they say here.

It's simply heavenly here to-day — warm, still, with wisps of cloud just here and there and le ciel deep blue. Everything is expanding and growing after the rain; the buds on the tea roses are so exquisite that one feels quite faint regarding them. A pink rose, "chinesy pink" in my mind, is out — there are multitudes of flowers and buds. And the freezias are up and the tangerines are turning. A painter whose ladder I see against the house across the valley has been singing ancient Church music — awfully complicated stuff. But what a choice! How much more suited to the day and the hour than — and now, I'm dished. For every song I wanted to find ridiculous seems somehow charming and appropriate and quite equally lovable.

> I put more whitewash on the old woman's face
> Than I did on the gar — den wall!

— for instance. That seems to me a thoroughly good song. You know the first two lines are:

> Up an' down, up an' down, in an' out the window
> I did no good at all.

Sam Mayo used to sing it. Things weren't so bad in those days. I really believe everything was better. The tide of barbarism wasn't flowing in.

I was all wrong about the house painter!! He's just come back from lunch — in a grey flannel suit — put on his overall and started singing in English! Elizabethan airs. He must be some sensible fellow who's taken the little house and is doing the job himself. He makes me think of you — but his singing is different — more difficult. . . .

Dream I.

I was living at home again in the room with the fire-escape. It was night: Father and Mother in bed. Vile people came into my room. They were drunk. B. led them. "You don't take me in, old dear," said she. "You've played the Lady once too often, Miss — coming it over me." And she shouted, screamed *Femme marquée* and banged the table. I rushed away. I was going away next morning so I decided to spend the night in the dark streets and went to a theatre in Piccadilly Circus. The play, a costume play of the

Restoration, had just begun. The theatre was small and packed. Suddenly the people began to speak too slowly, to mumble: they looked at each other stupidly. One by one they *drifted* off the stage and very slowly a black iron curtain was lowered. The people in the audience *looked* at one another. Very slowly, silently, they got up and moved towards the doors — stole away.

An enormous crowd filled the Circus: it was black with people. They were not speaking — a low murmur came from it — that was all. They were still. A white-faced man looked over his shoulder and *trying to smile* he said: " The Heavens are changing already; there are six moons! "

Then I realised that *our* earth had come to an end. I looked up. The sky was ashy-green; six livid quarters swam in it. A very fine soft ash began to fall. The crowd parted. A cart drawn by two small black horses appeared. Inside there were Salvation Army women doling tracts out of huge marked boxes. They gave me one! " Are you corrupted? "

It got very dark and quiet and the ash fell faster. Nobody moved.

Dream II.

In a café G. met me. " Katherine, you must come to my table. I've got Oscar Wilde there. He's the most marvellous man I ever met. He's splendid! " G. was flushed. When he spoke of Wilde he began to cry — tears hung on his lashes, but he smiled.

Oscar Wilde was very shabby. He wore a green overcoat. He kept tossing and tossing back his long greasy hair with the whitest hand. When he met me he said: " Oh Katherine! " — very affected.

But I did find him a fascinating talker. So much so that I asked him to come to my home. He said would 12.30 to-night do? When I arrived home it seemed madness to have asked him. Father and Mother were in bed. What if Father came down and found that chap Wilde in one of the chintz armchairs? Too late now. I waited by the door. He came with Lady M. I saw he was disgustingly pleased to have brought her. He said, " Katherine's hand — the same gentle hand! " as he took mine. But again when we sat down — I couldn't help it. He *was* attractive — as a curiosity. He was fatuous *and* brilliant!

"You know, Katherine, when I was *in that dreadful place* I was haunted by the memory of a *cake*. It used to float in the air before me — a little delicate thing *stuffed* with cream and with the cream there was something *scarlet*. It was made of pastry and I used to call it my little Arabian Nights cake. But I don't remember the name. Oh, Katherine, it was *torture*. It used to *hang* in the air and *smile* at me. And every time I resolved that next time *they let someone* come and see me I would ask them to tell me what it was but every time, Katherine, I was *ashamed*. Even now . . ."

I said, "Mille feuilles à la crême?"

At that he turned round in the armchair and began to sob, and M., who carried a parasol, opened it and put it over him. . . .

I'm not up to much to-day. Yesterday was dark and stormy: to-day is too. And in spite of my feelings the weather affects me physically. I fly so high that when I go down — it's a drop. Nothing serious; just a touch of cold, but with it to "bear it company" a black mood. Don't pay any attention to it. I expect it will have lifted utterly by the time this reaches you. And it's really caused by a queer kind of *pressure* — which is work to be done. *I am writing* — do you know the feeling? — and until this story is finished I am engulfed. It's not a tragic story either — but there you are. It seizes me — swallows me completely. I am Jonah in the whale and only you could charm that old whale to disgorge me. Your letters did for a minute but now I'm in again and we're thrashing through deep water. I fully realise it. It's the price we have to pay — we writers. I'm lost — gone — possessed and everybody who comes near is my enemy.

8.35 P.M.
November 3, 1920

Here it is under my hand — finished — another story about as long as *The Man Without a Temperament* — perhaps longer. It's called *The Stranger,* a "New Zealand" story. My depression has gone; so it was just this. And now it's here, thank God — and the fire burns and it's warm and tho' the wind is howling — it can howl. What a QUEER business writing is! I don't know. I don't believe other people are ever as foolishly excited as I am while I'm working. How could they be? Writers would have to live in trees. I've *been* this man, *been* this woman. I've stood for hours on the Auckland Wharf. I've been out in the stream waiting to be berthed — I've been a seagull hovering at the stern and a hotel porter whistling through his teeth. It isn't as though one sits and watches the spectacle. That would be thrilling enough, God knows. But one IS the spectacle for the time. If one remained oneself all the time like some writers can it would be a bit less exhausting. It's a lightning change affair, tho'. But what does it matter! I'll keep this story for you to read at Xmas. I only want to give it to you now. Accept my new story. Give it your blessing.

To Sydney Schiff   *November 4, 1920*

Yes, there are weak spots in *A Gift from the Dusk* but compared to the unworthy, stupifying, *untruthful* rubbish of to-day it did not do, I felt, to comment on them. The worst of it is, nowadays, that the majority of novels is so bad one becomes almost fearful of the strength of one's feeling for a " good " one. There were touches in that book that moved me tremendously. I felt that in the intimacy between Stephen and Mary — Prowse was, many times, speaking a language which I long in vain to hear spoken. The intimacy of two beings who are *essential* to each other — who is going to write that? And yet Love that is less than that — one wearies of hearing of it.

I wish there were six or seven writers who wrote for themselves and let the world go hang. But where are they?

To J. M. Murry   *Thursday*
         November 4, 1920

Thursday: I had about 1 inch of mouse's tail from you to-day, but it was the gay and wavy end so it didn't matter. 'Twas writ on Monday. . . . There's a debonair wind blowing to-day and a very pale, faint, jonquil sun. I send you Hugh Walpole's letter. He seems to me most awfully nice; and it is in reply to one which I sent him telling him what I really *did* think of his book — I mean as man to man — I said: "Just for once I'll be *dead frank*" and you know what that means. But I felt nobody else ever would and it was an opportunity. Besides his letter somehow called for one's deep sincerity. And instead of sending mine back with "This is outrageous" — he replies — so gently.

W. wrote yesterday too — touched one's heart. His wife has been very ill, she's had an operation and so on, and poor old W. is shattered. . . . His letter has actually "by the Grace of God" and "D. V." in it. What old Death can't shake out of us! But it's very touching to know how frail is one's hold on Picture Galleries and Editions de Luxe.

If the Last Trump ever *did* sound — would it frighten US? I don't think it would in the least. If God didn't take us both into Heaven I'd rather be in Hell and out of sight of anyone so stupid.

(I told poor old L. M. yesterday that after I died to PROVE there was no immortality I would send her a coffin worm in a match box. She was gravely puzzled.)

Friday
November 5, 1920

Oh, by the way, I had my photo taken yesterday — for a surprise for you. I'll only get des épreuves on Monday tho'. I should think it ought to be extraordinary. The photographer took off my head and then balanced it on my shoulders again at all kinds of angles as tho' it were what Violet would call an art pot. "Ne bougez PAS en souriant leggerreMENT — Bouche CLOSE." A kind of drill. Those penny studios fascinate me. I must put a story in one one day. They are the most *temporary shelters* on earth. Why is there always a dead bicycle behind a velvet curtain? Why does one always sit on a faded piano stool? And then, the plaster pillar, the basket of paper flowers, the storm background — and the *smell*. I love such endroits.

November 1920

I am awfully excited to-day. It's for this reason. I have made an offer to J. for this villa for one year from May 1st next and tho' the offer has not been accepted it has also not been refused.

Chances are even. *Oh dear, what torture!* Perhaps you don't know that my feelings towards this villa are so fearfully intense that I think I shall have to be evicted if she doesn't give it to me. It's the first real home of my own I have ever loved. Pauline — yes, it wasn't home tho', neither was Runcton, not even Hampstead. Not really, not with this thrill. This little place is and always will be for me — the one and only place, I feel. My heart beats for it as it beats for Karori. Isn't it awful? And for US it is made in every single particular. True there's no salle de bain. But there's a huge saucer bath and a spung as big as me. So what matters! The divine incomparable situation is the trick, I suppose. Heaven from dawn to dawn. Walking on the terrace by starlight looking through my vieux palmier I could weep for joy — running into the garden to see how many more buds are out in the morning is to run straight at — into — a blessing. The fires all burn — but not frightfully — the doors shut — the kitchen is big and the larder is down 10 steps that send a chill to one's knees. The garde-linge is immense, all fitted with cupboards and shelves. The luggage is kept there and the umbrellas and the flags that flew at my gate on the 11th. One gets one's parasol from the garde-linge. Your feltie would be there, too. There's enough garden for you to bien gratter in. At the back we could grow veg. In fack, it is the dearest, most ideal little corner. And private — just the next thing to an island.

Hold thumbs for me. Truly this is a great turning point. I'm trying to be calm, but it's not easy with such bliss in the balance — I had to offer an immense sum — 6000 francs.

Am I a little bit mad? You will find ISOLA BELLA in poker work on my heart. The baths are only ten minutes away from you in the summer, sea baths with splash boards — no, spring boards for you to plop off. I wait outside with a bun for you with big currant eyes (the bun I mean!).

November 1920

I've just finished a story called *The Ladies' Maid* which I'm sending for the paper. I do hope you will care to print it. It's what I meant when I said a Xmas story. Dear knows, Xmas doesn't come in it after all and you may think I'm a fraud. But I think, all the same, people might like to read it at Xmas time. The number of letters I've had about *Miss Brill!* I think I am very fortunate to have people like my stories — don't you? But I must say it does surprise me. *This* one I'd like you and de la Mare to like — other people don't matter.

It's *hell* to know one could do so much and be bound to journalism for bread. If I was a proper journalist I'd give the day to reviewing and so on — but no! Reviewing is on my chest — AND a sense of GUILT the whole week! However it can't be helped. I'll win out and then I don't want to read another novel for ——

But isn't it grim to be reviewing Benson when one might be writing one's own stories which one will never have time to write, on the best showing!

Personally I want to make money by my stories *now* — I can't live poor — can't worry about butter and cabs and woollen dresses and the chemist's bill and work too. I don't want to *live rich* — God forbid — but I must be free — and ça coûte cher aujourd'hui.

The story will go to you Wednesday morning. A typist has been found at 7 francs a 1000. *I* think she is mad as well. But I can't afford not to send corrected copies.

What a horrible note this is. And there's the evening star, like an emerald hanging over the palm. Forgive me, evening star. These are only sparks on my coat — they are not my real fur. But the ancien couteau burns faintly in my left lung to-night — and that makes me wicked. Wicked, but loving.

November 1920

Always examine *both sides.* In my house both sides are buttered.

Re your review of Mrs. Asquith. I thought it was *very good* but ... your feeling was really contained in your words: "The type it reveals is not very intriguing." She isn't your game. When all is said and done I feel that *you* haven't time for her and you don't care a Farthing Taster whether she made her horse walk upstairs or downstairs or in my lady's chamber. She would *weary* you. What is there really to get hold of? There's — nothing — in the sense you mean. The direct method (no, I can't for the life of me "see" the other) of examining the specimen isn't really much good except in so far as one can ... make certain deductions —

discover certain main weaknesses and falsities. But it's a bit like trying to operate on a diseased *mind* by cutting open a brain. The devil is — Oh the very devil is that you may remove every trace of anything that shouldn't be there and make no end of a job of it and then in her case, in the case of all such women — the light comes back into the patient's eyes and with it the vaguest of vague elusive *maddening* smiles. . . . Do you know what I mean? Here's, I think, the root of the matter. What IS Insensitiveness? We know or we could find out by examination what it is NOT but it seems to me the quality hasn't been discovered yet. I mean its *x* — it's a subject for research. It most certainly isn't only the *lack* of certain qualities: it's a kind of *positive unknown*. Does all this sound most awful nonsense to you? My vocabulary is awful, but I mean well and I faint, I thirst to talk. My landscape is terribly exciting at present. I never knew it contained such features or such fauna (they are animals various, aren't they?). But I do want a gentleman prepared to pay his own exes, to join me in my expedition. Oh, won't YOU come? No one else will do. But when you do it's a bit sickening —all my wild beasts get a bit funny-looking — they don't look such serious monsters any more. Instead of lions and tigers it's apt to turn into an affair of:

" The turkey ran pas' with a flag in his mas'
An' cried out: ' What's the mattah? ' "

Not that I think for one minute that you don't treat me au GRAND serieux or would dare to question my intelligence, of course not. All the same — there you are — Alone, I'm no end of a fillasoafer but once you join me in the middle of my seriousness — my deadly seriousness — I see the piece of pink wool I have put on your hair (and that you don't know is there).

I sometimes wonder whether the act of surrender is not one of the greatest of all — the highest. It is one of the (most) difficult of all. Can it be accomplished or even apprehended except by the *aristocrats* of this world? You see it's so immensely complicated. It " needs " real humility and at the same time an absolute belief in one's own essential freedom. It is an act of faith. At the last moments like all great acts it is *pure risk*. This is true for me as a human being and as a writer. Dear Heaven how hard it is to let go — to slip into the blue. And yet one's creative life depends on it and one *desires* to do nothing else. I shouldn't have begun on this in the corner of a letter, darling. It's not the place.

Letters 1920

To Richard Murry   *November 1920*

It's 7.15 A.M. and I've just had breakfast in a room lit with great gorse yellow patches of sunlight. Across one patch there's a feathery pattern that dances — that's from the mimosa tree outside. The two long windows are wide open — they are the kind that open in half — with wings, you know — so much more generous than the English kind. A wasp is paddling his pettitoes in the honey-glass and the sky is a sort of pale lapus lazuli. Big glancing silver ducks of light dive in and out of the sea.

This kind of weather has gone on for over a week without one single pause. I take a sun bath every morning — *costume de bain:* a black paper fan — and it has an awfully queer effect on one. I mean all this radiance has. You know those rare moments when it's warm enough to lie on your back and bask — it's a kind of prolongation of that. One tries to behave like a sober sensible creature and to say " thank you " to the postman and " no thank you " to the umbrella mender but all the time one is hiding broad beams. So I slink away out of sight of everybody, down the steps from the terrace and stand underneath a tree called a datura and there, privately, I gloat. This tree, Sir, is a sight for you. It has small, close, grey-green leaves; the buds in their first stage are soft green pods. They open and the flower, lightly folded, springs out and gradually it opens into a long bell-like trumpet about 8 inches long — gold coloured with touches of pale red. But the drawing in the buds and the petals! The gaiety of the edges — the freedom with which Papa Cosmos has let himself go on them! I have looked at this tree so long that it is transplanted to some part of my brain — for a further transplanting into a story one day.

You must come here one day, and live here for a bit. I don't see how you couldn't be happy. I appreciate your feeling that you would not care to work on a large canvas in England. I feel just the same about writing. I'm always afraid my feelings won't last long enough for me to have expressed all that I wanted to. There's something in the atmosphere which *may* blow cold. And there's always a sense of rush — a strain. If the Muse does deign to visit me I'm conscious all the time that she's got her eye on the clock, she's catching the funicular to Olympus at 5.30 or the special to

Parnassus at 5.15. Whereas here, one begins to tell the time by the skies again.

As for little K. M., she's a-going it as usual. The more I do the more I *want* to do, it will always be the same. The further one climbs the more tops of mountains one sees. But it's a matter for rejoicing — as long as one can keep the coffin from the door. I don't care a pin about the old *wolf*. I must get up and take the earwigs out of the roses. Why should they choose roses? But they do and I go against Nature in casting them forth.

November 1920

What you quote from Van Gogh is *very fine*.[1] I would give you it's twin sentence if I had Tchekhov's letters here. Tchekhov felt just *like that*. I, too, suspect and don't feel comfortable in this " art life." What I mean is when C. used to write me endless pages about good and bad art I always wanted to hang my head because I felt she wasn't *working*. She wasn't really *getting down to it* — (don't misunderstand me) humbly.

I don't believe there are any short cuts to Art. Victory is the reward of battle just exactly as it is in Life. And the more one knows of one's " soldiers " the better chance one has. That's not an absolutely true analogy tho'. The thing is more subtle.

But what I do believe with my whole soul is that one's *outlook* is the climate in which one's art either thrives or doesn't grow. I am dead certain that there is no separating Art and Life. And no artist can afford to leave out Life. If we mean to work we must go straight to Life for our nourishment. There's no substitute. But I am violent on this subjick. I must leave it.

I am stuck in bed — by my old doctor who says I must stay here another week at least. Pity poor little K. I hate bed. I shall never go to bed in Heaven or eat anything off a tray. If a cherubim and a seraphim come winging their way towards me with some toast and jelly I shall pop like a chestnut into Hell and be roasted.

[1] " . . . Nevertheless I find in my work a certain reverberation of what fascinated me. I know that Nature told me something, that she spoke to me, and that I took down her message in shorthand. Perhaps my transcript contains words that are undecipherable; belike there are faults and omissions in it too, — still it may possess something that the wood, the beach or the figures said."

To J. M. Murry

About the punctuation in *The Stranger*. No, my dash isn't quite a feminine dash. (Certainly when I was young it was.) But it was intentional in that story. I was trying to do away with the three dots. They have been so abused by female and male writers that I fight shy of them — *much* tho' I need them. The truth is — punctuation is infernally difficult. If I had time I'd like to write an open letter to the *A*. on the subject. It's boundaries need to be enlarged. But I won't go into it now. I'll try, however, to remember *commas*. It's a fascinating subject, ça, one that I'd like to talk over with you. If only there was time I'd write all one wants to write. There seems less and less time. And more and more books arrive. That's not a complaint. But it *is* rather cursed that we should have to worry about —— —— when we might be writing our own books — isn't it?

And about *Poison*[1] I could write about that for pages. But I'll try and condense what I've got to say. The story is told by (evidently) a worldly, rather cynical (not wholly cynical) man *against* himself (but not altogether) when he was so absurdly young. You know how young by his idea of what woman is. She has been up to now, only the *vision,* only she who passes. You realise that? And here he has put all his passion into this Beatrice. It's *promiscuous* love, not understood as such by him; perfectly understood as such by her. But you realise the vie de luxe they are living — the very table — sweets, liqueurs, lilies, pearls. And you realise? she expects a letter from someone calling her away? *Fully* expects it? That accounts for her farewell AND her declaration. And when it doesn't come even her *commonness* peeps out — the newspaper touch of such a woman. She can't disguise her chagrin. She gives herself away. . . . He, of course, laughs at it now, and laughs at her. Take what he says about her " sense of order " and the crocodile. But he also regrets the self who, dead privately, would have been young enough to have actually wanted to *Marry* such a woman. But I meant it to be light — tossed off — and yet through it — Oh, subtly — the lament for youthful belief. These are the rapid confessions one receives sometimes from a glove or a cigarette or a hat.

[1] See *Something Childish*, p. 250.

To Sydney Schiff *December 1, 1920*

About the Russians. I agree that translations are perfectly terrible. The peculiar *flatness* of them is so strange and it's just that flatness which the story or whatever it is mustn't have — One feels it's superimposed. And yet — and yet — though I hate to agree with so many silly critics I confess that Tchekhov does seem to me a marvellous writer. I do think a story like *In Exile* or *Missing* is frankly incomparable. (It's years since I read de Maupassant: I must read him again) — And then Tolstoy — well, you know, Anna's journey in the train when she finds Vronsky is travelling to St. Petersburg too and the whole figure of Anna — when I think how real, how vital, how vivid she is to me — I feel I can't be grateful enough to Tolstoy — by grateful — I mean full of praise to him for his works.

Will you lend me Marcel Proust when you come out this time? I don't feel qualified to speak of him.

I wonder what you'll think of this little Isola Bella. It's very small. The windows have got little cotton velveteen trousers put up by me in place of the dreadful little chemises that hung there on my arrival. And I have an old servant, a butter and sugar thief — who is an *artist* in her way — a *joy*. Her feeling for hot plates and for what dear Henry James might call the *real right* gravy is supreme. These things are so important. I don't think I could love a person who liked gravylene or browno or whatever they call it.

To J. M. Murry *December 1920*

Yesterday I had your letter *re* the finances of the *A*. Really, there is nothing to be said. —— has sat on the poor egg to some purpose. . . . The picture of you was lifelike. Your very legs were under the table. I would have known them among a million pairs. But you have a terrible pen for these small drawings. Dear! dear! they are so pathetical. When Mother came back from Switzerland, 1894, she bought me a tie-pin made like a violet and one shut one's eye and looked through it at the Lion of Lucerne!! Your tie-pins all are made of a diamond that's really a tear-drop. I shut one eye and look through at my own own little Lion — and my heart *faints* to see his sweet mane all in knots over his sums.

It's still freezing cold. Oh, I do feel the cold most cruelly. I *cannot* keep warm. Blankets over my knees, two pairs of everything that one has two of, a fire, soup — nothing saves me. And as soon as the sun so much as shakes his fiery head I feel better. Bogey, when I leave here, it will be to go farther south.

I confess since I've been away this time my need or my wish for people has absolutely fled. I don't know what it is to be *lonely,* and I love to be *solitary.*

If my book is to be reviewed in the paper, who is to do it? May I have a say? Of course you can't, and I don't want —— to, because I don't like her work at all at all at all. I'd prefer to have it done by someone who'll — oh, I don't know — Santayana, I prefer. Now I'm not being serious. I mean of course, that's only my wicked preference. But his idea of friendship and mine are alike — that *is* beaucoup, isn't it?

Did you read in the *Times* that Shelley left on his table a bit of paper with a blot on it and a flung down quill? Mary S. *had a glass case* put over same and carried it all the way to London *on her knees.* Did you ever *hear* such rubbish!! That's her final give away for me. Did she keep it on her knees while she ate her sandwiches — Did everybody know? Oh — *didn't* they just. I've done with her.

December 1920

Il fait beau, aujourd'hui. I am sitting in my long chair on the terrace. The wind of the last days has scattered almost the last of the fig leaves and now through those candle-shaped boughs I love so much there is a beautiful glimpse of the old town. Some fowls are making no end of a noise. I've just been for a walk on my small boulevard and looking down below at the houses all bright in the sun and housewives washing their linen in great tubs of glittering water and flinging it over the orange trees to dry. Perhaps all human activity is beautiful in the sunlight. Certainly these women lifting their arms, turning to the sun to shake out the wet clothes were supremely beautiful. I couldn't help feeling — and after they have lived they will die and it won't matter. It will be all right; they won't regret it.

A small, slender bird is pecking the blue bayberries. Birds are much milder here, much quicker, properly on the qui vive, you know. . . . Do you mind? I've done with England. I don't even want to see England again. Is that awful? I feel it is rather. I know you will always want to go back. I am collecting possessions at an awful rate. All my pennies go on them. . . . But they are all movables. They can all be carried up the mountains. Wander with me 10 years — will you? Ten years in the sun. It's not long — only 10 springs. If I manage to live for 10 years I don't think I'd mind dying at 42. . . . But as to starting a theatre for ——'s to come to — Lord, Lord — not I.

I suppose I haven't brought it off in *Poison*. It wanted a light, light hand — and then with that newspaper a sudden . . . let me see, *lowering* of it all — just what happens in promiscuous love after passion. A glimpse of staleness. And the story is told by the man who gives himself away and hides his traces at the same moment.

I realise it's quite a different kind to *Miss Brill* or *The Young Girl*. (She's not " little "; in fact, I saw her big, slender, like a colt.)

Will you tell me if you see my point at all? or do you still feel it's no go?

Here is an inside and an outside photograph of me in and out of my Isola Bella. Would you like some more? I have more here if you'd like them. And shall I tell you the conversation which just went on between Marie and the carpet woman? Oh, no, it's not interesting really without the voices. Even old Marie *attend Monsieur* now. " J'ai l'idée, Madame, d'acheter une belle tranche de veau — *alors* de faire une poche dedans et de la farcer avec un peu de jambon — *un* oeuf — " and so on and on and on — the song becoming more and more triumphant and ending " *mais* peut-être il vaudrait mieux que nous attendons l'arrivée de Monsieur pour ÇA. En effet un bon plat de nouilles est toujours un bon plat," and then she puts her head on one side and says, " Monsieur aime le veau? "

Pleased to tell you mice have made a nest in my old letters to

L. M. Would that I could always be certain of such behaviour. The mice in this house are upstarts.

To the Hon. Dorothy Brett   *December 22, 1920*

I wonder where you will be for Christmas. Having M. with me has turned it into a fête. My treasured Marie is determined that Christmas shall be kept well and bought The Mistletoe all in readiness for the arrival of Monsieur. The Kitchen is a progression of still lives from a poor dead bird leaning its tired head on a tuft of water-cress (oh, how awful it looks!) onwards. And because the weather is chill, blue and white weather, log fires roar in the chimleys. This little house is a perfect darling. It's not beautiful, it's shabby and the bedroom wall paper is baskets of pink flowers and in the dining room there is a big corpse of a clock that sometimes at dreadful intervals and for no reason begins to *chime* — never to tick. But there is a feeling over everything as though it were a real resting-place. I have taken it until the end of 1922 and even so I'm frightened at the idea of saying goodbye to it then. I love this country, too, more and more. It is winter now — many trees are bare, but the oranges, tangerines and lemons are all ripe; they burn in this clear atmosphere — the lemons with gentle flames, the tangerines with bright flashes, and the oranges sombre. My tiny peach tree still clings to a few exquisite leaves — curved like peaches — and the violets are just beginning.

More and more (for how long? no matter. A moment is for ever) one lives — really lives. . . .

Are you childish about the New Year? Do you feel it is a mystery and that if your friends wish you a happy one — happiness does come beating its beautiful wings out of the darkness towards you?

To Anne Estelle Rice   *December 26, 1920*

The parcel arrived on Xmas morning but it was a separate fête by itself, just your letter and the two enchanting sketches. I love them, Anne. They remind me of our spring together and the laburnum seems hung with little laughs. If you knew how often

I think of that time at Looe, our picnic, the white-eyed kaffir, the midget infant hurling large pieces of Cornwall into the sea on the beach that afternoon! It's all as clear as to-day.

But you know, don't you? that all the times we have ever spent together are clear like that. And here — I am always sending you greetings, always sharing things with you. I salute you in tangerines and the curved petals of *roses-thé* and the crocus colour of the sea and in the moonlight on the *poire sauvage*. Many, many other things. It will *always* be so with me, however seldom I see you. I shall just go on rejoicing in the fact of you. And loving you and feeling in that family where Monsieur Le Beau Soleil est notre père nous sommes des sœurs.

I am still hard at the story-writing and still feeling that only now do I begin to see what I want to do. I am sending you my book. It is not a good one. I promise the next will be better but I just wanted you to have a copy. Living solitary these last months with a servant who is a born artist and says, " Un ou deux bananes font plus *intrigant* le compotier," and who returns from market with a basket, which just to see on the kitchen table is *food* for the day, makes work a great deal easier to get at. The *strain* is removed. At last one doesn't worry any more. And fancy one's domestique having an idea of what work is! She won't even let a person talk at the front door if I am working. She whispers to them to go to la porte de la cuisine . . . " parceque c'est très énervant pour Madame d'entendre causer quelqu'un pendant qu'elle travaille! " It's like being in heaven with an ange gardienne.

To Richard Murry   January 1, 1921

I have written a huge long story of a rather new kind.[1] It's the outcome of the *Prelude* method — it just unfolds and opens — But I hope it's an advance on *Prelude*. In fact, I know it's that because the technique is stronger — It's a queer tale, though. I hope you'll like it. . . .

We had a marvellous drive up into the mountains here the other day to a very ancient small village called Castellar. These roads wind and wind higher and higher — one seems to drive through

---
[1] *The Daughters of the Late Colonel.*

the centuries too, the boy with the oxen who stands on the hillside with a green branch in his hand, the old women gathering twigs among the olives — the blind peasant with a wild violet pinned to his cap — all these figures seem to belong to any time — And then the tiny walled village with a great tree in the cobbled square and the lovely young girl looking out of the window of flower pots in the Inn — it's all something one seems to have known for ever. I could live here for years and years — I mean away from what they call " the world."

January 17, 1921

If you knew how I love hearing from you and how honoured I am by your confidences! Treat me as a person you have the right to ask things of. Look here — if you want anything and you haven't the dibs — come to me *bang* off and if I have the money you're welcome to it — without a single hesitation.

Why I am saying all this is (I see your eyes rolling and your hair rising in festoons of amazement and I don't care!) well, why I am saying it is that we " artists " are not like ordinary people and there are times when to know we have a fellow workman who's ready to do all in his power, because he loves you and believes in you, is a nice comfortable feeling. I adore *Life,* but my experience of the world is that it's pretty terrible. I hope yours will be a very different one, but just in case . . . you'd like to shout Katherine at any moment — here she is — See?

Having got that off my chest (which is at this moment more like a chest of super-sharp edged cutlery) let me say how I appreciate all you feel about *craft*. Yes, I think you're absolutely right. I see your *approach* to painting as very individual. Emotion for you seems to grow out of deliberation — looking long at a thing. Am I getting at anything right? In the way a thing is made — it may be a tree or a woman or a gazelle or a dish of fruit. You get your inspiration. This sounds a bit too simple when it is written down and rather like " Professor Leonard The Indian Palmist." I mean something, though. It's a very queer thing how *craft* comes into writing. I mean down to details. *Par example*. In *Miss Brill* I choose not only the length of every sentence, but even the sound of every sentence. I choose the rise and fall of every paragraph to fit her, and to fit her on that day at that very moment. After I'd written it I read it aloud — numbers of times — just as one would *play over* a musical composition — trying to get it nearer and nearer to the expression of Miss Brill — until it fitted her.

Don't think I'm vain about the little sketch. It's only the method I wanted to explain. I often wonder whether other writers do the same — If a thing has really come off it seems to me there mustn't be one single word out of place, or one word that could be taken out. That's how I AIM at writing. It will take some time to get anywhere near there.

But you know, Richard, I was only thinking last night people have hardly begun to write yet. Put poetry out of it for a moment and leave out Shakespeare — now I mean prose. Take the very best of it. Aren't they still cutting up sections rather than tackling the whole of a mind? I had a moment of absolute terror in the night. I suddenly thought of *a living mind* — a whole mind — with absolutely nothing left out. With *all* that one knows how much does one not know? I used to fancy one knew all but some kind of mysterious core (or one could). But now I believe just the opposite. The unknown is far, far greater than the known. The known is only a mere shadow. This is a fearful thing and terribly hard to face. But it must be faced.

To Lady Ottoline Morrell   *Wednesday*
February 2, 1921

M. is still here. He came back suddenly and now he is going to England to-morrow only to arrange to leave for good. . . . I *don't* know. I hope he will be happy. When he is away — yes — I do miss his *companionship*. I miss talking with a man — and its very lonely here when he's in London — for the Mountain and I only agree when we are silent or out of each other's sight!! But I mean to leave the Riviera as soon as possible. I've *turned* frightfully against it and the French. Life seems to me ignoble here. It all turns on money. Everything is money. When I read Balzac I always feel a peculiar odious exasperation because according to him the whole of life is founded on money. But he is right. It is

—for the French. I wish the horrid old Riviera would fall into the sea. It's just like an exhibition where every single side show costs another sixpence. But I paid goodness knows what to *come in*.

Where can one go, I wonder. Italy?

Do tell me if you find a lovely place in Italy. . . . As to England—I never want to see it again. I read M.'s letters from —— and Co. and they horrify me. Did one know all the wrong people? Is that why nobody remains to me—not one—except de la Mare whom I never knew when I was there. . . .

However, one goes on believing. Life *might be* marvellous. One keeps faith with that belief in one's work. I've been writing of a dance this afternoon and remembering how one polished the floor was so thrilling that everything was forgotten. . . .

To Richard Murry *February 3, 1921*

I don't suppose you really realise what your two last letters to me have been like. Well, I must say I've *never* had any letters to beat them, and when you are in Paradise I hope the Lord will present you with two brushes of comets hair in token of appreciation for same. Paint brushes, of course, I mean. In the meantime je vous serre le main bien fort, as they say, for them. . . . I'll take 'em in order.

The first, I must say, was what the French newspapers call un espèce de bowl-over! Your interview with Fate (not forgetting his Secretary) written on that beautiful leming coloured paper was simply a proof of what you could do at this imaginative short story writing if you really got going. Richard Murry enters the ring and shows Kid Mansfield How to Do it. I leave the drawing of the scene to you—me—in black velvet shorts with a crochet lace collar and you in a kind of zebra tights costume. . . . Well, dear old boy, you wiped the ring with me. Not only that I do really think that things have taken a Turn and that J. and I have seen our worst days. Hope so, at any rate. I think your Easter plan is a first-rate one. It's down in my diary as a certainty. Do let's bring it off! Don't worry about the fare. When the time comes just put your toospeg brush, pyjamas and a collar (for Sundays and fête days) into a handkerchief and I'll send along the ticket and a dotted line for you to follow. Seriously a rucksack is all you'll need. My grandpa said a man could travel all over the world with a clean pair of socks and a rook rifle. At the age of 70 odd he started for England thus equipped but Mother took fright and added a handkerchief or two. When he returned he was shorn of everything but a large watering can which he'd bought in London for his young marrows. I don't suggest him as a Man to be Followed, however. Already, just with the idea of you coming I've seen you on the terrace — the three of us, talking. I've packed picnic basket and we've gone off for the day. Lunch under the olive trees . . . and so on . . . it will be awful if it doesn't come true! We must make it. J. has a scheme to meet you in Paris and convey you to and from the Louvre on your way.

Well, I now come to your Letter II. containing your photograph. I love having it. You have, as Koteliansky used to say, an "extremely nice face," Richard. Being fond of you as I am I read into it all sorts of signs of the future painter . . . I believe they are all there.

My honest opinion is that if there is a person going on the right lines — you are he. I can't tell you how right I feel you are. It seems to me like this. There is painting and here is life — we can't separate them. Both of them have suffered an upheaval extraordinary in the last few years. There is a kind of tremendous agitation going on still, but so far anything that has come to the surface seems to have been experimental, or a fluke — a lucky accident. I believe the only way to *live* as artists under these new conditions in art and life is to put everything to the test for ourselves. We've got, in the long run, to be our own teachers. There's no getting away from that. We've got to win through by ourselves. Well, as I see it, the only way to do that honestly, dead truthfully, shirking nothing and leaving nothing out, is to put everything to the test; not only to face things, but really to find out of what they are composed. How can we know where we are, otherwise? How can we prevent ourselves being weak in certain places? To be *thorough* — to be *honest*. I think if artists were really thorough and honest they would save the world. It's the lack of those things and the reverse of them that are putting a deadly blight on life. Good work takes upon itself a Life — bad work has death in it.

Well (forgive me if I'm dull, old boy), your longing for

technical knowledge seems to me profoundly what an artist *ought* to feel to-day. It's a kind of deep sign of the times — rather the Zeitgeist — that's the better word. Your generation, and mine too, has been "put off" with imitations of the real thing and we're bound to react violently if we're sincere. This takes so long to write and it sounds so heavy. Have I conveyed what I mean to even. You see I too have a passion for technique. I have a passion for making the thing into a *whole* if you know what I mean. Out of technique is born real style, I believe. There are no short cuts.

But I wish you were not so far away. I wish the garden gate flew open for you often and that you came in and out and we talked — not as in London — more easily and more happily. I shall pin the sun into the sky for every day of your holiday and at night I shall arrange for a constant supply of the best moonlight.

To Sylvia Lynd   *January 1921*

Your letter and your book made a sort of *Fête de Saint Sylvie* of yesterday. Your lovely little letter brought you back to me so clearly — very radiant, in air blue and primrose, sitting for a moment in time on my small sofa — the one which in private life is known as "the stickleback."

Thank you very much indeed, please, for *The Swallow Dive*. It is full of the most beautiful things. You turn to Beauty like a flower to the light. (I must put it in the third person. It's easier to say.) She fills and glows with it and is like a shining transparent cup of praise. . . . Early morning light, I feel, with the grass still pearled and long, slender shadows. . . . If you were here I should like to say . . . "Caroline crying after she had heard of Ethel's engagement"; "her moment of leaving her Aunt Mildred's house for ever. . . ."; "her top of the 'bus ride"; her pink cotton frock drifting through July in London. As to the Fall of Antioch, I *hear* it, *smell* it, *know* it as if I had played in it. But above all, *Ashleem!* Your early morning description of Ashleem, Miss, took away my breff.

Forgive an impudent woman. She's very, very serious really. And because we are *fellow-workmen,* may I say I think you sometimes know more than you say, and sometimes you say less than you know. . . . Does that convey anything?

I find my great difficulty in writing is to learn to submit. Not that one ought to be without resistance — of course I don't mean that. But when I am writing of 'another' I want so to lose myself in the soul of the other that I am not. . . .

I wish we could have a talk about writing one of these days.

Was there really a new baby in your letter? Oh dear, some people have all the babies in this world. And as sometimes happens to us women just before your letter came, I found myself tossing a little creature up in the air and saying, "Whose boy are you?" But he was far too shadowy, too far away to reply.

So tell me about *your* baby, will you? And when I do get out of this old bed I shall drive to the lace shop and buy a cobweb to make a cap for himher. Farewell. May the fairies attend you. No, dear woman, it is grim work — having babies. Accept my love and my sympathy.

To Sydney Schiff   *February 1921*

Let me add one word to our all too brief conversation this afternoon. Alas! what a plague is Time. No sooner has one begun to *appreciate* what the other is seeing than — it's as though, at a turn of the planet — he is whirled away.

The question of the Artist and his Time is, I am sure, the Question of Questions. The artist who denies his Time, who turns away from it even so much as the fraction of a hair is false. First, he must be free; that is, he must be controlled by none other than his deepest self, his truest self. And then he must accept Life, he must submit — give himself so utterly to Life that no personal *quâ* personal self remains. Does that convey anything? It's so hard to state. " Bitterness " is a difficult word for me to disentangle from a sense of personal wrong — a " this is what Life has done to me." But I know you don't mean that. You mean a bigger thing — the gesture with which one turns aside to-day from what might have been — what ought to have been. There is humour in it, of a kind, and inevitable sadness. . . .

But let me confess, Sydney. I feel something else as well — and that is *Love*. But that's so difficult to explain. It's not pity or rainbows or anything up in the air — Perhaps it's *feeling, feeling, feeling*.

Letters 1921

To S. S. Koteliansky *February 19, 1921*

What has happened to the inkstand with the elephants on it — mother-of-pearl, inlay — or was it ivory? Some of the inlay had begun to come off; I fancy one of the elephants had lost an eye.

And that dim little picture of a snowy landscape hanging on the wall in your room. Where is it now? And where are the kittens and the children and Christ, who looked awfully like a kitten, too, who used to hang in the dining room? And that leather furniture with the tufts of horse-hair stuffing coming out?

Where are all the hats from the hatstand? And do you remember for how long the bell was broken. . . . Then there was the statue on the stairs, smiling, the fair caretaker, always washing up, the little children always falling through her door.

And your little room with the tiny mirror and the broken window and the piano sounding from outside.

Those were very nice teacups — thin — a nice shape — and the tea was awfully good — so hot.

"At the Vienna Café there is good bread."

And the cigarettes. The packet done up in writing paper you take from your pocket. It is folded so neatly at the ends like a parcel from the chemists.

And then Slatkovsky — his *beard*, his "glad eye" — his sister, who sat in front of the fire and took off her boot. The two girls who came to see him the Classic Day his Father died. And the view from your window — you remember? The typist sits there and her hat and coat hang in the hall. Now an Indian in a turban walks up that street opposite to the British Museum *quartier*.

It begins to rain. The streets are very crowded. It is dusky. Now people are running downstairs. That heavy outer door slams. And now the umbrellas go up in the street and it is much darker, suddenly. Dear friend — do not think evil of me — forgive me.

To ——— *March 1, 1921*

Don't blame your parents too much! We *all* had parents. There is only one way of escaping from their influence and that is by going into the matter with yourself — scanning yourself and mak-

= 366 =

ing perfectly sure of their share. It can be done. One is NEVER free until one has done blaming somebody or praising somebody for what is bad and good in one. Don't you feel THAT? By that I don't mean we ought to live, each of us on our own island. On the contrary — Life is relationship — it's giving and taking — but that's not quite the same thing as making others *responsible* — is it? There is the danger. Don't think I underestimate the enormous power parents can have. I don't. It's staggering, it's titanic. After all, they are real giants when we are only table high and they act according. But like everything else in life — I mean all suffering, however great — we have to get over it — to cease from harking back to it — to grin and bear it and to hide the wounds. More than that, and far more true is we have to find the *gift* in it. We can't afford to waste such an expenditure of feeling; we have to learn from it — and we *do,* I most deeply believe, come to be thankful for it. By saying we can't afford to . . . waste . . . feeling! I sound odious and cynical. I don't feel it. What I mean is. *Everything must be accepted.*

I am only on nodding acquaintance with Spring. We talk from the window. But she looks from this distance fairer than ever, more radiant, more exquisite. It is marvellous to know the earth is turned to the light.

To Lady Ottoline Morrell   Monday
                                                March 14, 1921

I have been in bed for six weeks with my lungs and heart; then "They" have decided that my heart trouble is caused by a very swollen gland which presses, with intense pain, on an artery. This the surgeon tapped on Saturday and intends to tap 2 or 3 times again. And so on and so on and so on. L. M. is in England pendant cette crise — But I'll not go on.

The weather is really exquisite. To-day was perfection. Radiant, crystal clear, one of those days when the earth seems to pause, enchanted with its beauty, when every new leaf whispers: "Am I not heavenly fair!" The sun is quite warm. It is tame again. It comes and curls up in your arms — Beautiful Life! In spite of everything one cannot but praise Life. I have been watching the peach tree outside my window from the very first moment, and now it is all in flower and the leaves are come, small shy clusters like linnets' wings.

Even now I can't explain. Something happened, a kind of earthquake that shook everything and I lost faith and touch with everybody. I cannot write what it was. And perhaps I shall never meet you again so that I can tell you. This is sad. Blame me if you must. How can you do otherwise? I expect this all sounds fantastic. I hate people who hint at secrets in letters. You will hate this. Let me say I was almost out of my mind with misery last year —

M. is here for the moment. He goes back to England at the end of April. His typewriter ticks away here. I have just been looking at the Keats Memorial Volume. It is simply *indescribable* in its vulgarity. But there's a letter by Keats in it — so full of power, gaiety, "fun" that it mocks the book as he would have mocked it!

To the Hon. Dorothy Brett   *April 20, 1921*

We are wondering if that strike has really struck. There is no way of knowing here. It must be horrible in London. Bernard Shaw had a letter in the *D.N.* which explained it all away. It's a pity he's not King. But the very sound of soldiers fills me with horror, and as to all these pictures of young giants joining up and saying goodbye to Daddy — the falsity of it! The waste of life — even if not a man is killed — is appalling. And all the while the trees come out and the year begins to ripen. . . . If there were a God, he'd be a queer fellow.

Here it is so cold that it might be November. We are both frozen, we shiver all day. I get up from 11 — 5.30 and turn the clock round so as to get back to bed more quickly. I've been spitting blood since last Tuesday too — which is horrid. It makes one feel that while one sits at the window the house is on fire. And the servants have gone mad or bad or both. One has completely disappeared, only her feather duster remains. She wasn't a little one either. But I expect we shall come across her one day. I have a fancy she is in one of the chimneys. All our flags are pinned on Switzerland. Meadows, trees, mountings, and kind air. I hope we shall get there in time.

To J. M. Murry   *Saturday*
Baugy, Switzerland
May 7, 1921

I have been walking round and round this letter, treading on my toes and waving my tail and wondering where to settle. There's *too* much to say! Also, the least post card or letter penned within view of these mountains is like presenting one's true account of one's Maker. Perhaps their effect will wear off. But at present ... one keeps murmuring that about cats looking at Kings, but one feels a very small cat, sneezing, licking one's paw, making a dab or two at one's tail in the eye of Solemn Immensities. However, the peasants don't mind, so why should I? They are cutting the long brilliant grass; they are wading waist high through the field with silver stars — their scythes, winking bright in the sun — over their shoulders. A cart drawn by a *cow* (I'm sure it is a cow) drags over a little bridge, and the boy driver, lying like a drunken bee on his fresh green bed, doesn't even try to drive. It's a perfect, windless day. I'm, as you have gathered, sitting on the balcony outside my room. The sun is wonderfully warm, but the air is just a little too clean not to be chill. The cleanliness of Switzerland! It is frightening. The chastity of my lily-white bed! The waxy-fine floors! The huge bouquet of white lilac, fresh, crisp from the laundry, in my little salon! Every daisy in the grass below has a starched frill — the very bird-droppings are dazzling.

"But ... this is all jolly fine, but why don't you tell me things? Get down to it!"

I'm sorry; I'll have another try. You got my telegram? The journey was excellent. The *lits salons* were horrid — when they unfolded they were covered thickly with buttons so that one felt like a very sensitive bun having its currants put in. But it was soon morning, and my mountains appeared as of yore with snow, like silver light, on their tops, and beautiful clouds above, rolling solid white masses. We passed little watery villages clinging to the banks of rivers, it was raining, the trees dripped, and everybody carried a gleaming umbrella. Even the fishers fished under umbrellas, their line looked like the huge feeler of a large water beetle. And then the rain stopped, the cows began to fatten, the houses had broad eaves, the women at the bookstalls got broader and broader, and it was Switzerland.

I sat on a neat green velvet chair in Geneva for three hours. L. M. brought tea on a tray. Do you see her, coming from afar, holding the tray high, her head bent, a kind of reverent beam on her face, and the smoke of the teapot rising like the smoke of sacrifices?

Then we mounted an omnibus train and *bummelted* round the Lake. The carriage was full of Germans; I was imbedded in huge ones. When they saw a lilac bush, Vater und die Mamma and even little Hänse all cried: " Schön." It was very old-world. Also they each and all read aloud the notice in the carriage that a cabinet was provided for the convenience of passengers! (What other earthly reason would it have been there for?) We reached Clarens at 7. The station clock was chiming. It was a cuckoo clock. Touching — don't you think? I was *very* touched. But I didn't cry. And then a motor car, like a coffee-mill, flew round and round the fields to Baugy. The manager, who is very like a goldfish, flashed through the glass doors and our journey was over. . . .

This hotel is admirable. The food is prodigious. At breakfast one eats little white rolls with butter and fresh plum jam and cream. At lunch one eats — but no, I can't describe it. It could not be better though. I suppose, in the fullness of time, I shall take soup at midday, too. But at present I can only watch and listen. . . . My rooms are like a small appartement. They are quite cut off and my balcony is as big as another room. The sun rises in the morning vers les sept heures, and it sets, or it begins to set (for it takes its setting immensely seriously here) at seven in the evening. It has no connection whatever with the South of France sun. This is le soleil père — and she's a wanton daughter whose name is never mentioned here.

The air is all they say. I am posing here as a lady with a weak heart and lungs of Spanish leather-o. And so far, I confess I hardly cough except in the morning. One mustn't be too enthusiastic though. Perhaps it is the hypnotic effect of *knowing* one is so high up. But the air is amazing!

It's all very German. Early German. Fat little birds, tame as can be — they look as though their heads unscrewed and re-

vealed marzipan tummies — fat little children, peasants, and
— I regret to say — ugly women. In fact, everybody seems to me
awfully ugly. Young men with red noses and stuffy check suits
and feathers in their hats ogling young females in mackintoshes
with hats tied with ribbon under the chin! *Oh Weh! Oh Weh!*
and if they try to be "chic" — to be French — it's worse still.
Legs — but legs of mutton in silk stockings and powder which
one feels sure is die Mamma's icing sugar.

Of course, I quite see the difficulty of being chic in this landscape. I can't quite see . . . yet. Perhaps a white woollen dress, a Saint Bernard, a woollen Viking helmet with snowy wings. And for your . . . ? More wool, with your knees bare, and boots with fringèd tongues. . . . But I don't know — I don't know. . . .

I am sure you will like Switzerland. I want to tell you nicer things. What shall I tell you? I should like to dangle some very fascinating and compelling young carrots before your eminent nose. . . . The furniture of my salon is green velvet inlaid with flesh pink satin, and the picture on the wall is *Jugendidylle*. There is also an immense copper jug with lovely hearts of imitation verdigris. . . .

                                                    Monday
                                                May 9, 1921

It was a great pleasure to hear from you to-day and get your post cards of Bandol and Arles. *This* time I am numbering and keeping your letters. . . . You took me back to Graviers — especially those big pebbles. They are so plain in my memory, big, round, smooth. I see them. I am glad you saw the Allègres, even tho' it was sad. The post cards are very impressive. So was your desire to see a bull-fight. I rolled my eyes.

After my hymn in praise of the weather it changed on Saturday night, to heavy rolling mists and thick soft rain. The mountains disappeared very beautifully, one by one. The lake became grave and one felt the silence. This, instead of being depressing as it is in the South, had a sober charm. I don't know how it is with you; but I feel the South is not made pour le grand travail. There is *too much light*. Does that sound heresy? But to work one needs a place (or so I find) where one can spiritually dig oneself in. . . . And I defy anybody to do that on the Riviera. Now this morning the mist is rolling up, wave on wave, and the pines and firs, exquisitely clear, green and violet-blue, show the mountain sides. This grass, too, in the foreground, waving high, with one o'clocks like bubbles and flowering fruit trees like branches of red and white coral. One looks and one becomes absorbed. . . . Do you know what I mean? This outer man retires and the other takes the pen. In the South it is one long fête for the outer man. But perhaps, after your tour in Provence, you won't be inclined to agree (I mean about its not being ideal for working).

I feel, at present, I should like to have a small chalêt, high up somewhere, and live there for a round year, working as one wants to work. The *London Mercury* came on Saturday with my story.[1] Tell me if anybody says they like it, will you? That's not vanity. Reading it again, I felt it might fall dead flat. It's so plain and unadorned. Tommy and de la Mare are the people I'd *like* to please. But don't bother to reply to this request, dearest. It's just a queer feeling — after one has dropped a pebble in. Will there be a ripple or not? . . .

What do you feel about Broomies now? This weather, so soft, so quiet, makes me realise what early autumn there might be. It's weather to go and find apples — to stand in the grass and hear them drop. It's Spring and Autumn with their arms round each other — like your two little girls in Garavan.

The packet arrived safely, thank you. Your remark about Tiz reminded me that in a paper here I read a little letter by Gaby Deslys[2] saying that Reudel's Bath Saltrates made her feet "feel so nice." A little laughing picture and a bright string of bébé French. I felt, if I went on reading there'd come a phrase, " Quand on est mort, tu sais. . . ."

To Anne Estelle Rice   *May 1921*

If I were in Paris wouldn't I fly to where you were! It's so perfect of you even to think I'm there. I feel as though I was.

[1] *The Daughters of the Late Colonel.*
[2] Gaby Deslys had died shortly before.

Or at least that for two quite inferior pins I could pack up and go. But—chère—at the moment I can only walk from the kerridge. Can't mount a stair—can't do *anything,* but lie in a chaise longue looking at mountains that make one feel one is living in the Eye of the Lord. It is all temporary—I am full of beans and full of fight—but unfortunately, darling, I'm full of bacilli too. Which is a bother. If you came here I'd simply have such a laugh about it that this rotten old chaise longue would break its Swiss legs. Instead, I'm waiting for Docteur Figli (good name, that!) and I've got a very nice booklet of information to give him about two little guineas that have just died for my sake. The number of guinea pigs, Anne, that I've murdered! So that, my precious dear, is *that.* Paris might be—might very *well* be, la pleine lune for me.

I left my dear little Isola Bella last week. The South of France is fever to the feverish. That's my experience. Adorable pays. I'll go back there one day but sans un thermomètre. Switzerland, which I've always managed to avoid, is the very devil. I knew it would be. I mean, the people are so UGLY; they are simply hideous. They have no shape. All the women have pear-shaped derrières, ugly heads, awful feet. All the men wear ready-made check flannelette suits, six sizes too small and felt hats another six sizes too small, with a little pre-war feather sticking up behind. Curse them. And the FOOD. It's got no nerves. You know what I mean? It seems to lie down and wait for you; the very steaks are meek. There's no contact between you and it. You're not attracted. You don't feel that keenness to meet it and know more of it and get on very intimate terms. The asparagus is always stone dead. As to the purée de pommes de terre, you feel inclined to call it "uncle." Now I had food in the South that made me feel—should there be a Paradise—you and I shall have one lunch cooked by my old Marie which will atone for years of not meeting. And then, Anne, Switzerland is revoltingly clean. My bed—it's enough to unmake any man, the sight of it. Dead white—tucked in so tight that you have to insert yourself like a knife into an oyster. I got up the first night and almost whimpering, like Stepan in *The Possessed,* I put my old wild jackall skin over the counterpane. But this cleanliness persists in everything. Even the bird-droppings on the terrasse are immaculate and every inch of lilac is crisp home from the laundry. It's a cursed country. And added to this there are these terrific mountains.

However, darling, I believe it is the only place where they do give one back one's wings. And I can't go on crawling any longer. It's beyond a joke.

I shan't stay here at this hotel long, so my London address is best. The sight of distant Montreux is altogether too powerful. As to the people in this hotel, it is like a living cemetery. I never saw such deaders. I mean belonging to a bygone period. Collar supports (do you remember them?) are the height of fashion here and hairnets and silver buckles and button boots. Face powder hasn't been *invented* yet.

It's a queer world, but in spite of everything, darling, it's a rare, rare joy to be alive and I salute you — and it — and kiss you both together — but you I kiss more warmly.

To J. M. Murry   *May 1921*

Read this criticism. It takes the bisquito. But why a half-brick at me? They do hate me, those young men. The *Sat. Review* said my story [*The Daughters of the Late Colonel*] was "a dismal transcript of inefficiency." What a bother! I suppose that, living alone as I do, I get all out of touch and what seems to me even *lively* is ghostly glee. . . .

I like these two torn pages written at such a terrific lick — funny long y's and g's tearing along like fishes in a river when you are wading.

I was not honest about "not facing facts." Yes, I *do* believe one ought to face facts. If you don't, they get behind you and may become terrors, nightmares, giants, horrors. As long as one faces them one is top-dog. The trouble is not to steel oneself — to face them calmly, easily — to have the habit of facing them. I say this because I think nearly all my falsity has come from not facing facts as I should have done, and it's only now that I am beginning to learn to face them.

Thursday
May 12, 1921

The inventory came from Pope's last night. . . . The list of our furniture would make any *homme de cœur* weep.

    1 Tin Box Doll's Tea Service.
    1 China Figure of Sailor.
    2 Liqueur decanters.
    1 Liqueur glass.
    3 Light Dresden Girandole.
    1 Glass Bowl.
    9 Paper Knives.

Doesn't it sound a heavenly dustbin? Did you know there was a Fluted Compot? and a Parian Flower Jar?

Since my first letter the mountains have been mobled kings. They have un-mobled themselves to-day. . . . Is it to be post cards, post cards all the way?

Saturday Evening
May 1921

I am rather conscious that my letters have fallen off just these last days. Specially so since this evening I have read yours written at Oxford on Thursday. You know how it is when just the letter you get is the letter you would love to get. That was my experience with this one of yours. I dipped into that remote Oxford and discovered you there. Heard that click of the cricket ball and I saw the trees and the grass. I was with you, standing by you, not saying anything, but happy.

The reason why I haven't written is that I am fighting a kind of Swiss chill.

All day, in the sun, the men have been working in the vineyards. They have been hoeing between the vines, and then an old man has been dusting certain rows with powder out of a Giant Pepper-pot. The heat has been terrific. The men have worn nothing but cotton trousers. Their bodies are tanned almost red brown — a very beautiful colour. And every now and then they stop work, lean on their pick, breathe deeply, look round. I feel I have been watching them for years. Now the day is over; the shadows are long on the grass. The new trees hold the light and wisps of white cloud move dreamily over the dreaming mountains. It is all very lovely. . . .

How hot is it in England? Here it is really — as C. would say — almost tropical. The nights are hot too. One lies with both windows open, and my toes as usual, get thirsty. . . .

Thank you for Tchekhov. Came to-night, I am simply captivated by Chaucer just now. I have had to throw a bow window into my cœur petit to include him with Shakespeare. Oh, dear! His *Troilus and Cressid!!* And my joy at finding your remarks and your pencil-notes.

I read to-day *The Tale of Chaunticleer and Madame Perlicote:* it's the Pardouner's tale. Perfect in its way. But the *personality* — the *reality* of the man. How his impatience, his pleasure, the very tone rings through. It's a deep delight to read. Chaucer and Marlowe are my two at present. I don't mean there's any comparison between them. But I read *Hero and Leander* last night. That's incredibly lovely. But how extremely amusing Chapman's *finish* is! Taking up that magical poem and putting it into a bodice and skirt. It's v. funny.

Thursday
May 1921

Of course, I remember old Grundy. It was Goodyear's laugh I heard when I read his name — a kind of snorting laugh, ending in a chuckle and then a sudden terrific *frown* and he got very red. Do you remember? And you remember the stick he brought from Bombay? He was very pleased with that stick. Your mention of G. gave me Goodyear again — living, young, a bit careless and *worried,* but enjoying the worry, in the years before the war, when a pale moon shone above Piccadilly Circus and we three stood at the corner and didn't want to separate or to go home. . . .[1]

I went out yesterday in a Swiss kerridge to see M. The Swiss kerridge was a rare old bumper, and the driver who weighed about eighteen stone leaped into the air and then crashed back on to the seat. It was raining. A massive hood was down. I could

[1] For Frederick Goodyear see the *Journal*, p. 58.

just put forth a quivering horn from beneath it. Montreux is *very ugly* and quite empty. But in the shops the people are awfully nice. They are simple, frank, honest beyond words and kind in the German way. The thing about Switzerland is that there is absolutely no *de luxe*. That makes an enormous difference. It's simply not understood. And one is not expected to be rich. One isn't expected to spend. This is very pleasant indeed. I suppose there is a sort of surface scum of what the *Daily Mail* calls the " Jazzing World," but it doesn't touch the place. To put it into a gnut shell, there simply is no *fever* — no fret. The children are really beautiful. I saw a baby boy yesterday who took my breath away. He was a little grub in a blue tunic with a fistful of flowers — but his *eyes!* his *colour!* his *health!* You want to lie in the grass here and have picnics. Monte Carlo is not in the same world. It's another planet almost.

Sunday
May 1921

I got back from Sierre at about 7.30 last night. I rather wish I hadn't sent you that little note from there. It was no confused. Tear it up.... While I write a man is playing the zither so sweetly and gaily that one's heart dances to hear. It's a very warm, still day.

Will you please look at this picture of the lake at Sierre? Do you like it? It's lovely — really it is. If we spend a year here in Switzerland I don't think you will regret it. Yesterday gave me such a wonderful idea of it all. I feel I have been through and through Switzerland. And up there, at Sierre, and in the tiny mountain towns on the way to Sierre it is absolutely unspoilt. I mean it's so unlike — so remote from — the Riviera in that sense. There are *no* tourists to be seen. It is a whole complete life. The only person I could think of meeting was Lawrence before the war. The only thing which is modern (and this makes me feel the Lord is on our side) is the postal service: it is excellent everywhere in Switzerland, even in the villages. There are two posts a day everywhere. As to telegrams, they simply fly — and your letter posted 8.30 P.M. on May 12th arrived here 9.30 A.M. May 14th. All these remarks are, again, of the carrot family.

I heard there are any number of small chalêts to be had in Sierre and in Montana. We should take one — don't you think? and have a Swiss bonne. As to cream-cows, they abound. And the whole country-side is full of fruit and of vines. It's famous for its small grapes, and for a wine which the peasants make. The father brews for his sons, and the sons for their sons. It's drunk when it's about 20 years old, and I believe it is superb.

Queer thing is that all the country near Sierre is like the Middle Ages. There are ancient tiny castles and small round wooded knolls, and the towns are solid, built round a square. Yesterday as we came to one part of the valley — it was a road with a *solid* avenue of poplars, a green wall on either side — little wooden carts came spanking towards us. The man sat on the shafts. The woman, in black, with a flat black hat, earrings and a white kerchief, sat in front with the children. Nearly all the women carried huge bunches of crimson peonies, flashing bright. A stream of these little carts passed, and then we came to a town and there was a huge fair going on in the market square. In the middle people were dancing, round the sides they were buying pigs and lemonade, in the cafés under the white and pink flowering chestnut trees there were more people, and at the windows of the houses there were set pots of white narcissi and girls looked out. They had orange and cherry handkerchiefs on their heads. It was beyond words gay and delightful. Then further on we came to a village where some fête was being arranged. The square was hung with garlands and there were cherry-coloured masts with flags flying from them and each mast had a motto framed in leaves — AMITIE — TRAVAIL — HONNEUR — DEVOIR. All the men of the village in white shirts and breeches were stringing more flags across and a very old man sat on a heap of logs plaiting green branches. He had a huge pipe with *brass fittings*.

Oh dear — in some parts of the Rhone valley there are deep, deep meadows. Little herd boys lie on their backs or their bellies and their tiny white goats spring about on the mountain slopes. These mountains have little lawns set with trees, little glades and miniature woods and torrents on the lower slopes, and all kinds of different trees are there in their beauty. Then come the pines and the firs, then the undergrowth, then the rock and the snow. You meet tiny girls all alone with flocks of *black* sheep or herds of huge yellow cows. Perhaps they are sitting on the bank of a stream with their feet in the water, or peeling a wand. And the houses are so few, so remote. I don't know what it is, but I think you would feel as I did, *deeply pleased* at all this. I like to imagine (am I right?) that you will muse as you read: Yes, I could do with a year there. . . . And you must know that from Sierre we can go far and wide — in no time. I believe the flowers are in their perfection in June and July, and again the *Alpine flora* in September and October.

I see a small white chalêt with a garden near the pine forests. I see it all very simple, with big white china stoves and a very pleasant woman with a tanned face and sun-bleached hair bringing in the coffee. I see winter — snow and a load of wood arriving at our door. I see us going off in a little sleigh — with huge fur gloves on, and having a picnic in the forest and eating ham and fur sandwiches. Then there is a lamp — *très important* — there are our books. It's very still. The frost is on the pane. You are in your room writing. I in mine. Outside the Stars are shining and the pine trees are dark like velvet.

I was not surprised at ——. He's so *uncertain* at present, I mean in his own being, that it will come natural to him to pose. I don't know how far you realise that you *make* him what he is with you — or how different he is with others. Also at present he has no real self-respect and that makes him *boast*. Like all of us he wants to feel important and that's a *right* feeling — we *ought* to feel important — but while he remains undisciplined and dans le vague he *can't be* important. So he has to boast. I mustn't go on. You are calling me a schoolmistress. . . .

To Anne Estelle Rice Thursday
  May 19, 1921

I must write to you once again, darling woman, while you are in Paris. Anne, if I were not to hear from you again ever I could live on your last letter. To have taken the trouble — I know what writing means — to have sent me that whole great piece of Paris — complete, with yourself and the traffic (I'd love to be somewhere where taxis ran one over) and marble tops and Louise avec son plumeau, and the shops with the flowery saucissons, and that getting le petit déjeuner, and Wyndham Lewis and — well — I walked through your letter once and then I just idled through it again and took my time and stopped to look and admire and *love* and smell and hear it all. It was a great gift, my dearest Anne — it was un cadeau superbe pour moi. How I *love* you for doing just that! Do you feel I do? You must. Now I've been to Paris — and even to St. Cloud. For your idea of a house there started me dreaming of the house next door. Charming houses — two storied with lilac bushes at the gate. I made a hole in my fence big enough for an eye to flash through — and in the morning I spied through and called to the petit who was *gardening,* "David," and he said, rather off hand, "Quoi?" And I said, "Will you come to tea with me to-day?" And he turned his back on me and shouted up at his own house, "She wants me to go to tea." At that your head appeared at a window and you said: "Well, do you want to go?" David replied: "Well, what have we got for tea here?" . . . It was an *awfully* sweet dream. I wish it would come true. What fun we should have! In the evening there would be a lamp on the garden table. I see a whole, lovely life — and more my life than cafés nowadays.

All the same, Paris and London have their appeal. It's very good to talk at times and I love *watching* and *listening*. These mountains are crushing table companions. But all the same I lie all day looking at them and they are pretty terrific. . . . If you could get them into the story, you know — get them "placé."

I saw the biggest specialist in Switzerland on Saturday, Anne. That's what made your letter so wonderfully good just at the moment. It seemed to bring Life so near again. After I'd seen this man it was just as if the landscape — everything — changed a little — moved a little *further off*. I always expect these doctor men to say: "Get better? Of course you will. Will put you right in no time. Six months at the very most and you'll be fit as a fiddle again." But though this man was extremely nice he would not say more than "I still had a chance." That was all. I tried to get the word "Guéri" but it was no good. All I could wangle out of him was "If your digestion continues good, you still have a chance."

It's an infernal nuisance to love life as I do. I seem to love it more as time goes on rather than less. It never becomes a habit to me — it's always a marvel. I do hope I'll be able to keep in it long enough to do some really good work. I'm sick of people dying who promise well. One doesn't want to join that crowd at all. So I shall go on lapping up jaunes d'œufs and de la crême. . . .

It's evening now. I expect the lights are just out in the streets. I see the round shadows of the trees, the warm white of the pavement. I see the people flitting by. And here in the lake the mountains are bluish — cold. Only on the high tops the snow is a faint apricot colour. Beautiful Life! " To be alive and that is enough." I could almost say that, but not quite.

To Sydney and Violet Schiff   *Saturday*
May 21, 1921

Many thanks for your letter. I want to write to you; I shall as soon as I've got over this chill. At present I am in the very middle of it.

The *place* is marvellous; the doctors incredibly, fantastically, too hopelessly maddening. They will speak English, too. If I could only give you an imitation of the one who has just left me. " Dere is nudding for it but lie in de bed — *eat* — and tink of naice tings " . . . He wore a little tiny straw hat too, and brown cotton gloves. . . . What is one to do — dearest? To shoot or not to shoot. . .

To J. M. Murry   *May 1921*

You ask me how I am. . . . I am much the same. This chill has been the worst I have ever had since I was ill, and so I feel weak and rather shadowy — physically. My heart is the trouble. But otherwise I feel . . . well . . . it's difficult to say. No, one can't believe in *God*. But I must believe in something more *nearly* than I do. As I was lying here to-day I suddenly remembered that: " O ye of little faith! " Not faith in a God. No, that's impossible. But do I live as though I believe in anything? Don't I live *in glimpses* only? There is something wrong, there is something small in such a life. One must live more fully and one must have more *power* of loving and feeling. One must be true to one's vision of life — in every single particular — and I am not. The only thing to do is to try again from to-night to be stronger and better — to be *whole*.

That's *how I am*. . . . Goodnight.

May 1921

The people whom we read as we read Shakespeare are part of our *daily lives*. I mean it doesn't seem to me QUEER to be thinking about Othello at bregchick or to be wondering about the Phœnix and the Turtle in my bath. It's all part of a whole. Just as that vineyard below me is the vineyard in the Song of Solomon, and that beautiful sound as the men hoe between the vines is almost part of my body, goes on in me. I shall never be the same as I was *before* I heard it, just as I'll never be the same as I was before I read the Death of Cleopatra. One has willingly *given* oneself to all these things — one is the result of them all. Are you now saying "intellectual detachment"? But I've *allowed* for that.

Other people — I mean people to-day — seem to look on in a way I don't understand. I don't want to boast. I don't feel at all arrogant, but I do feel they have not perhaps lived as fully as we have. . . . However. . . . Did you know that Turgenev's brain *pesait deux mille grammes?* Horrible idea! I couldn't help seeing it *au beurre noir* when I read that. I shall never forget that brain at Isola Bella. It was still *warm from thinking*. Ugh!

I shall be very, very glad to see you. I have a mass of things to talk about. "The great artist is he who exalts difficulty" — do you believe that? And that it's only the slave (using slave in our mystical sense) who pines for freedom. The free man, the artist, seeks to bind himself. No, these notes aren't any good. But I have been finding out more and more how true it is that it's only the difficult thing that is worth doing; it's the difficult thing that one deliberately chooses to do. I don't think Tchekhov was as aware of that as he should have been. Some of the stories in *The Horse-Stealers* are — rather a shock.

Tell me (I've changed my pen and my *sujet*), how is this? There is no Saint Galmier here, only Eau de Montreux, which, according to the bottle, is saturated with carbonic acid gas. But my physiology book said that carbonic acid gas was a deadly poison: we only breathed it out, but never, except at the last desperate moment, took it in. And here are Doctors Schnepsli, Rittchen and Knechloo saying it's a sovereign cure for gravel. It is all so very difficult, as Constantia would say.

Don't walk on both sides of the street at once. It distracts people and makes it difficult for them to continue the conversation.

Tuesday, 4.30 P.M.
May 1921

I never read anything about a child more exquisite than your little girl's remark " Il pleut " when someone put a sunshade up. It's the most profound thing about a very young baby's vision of the world I've ever struck. *It's what babies in prams think*. It's what you say long before you *talk*. She's altogether a ravishing person — no, so much more than that. She is a tiny vision there in those gardens for ever. The tenderness is perfect — it's so true.

I am writing in the thick of a thunder-storm. They are regular items now in the late afternoon. It gets misty, the birds sound loud, it smells of irises and then it thunders. I love such summer storms. I love hearing the maids run in the passages to shut the windows and draw up the blinds, and then you see on the road between the vineyards people hurrying to take shelter. Besides, I've such a great part of the sky to see that I can watch the beginning, the middle and the end.

Tuesday

Know that goldfinch I have tamed? He comes right into my bedroom now and eats breakfast crumbs beside the bed. He is a ravishing little bird. If only he were carpet-trained. But I'm afraid you can't train birds. He seems just as surprised as I am. The sparrows, now that he has come in, grow bold and come as far as the parquet, too. But I won't have them. I aspire to having taught this goldfinch to present arms with my founting pen by the time you come — to do you honour. I also dream of its singing an address of welcome — holding the address, you know, in one claw.

During the past two nights I have read *The Dynasts.* Isn't it queer how a book eludes one, and then suddenly opens for you? I have looked into this book before now. But the night before last when I opened it I suddenly understood what the poet meant, and how he meant it should be read! *The point of view* which is like a light streaming from the imagination and over the imagination — over one's head as it were — the chorus and the aerial music. I am talking carelessly, because I am talking to you, and I am relying on you to more than understand me. But it did seem to me that if the *poetic drama* is still a possible "form" it will be, in the future, like *The Dynasts* — *As if* for the stage and yet not to be played. That will give it its freedom. Now when one reads *The Dynasts* it's always as though it were on the stage. . . . But the stage is a different one — it is within us. This is all *très vague.* . . . I long to talk about it.

Here I stopped. The doctor came. It's really funny. I must tell you. My chill is slightly better, but I have symptoms of whooping cough! *Il ne manquait que ça.*

To Lady Ottoline Morrell   *May 1921*

One can't be really happy if one's body refuses to "join in," if it persists in going its own way and *never* letting one forget it. But how is one to get cured? As to doctors — there aren't any. I have just paid little B. 2,000 francs for looking after me and I'm 50 times worse than I was at Christmas. They know nothing. I had two really deadly experiences here with perfect fools and after all this long time they depressed me so much that I felt desperate and I motored off to Montana to see the specialist there. He's supposed to be the best man in Switzerland for lungs. He was better than the others and I am going to be under him in future. I don't know for how long. It's very vague. He would not say I can get better. All he would say was I still have a chance and he has known patients with lungs as far gone as mine who have recovered. I really don't mind a straw. It was a divine day — the day I met him — and the strange ancient room in an old hotel where we talked was so beautiful that the moment was enough. One must live for the moment, that is all I feel now. When he explained how the left lung was deeply engaged but the right was really the dangerous one I wanted to say: " Yes, but do listen to the bees outside. I've never heard such bees. And there's some delicious plant growing outside the window. It reminds me of Africa — "

But my health is such a frightfully boring subject that I won't talk about it.

Life in this hotel is a queer experience. I have two rooms and a balcony — so I am — thank Heaven — quite cut off. They are corner rooms, too. But I descend for the meals — step into the whirlpool — and really one sees enough, hears enough at them, to last one for ever. I have never *imagined* such people. I think they are chiefly composed of Tours — they are one composite person, being taken round for so much a week. It's hard to refrain from writing about them. But my balcony looks over Montreux and Clarens. Anything more hideous!! I think Switzerland has the very ugliest houses, people, food, furniture, in the whole world. There's something incredible in the solid ugliness of the people. The very newspapers full of advertisements for a "magnificent *porc*" or a batterie de cuisine comprising 75 pieces are typical. And the grossness of everything. I can't stand the narcissi even. I feel there are too many and the scent is too *cheap*. Yesterday L. M. who is staying at a place called Blonay brought me a bunch of lilies of the valley — an immense cauliflower it looked like, and smelt like.

But I must say the country round Sierre is simply wonderful. That's where I'd like to be. It's so unspoilt, too. I mean there are no Casinos, no *tea shops* and as far as I could see from my glimpse not a tourist to be seen. I shall go there at the end of June when Murry has joined me. I feel so remote, so cut off from everything here. . . . I can't walk at all. I lie all day in the shade and write or read and that's all. Work is the only thing that never fails. Even if people don't like my stories I don't mind. Perhaps they will one day — or the stories will be better. I've been reading Chaucer. Have you read his *Troilus and Cressid* lately? It is simply *perfect*. I have a passion for Chaucer just now. But England seems to think Miss Romer Wilson is so much the greatest writer that ever was born. She *does* sound wonderful, I must say. Is it all true?

June 1921

I am leaving here to-morrow. If I look down upon Montreux another day I shall fly into pieces with rage at the ugliness of it all. It's like a painting on a mineral water bottle — *Bâtiment des Eaux.* And then along the road that winds through (I must say lovely) vines go these awful, ugly people, and one can't help looking at them. Never have I seen such ugliness. Father, with a straw hat on the back of his head, coat off, waistcoat unbuttoned and stiff shirt showing, marches ahead and Mother follows — with her enormous highly respectable derrière and after them tag the little Swisses — Oh! Oh!! Oh!!!

Matters have reached a crisis too, as these last two days there has been the Fête des Narcisses. Hoards of uglies rushing by on bicycles with prodigious bunches of these murdered flowers on the handle-bars, all ready for the fray. Happily, it rained and became a Fête des Ombrelles instead. I think from the expression of the company homeward bound the umbrellas had been thrown as well!

To me, though, the symbol of Switzerland is that large middle-class female *behind*. It is the most respectable thing in the world. It is Matchless. Everyone has one in this hotel; some of the elderly ladies have two.

I think Sierre may be better and there one is, at least, in reach of forests and tumbling rivers. The man from Montana who is going to keep an Eye on me is near too, but thinking him over (as one does), I believe he's no better than the rest of them and he overcharged me *horribly*. I shall pin my faith on forests. Bother all doctors!

I know I *ought* to love —— and she is such a " brick," as they say. But when that brick comes flying in my direction — Oh, I DO want to dodge it!

I read less and less, or fewer and fewer books. Not because I don't want to read them, I do — but they seem so high up on the tree. It's so hard to get at them and there is nobody near to help. . . . On my bed at night there is a copy of Shakespeare, a copy of Chaucer, an automatic pistol and a black muslin fan. This is my whole little world.

I have just finished a new story which I'm going to send on

speck to the *Mercury*. I hope someone will like it. Oh, I *have* enjoyed writing it.

To Richard Murry *Chateau Belle Vue,*
Sierre, Valais
June 20, 1921

I answer your letter bang off. But so many thoughts go chasing through my head (do you see them? the last thought, rather slow, on a tricycle!) and there are so many things I'd like to talk over that it's not as easy as it sounds. . . . You know — it's queer — I feel so confident about you always. I feel that, the way you are building your boat, no harm can come to it. It will sail. You're building for the high seas, and Once you *do* take her out nothing will stop her.

About the old masters. What I feel about them (all of them — writers too, of course) is the more one *lives* with them the better it is for one's work. It's almost a case of living *into* one's ideal world — the world that one desires to express. Do you know what I mean? For this reason I find that if I stick to men like Chaucer and Shakespeare and Marlowe and even Tolstoy I keep much nearer what I want to do than if I confuse things with reading a lot of lesser men. I'd like to make the old masters my *daily* bread — in the sense in which it's used in the Lord's Prayer, really — to make them a kind of essential nourishment. All the rest is — well — it *comes after*.

I think I understand exactly what you mean by "visionary consciousness." It fits the writer equally well. It's mysterious and it's difficult to get into words. There is *this* world, and there is the world that the artist creates in this world, which is nevertheless *his* world, and subject to *his* laws — his "vision." Does that sound highflown? I don't mean it to be. It's difficult to get over, in a letter, a smile or a look or a something which makes it possible to say these things when one's with a person without that person feeling you are a bit of a priglet. . . .

J. told me you were working at technique. So am I. It's extraordinarily difficult — don't you find? My particular difficulty is a kind of fertility — which I suspect very much. It's not solid enough. But I go at it every day. It's simply endlessly fascinating.

We are leaving here at the end of this week and creeping by funicular up to Montana. There I hope we shall stay for the next two years. We have our eye on a chalêt called Les Sapins which is in the midst of the forests — pine forests — there's not even a fence or a bar between it and the trees. So you picture the wolves breathing under the front door, the bears looking through our keyhole and bright tigers dashing at the lighted window panes. Montana is on a small plateau ringed round by mountains. I'll tell you more about it when we get there. J. has been up twice. He says it's the best place he's ever seen.

This place, Sierre, is in a valley. It's only 1,500 feet high — very sheltered. Fig trees grow big, vines are everywhere; large flowery trees shake in the light. Marvellous light — Richard — and small lakes, bright, clear blue, where you can swim. Switzerland makes us laugh. It's a comic country: the people are extraordinary, like comic pictures and they are dead serious about it all. But there is something fine in it, too. They are " simple," unspoilt, honest and real democrats. The 3rd-class passenger is just as good as the 1st-class passenger in Switzerland and the shabbier you are the *less* you are looked at. No one expects you to be rich or to spend money. This makes life pleasant — very. They are not at all beautiful people; the men are very thick, stiff, ugly in the German way, and the women are nearly all *dead plain*. But seen from afar, in the fields, against mountains, they are all well in the picture. The Spring is a good time here. I arrived just as the field flowers were out; now the hay is gathered and the grapes are formed on the vines. I can't say, Richard, how I *love* the country. To watch the season through, to lose myself in love of the earth — that is life to me. I don't feel I could ever live in a city again. First the bare tree then the buds and the flowers, then the leaves, then the small fruit forming and swelling. If I only watch one tree a year one is richer for life.

To William Gerhardi   June 23, 1921

I cannot tell you how happy I am to know that *The Daughters of the Late Colonel* has given you pleasure. While I was writing that story I lived for it but when it was finished, I confess I hoped very much that my readers would understand what I was trying to express. But very few did. They thought it was " cruel "; they thought I was " sneering " at Jug and Constantia; or they thought it was " drab." And in the last paragraph I was " poking fun at the poor old things."

It's almost terrifying to be misunderstood. There was a moment when I first had " the idea " when I saw the two sisters as *amusing;* but the moment I looked deeper (let me be quite frank) I bowed down to the beauty that was hidden in their lives and to discover that was all my desire. . . . All was meant, of course, to lead up to that last paragraph, when my two flowerless ones turned with that timid gesture, to the sun. " Perhaps *now* . . ." And after that, it seemed to me, they died as surely as Father was dead.

To Lady Ottoline Morrell   *Châlet des Sapins*
Montana-sur-Sierre
July 24, 1921

Here it is simply exquisite weather. We are so high up (5,000 feet above the sea) that a cool breeze filters through from Heaven, and the forests are always airy. . . I can't imagine anything lovelier than this end of Switzerland. Once one loses sight of that hideous Lac Leman and *Co.* everything is different. Sierre, a little warm sunripe town in the valley, was so perfect that I felt I would like to live there. It has all the flowers of the South and it's gay and " queynt " and full of nightingales. But since we have come up the mountains it seems lovelier still. We have taken a small — not very small — châlet here for two years. It is quite remote — in a forest clearing; the windows look over the tree tops across a valley to snowy peaks the other side. The air feels wonderful but smells more wonderful still. I have never lived *in* a forest before, one steps out of the house and in a moment one is hidden among the trees. And there are little glades and groves full of flowers — with small ice-cold streams twinkling through. It is my joy to sit there on a tree trunk; if only one could make some small grasshoppery sound of praise to *someone* — thanks to *someone*. But who?

M. and I live like two small time-tables. We work all the morning and from tea to supper. After supper we read aloud and smoke; in the afternoon he goes walking and I crawling. The days seem to go by faster and faster. One beaming servant who wears peasant "bodies" and full skirts striped with velvet looks after everything. And though the chalêt is so arcadian it *has* got a bathroom with hot water and central heating for the winter and a piano and thick carpets and sunblinds. I am too old not to rejoice in these creature comforts as well.

The only person whom we see is my Cousin Elizabeth who lives half an hour's scramble away. We exchange Chateaubriand and baskets of apricots and have occasional lovely talks which are rather like what talks in the after-life will be like, I imagine ... ruminative, and reminiscent — although dear knows what it is really all about. How strange talking is — what mists rise and fall — how one loses the other and then thinks to have found the other — then down comes another soft final curtain. ... But it is incredible — don't you feel — how mysterious and isolated we each of us are — at the last. I suppose one ought to make this discovery once and for all, but I seem to be always making it again.

It seems to me that writers don't acknowledge it half enough. They pretend to know all there is in the parcel. But how *is* one to do it without seeming vague?

Some novels have been flying up our mountain side lately. ... I wish a writer would rise up — a new one — a really good one.

I keep on with my short stories. I have been doing a series for *The Sphere,* because it pays better than any other paper I know. But now they are done I don't believe they are much good. Too simple. It is always the next story which is going to contain everything, and that next story is always just out of reach. One seems to be saving up for it. I have been reading Shakespeare *as usual. The Winter's Tale* again. All the beginning is very dull — isn't it? That Leontes is an intolerable man and I *hate* gentle Hermione. Her strength of mind, too, in hiding just round the corner from him for 15 years is terrifying! But Oh — the Shepherd scene is too perfect. Now I am embedded in *Measure for Measure.* I had no idea it was so good. M. reads aloud in the evenings and we *make notes.* There are moments when our life is rather like a school for two! I see us walking out crocodile for two and correcting each other's exercises. But no — not really.

Is this a Fearfully dull letter? I'm afraid it is. I'm afraid "Katherine has become so boring nowadays."

Letters 1921

To the Hon. Dorothy Brett   *July 29, 1921*

I tremendously enjoyed that long letter. I had been out with M. down the road a little way and then across a stream and into the forest. There are small glades and lawns among the trees filled with flowers. I sat under a big fir and he went gathering. It was a dazzling bright day, big silvery clouds pressing hard on the mountain tops, not even the cotton grass moving. Lying on the moss I found minute strawberry plants and violets and baby fir cones, all looked faery — and M. moved near and far — calling out when he found anything special. . . . Then he disappeared down into a valley and I got up and explored the little fir parlours and sat on the stumps and watched ants and wondered where that apricot stone had come from. These forests are marvellous: one feels as though one were on a desert island somehow. As to the butterflies and golden and green dragon-flies and big tawny bumble bees, they are a whole population. M. came back with a huge bunch of treasures and I walked home and found your letter in the hall. So I sat down on the bottom step of the stairs with the flowers in a wet hanky beside me and read it. Don't you think the stairs are a good place for reading letters? I do. One is somehow suspended — one is on neutral ground — not in one's own world, not in a strange one. They are an almost perfect meeting place — oh Heavens! how stairs do fascinate me when I think of it. Waiting for people — sitting on strange stairs hearing steps from above, watching the light *playing* by itself — hearing — far below a door, looking down into a kind of dim brightness, watching someone come up. But I could go on for ever.

Must put them in a story though! People come out of themselves — on stairs — they issue forth, unprotected. And then the window on a *landing*. Why is it so different to all other windows? I must stop this . . .

I am deeply interested in what you feel about Manet. For years he has meant more to me than any other of those French painters. He satisfies something deep in me. There is a kind of beautiful real *maturity* in his painting, as though he had come into his own, and it is a rich heritage. I saw a reproduction of a very lovely Renoir the other day, a young woman — profile — a three-quarter with the arm lazily outstretched, lovely throat, bosom, shoulder —

such grace. But I think that in his later paintings he is so often muzzy. I can't appreciate the queer woolly outline, and I feel it was so often as like as not *rheumatism* rather than *revelation*. But I don't know. I'd like to have a feed of paintings one day — go from here to Madrid, say, and have a good look. I shall. Once one is out of England I always feel every *thing* and *place* is near. We are only four hours from Milan here. Well, even tho' we don't go — there it *is*. One *could* start on Saturday morning and be there for the opera that evening. It's the channel which is such a dividing line. It frightens me. It is so terrifically wide, really. And once one is across it one is *on the island*.

While I remember. Have you read *The Three Mulla-Mulgars* by de la Mare? If you haven't, *do* get it and read it to any infants you know. It's about three monkeys.

One seems to read a lot here. It's the kind of house in which you go into a room to comb your hair, find *Gulliver's Travels* on the shelf behind the door and are immediately lost to the world. The bedroom walls are of wood; there are thick white carpets on some of the floors — outside the windows wide balconies and thick striped cotton blinds shut out the midday glare. A great many flowers everywhere — generally apricots ripening on the balcony ledge and looking rather gruesome like little decapitated chickens. If only I can make enough money so as never to leave here for good! One never gets old here. At 65 one is as spry as a two-year-old — and (I suppose it is the climate) all is so *easy*. The strain is gone. One hasn't that feeling of dragging a great endless rope out of a dark sea. Do *you* hate London? No, I do see it has its beauty and its charm, too. But all the same one feels so like the swollen sheep that looks up and is not fed. It is so hard — to put it " stuffily " — to live from one's centre of being in London.

Tell me what you are doing, if you are so inclined. Don't lose any more half stones! For Heaven's sake put the half back again. Look at the Sargol advertisements and be wise in time. God only loves the Fat; the thin people he stick pins into for ever and ever.

August 8, 1921

Forgive this paper. I am at the top of the house and there is no other here. I am on the wide balcony which leads out of my dressing room. It's early morning. All the tree-tops are burnished gold, a light wind rocks in the branches. The mountains across the wide valley are still in sunlight: on the remote drowsy peaks there are small cloud drifts — silvery. What I love to watch, what seems to become part of one's vision, though, are the deep sharp shadows in the ravines and stretching across the slopes. But one couldn't imagine a more marvellous view or one more perfect to live by. I watch it from early morning until late at night, when bats are out and booming moths fly for one's hair. With intervals. . . .

Please *please* never think I need money like that. I can always get money. I can always go into some wonder place and hold out my hat or sell 1d. worth of boracic ointment for 2/6, net profit 2/5, or —— money has no terrors for me nowadays. And besides I am making some — and it's only a question of my own activity how much I make. At present I am £30 *down* — and two nuns have just come with needlework made by infants in their convent. The dear creatures (I have a romantic *love* of nuns) my two gentle columbines, blue-hooded, mild, folded over — took little garments out of a heavy box and breathed on them and I spent £2 7/- on minute flannel jackets and pinnies for Ernestine's sister's first not-yet-born baby.

The butcher's bill on *red* slaughtered butcher's paper is quite unpaid, and now I can't pay it. But you see that's what I am like about money, never to be pitied or helped!

What is your picture, the one you thought of in your bath? Yes, I find hot baths very inspiring, so does my Cousin Elizabeth. She reads Shakespeare in hers. Her love of flowers is really her great charm. Not that she says very much, but every word *tells*. A man couldn't discover it in her — he wouldn't realise how deep it is. For no man loves flowers as women *can*. Elizabeth looks coolly at the exquisite petunias and says, in a small far away voice, "They have a very perfect scent." But I feel I can hear oceans of love breaking in her heart for petunias and nasturtiums and snapdragons.

I must stop this letter and get on with my new story. It's called

At the Bay and it's (I hope) full of sand and seaweed, bathing dresses hanging over verandas, and sandshoes on window sills, and little pink " sea " convolvulus, and rather gritty sandwiches and the tide coming in. And it smells (oh I *do* hope it smells) a little bit fishy.

To Richard Murry   *August 9, 1921*

We have just been doing the flowers — before we start work. Scene: the salle à manger — with windows wide open and pink curtains flapping. The table bare and heaped with petunias, snapdragons and nasturtiums. Glass vases and bowls full of water — a general sense of buds and wetness and that peculiar stickiness of fresh stalks. J. — white shirt with sleeves up to his shoulders, white duck trousers and rope shoes, snipping with a large pair of wet scissors — me — blue cotton kimono and pink slippers, a-filling of the vases. . . . J. is *terribly* keen on petunias. I wish I could send you a whole great bastick full. They are wonderful flowers — almost pure light — and yet an exquisite starry shape. We have every colour from pale pink to almost blackish purple. And do you know the smell of snapdragons? My dear boy, I must here pause or you will walk away. But tell me — why do people paint forever bottles and onions? A white snapdragon, for instance, just for a change would be worth it, surely — Richard. I wish I could unobtrusively give you these things — leave flowers instead of foundlings on your studio doorstep, in fact. Perhaps one day I shall be able to. . . .

I have been looking at a good deal of modern " work " lately, and it almost seems to me that the blight upon it is a kind of *fear*. Writers, at any rate, are self-conscious to such a pitch nowadays that their feeling for life seems to be absolutely stopped — arrested. It is sad. They know they oughtn't to say " driving fast, eh ? " and yet they don't know what they ought to say. If I am dead sincere I'd say I think it is because people have so little love in their hearts for each other. " Love casteth out Fear," is one of those truths that one goes on proving and proving. And if you are without fear you are free; it's fear makes us slaves — But this sounds so prosy. You know it as well as I do. I hate to bore you.

J. had a birthday on Saturday. His presents were (1) a panama hat; (2) some coloured blotting paper; (3) a cake; (4) a ruler. We had a tea with candles complete and liqueur chocolates that were positively terrifying. The moment of agonizing suspense when you had the chocolate in your mouth and had to bite through to the *mysterious* liqueur. However, we survived.

The weather is superb, here. There has been a Battle of the Wasps. Three hosts with their citadels have been routed from my balcony blind. In the swamps, still white with cotton grass, there are hundreds of grasshoppers. J. saw an *accident* to one the other day. He jumped by mistake into a stream and was borne away. Body not recovered. When we thought about it — it was the first real accident to an insect that we remembered. Richard, I must start work.

I still have so much to tell you. I've only unpacked the little small things on top. All the big heavy ones are underneath.

L. M., who lives about 2 miles from here, is going to England this month and is going to bring back Wingley. Athy is married to an elderly lady in Hampstead, I believe, a *widow*. She lost her first husband — a lovely tabby — some time ago.

August 1921

It's Sunday — my day for writing letters. But I don't write them. You are one of the very very few people whom I *want* to write to. I think of you and I straightway long to " clasp hands across a vast " ... and more. I want to talk and to listen — (that first) and to have a good long look at you. When I'm fond of people their appearance is very valuable to me too. Do you feel like that? But *re people*. It's queer how unimportant they seem to become as one goes on. One feels as tho' one has seen them enough — got what one wants from them and so — to work. I don't mean that in a cold-blooded way. Perhaps the truth is one has less and less time away from work. It gets more engrossing every day here, and we live like a pair of small time-tables. The hours away from it we read Shakespeare aloud, discuss what has been written. J. goes flower finding — then the specimens have to be sorted, pressed, examined. While he's out I play the piano or go for a small snail crawl myself. And before one can say knife it's time to go to bed. We get up at 7.30 — both of us — and breakfast on a balcony all windows with a ring of snow mountains to look at across the valley.

Come here, one day. It's a very good place. I am determined to make enough money to build a small shack here and make it my winter perch for as long as I need perches. The point about this place is it is not spoilt. There never can be a railway here. There is nothing to do except look at the mountains, climb them and explore the forests and paddle in the streams. Motor cars can't do these things so the rich and great will never come. The very flowers seem to me to know this — there is a brightness upon them — and they are careless — even the wild strawberry doesn't bother to hide — And there's a delicate creature (the Bell Flower, J.'s favourite) that grows everywhere — as fine as a harebell and a very clear almost glassy blue. It would not dare to grow in more civilised places. Oh, Richard — I do love the earth! When I go off by myself here — one slips through the tree trunks and one is out of sight at once — hidden from every eye. That's my joy. I sit on a stump or on the fir needles and my only trouble is that I can't make some small grasshoppery sound now and then — one wants to praise someone or give thanks to someone.

Down below our windows in that rocky clearing before the trees begin there is a flock of goats feeding as I write. The sound of their bells is very pleasant. I look at them and wish I could put one in an envelope (a goat, I mean) for you to draw. Small, fine, flattish head, delicate legs, lean springing haunches. I'd like also to post you our maid-servant Ernestine to paint. She looks like a sunflower. She's in the kitchen now, shelling peas, and she wears a Sunday bodice, yellow with black velvet stripes and rather big sleeves. (She always dresses in the peasant costume.) As I write it seems to me I've told you all this before. Have I? Forgive me if I have.

To the Hon. Dorothy Brett *August 29, 1921*

I would have written before but the Furies have had me until to-day. Something quite new for a change — high fever, deadly sickness and weakness. I haven't been able to lift my head from the pillow. I think it has been a break-down from too much work. I have felt exhausted with all those stories lately and yet — couldn't stop. Well, there has been a stop now and I am just putting forth my horns again and thinking of climbing up the hill. . . . How I do abominate any kind of illness! . . . Oh God, what it is to live in such a body! Well, it doesn't bear thinking about. . . .

As soon as I can get well enough to go downstairs I shall engage our one original cab and go for a drive behind the old carthorse with his jingle-bells. The driver — as a great honour — throws the footmat over the back when one goes for a party of pleasure. He seems to think that is *very* chic! But this is such a beautiful country — Oh! it is so marvellous. Never looks the same — the air like old, still wine — sound of bells and birds and grasshoppers playing their fiddles and the wind shaking the trees. It rains and the drops on the fir trees afterwards are so flashing — bright and glowing that one feels all is enchanted. It is cloudy — we live in fine white clouds for days and then suddenly at night all is crystal clear and the moon has gold wings. They have just taken the new honey from the hives, I wish I could send you a jar. All the summer is shut up in a little pot.

But summer is on the wane — the wane. Now M. brings back autumn crocuses, and his handkerchief is full of mushrooms. I love the satiny colour of mushrooms, and their *smell* and the soft stalks. The Autumn crocuses push above short, mossy grass. Big red pears — monsters — jostle in Ernestine's apron. Yes, ça commence, ma chère. And I feel as I always do that Autumn is loveliest of all. There is such a sharpness with the sweetness — there is the sound of cold water running fast in the streams in the forest. M. says the squirrels are tamer already. But Heavens, Brett — Life is so marvellous — it is so rich — such a store of marvels that one can't say which one prefers. . . . I feel with you — most deeply and truly that it's not good to be " permanent." It's the old cry: " Better be impermanent movables!" Now here, for instance — we are only 4 hours from Italy — one can run into Italy for tea. M. went down to see Elizabeth last week and she had so done. She had waked with a feeling for Italy that morning and behold she was flown. And that night she sat in the opera house in Milan. . . . That is *right* — I am sure. That's why I hate England. I can't help it, Miss, Downs or no Downs. There is that channel which lies like a great cold sword between you and your dear love, Adventure. And by Adventure I mean — yes — The wonderful feeling that one can lean out of heaven knows what window to-night — one can wander under heaven knows what flowery trees. Strange songs sound at the windows. The wine bottle is a new shape — a perfectly new moon shines outside. . . . No, don't settle. Don't have a convenient little gentlewoman's residence. Hot baths in one's own bathroom are fearfully nice — but they are too *dear*. I prefer to bathe in a flower-pot as I go my way. . . .

Renoir — at the last — bores me. His feeling for flesh is a kind of super-intense feeling about a lovely little cut of lamb. I am always fascinated by lovely bosoms but not without the heads and hands as well, and I want in fact the feeling that all this beauty is in the deepest sense attached to life. Real life! In fact I must confess it is the spirit which fascinates me in flesh. That does for me as far as modern painters are concerned, I suppose. But I feel bored to my last groan by all these pattern-mongers. Oh, how weary it is! I would die of it if I thought. And the writers are just the same. But they are worse than the painters because they are so many of them dirty-minded as well.

What makes Lawrence a *real* writer is his passion. Without passion one writes in the air or on the sand of the seashore. But L. has got it all wrong, I believe. He is right, I imagine — or how shall I put it . . . ? It's my belief that nothing will save the world but love. But his tortured, satanic demon love I think is all wrong. The whole subject is so mysterious, tho'; one could write about it forever. But let me try to say something. . . .

It seems to me there is a great change come over the world since people like us believed in God, God is now gone for all of us. Yet me must believe and not only that we must carry our weakness and our sin and our devilish-ness to somebody. I don't mean in a bad, abasing way. But we must feel that we are *known,* that our hearts are known as God knew us. Therefore love to-day between " lovers " has to be not only human, but divine to-day. They love each other for everything and through everything and their love is their religion. It can't become anything less — even affection — I mean it can't become less supreme, because it is an act of faith to believe! But oh, it is no good. . . .

I can't write it all out. I should go into pages and pages.

My stories for *The Sphere* are all done — thank the Lord! I have had copies with ILLUSTRATIONS! Oh, Brett! such fearful horrors. All my dear people looking like — well — Harrod's 29/6 crêpe de chine blouses and young tailors' gents, and my old men — stuffy old woolly sheep. It's a sad trial. I am at present embedded in a terrific story, but it still frightens me.

To Richard Murry   *September 5, 1921*

I have been too long in answering your last letter. Forgive me. They varnished the outside of this châlet and the " niff " gave me white lead poisoning and I felt an awful worm with it. The whole world seemed varnish. Everything I ate had varnish sauce. Even J. was overcome for a day. But it's over now, and we appear to be living in a house beautifully basted with the best brown gravy — and the factory is in full blas' again. I must say we do manage to get through a great deal of work here, and there are always side issues — such as jam-making, sewing on our buttings, cutting each other's hair, which fill up the margin of the days. We *try* to make it a rule not to talk in bed. It's queer how full life is once one gets free of wasted time. . . .

My ambition is to make enough money to build a small house here, near where we are — on a grassy slope with a wood behind and mountains before. It will take about five years to do it — get the money together. But it would be a very great satisfaction to design a really good place to work in — down to the last cupboard. But who am I to talk so lofty? When — if — the time comes and you're not too famous I'll beg you to lay aside your laurels and do it for us. I'll only look over your shoulder and breathe very hard when you make those lovely little lines that mean stairs.

Since I last wrote summer has gone. It's autumn. Little small girls knock at the door with pears to sell and blue-black plums. The hives have been emptied; there's new honey and the stars look almost frosty. Speaking of stars reminds me — we were sitting on the balcony last night. It was dark. These huge fir trees " take " the darkness marvellously. We had just counted four stars and remarked a light; high up — what was it? — on the mountain opposite, when suddenly from far away a little bell began ringing. Someone played a tune on it — something gay, merry, *ancient,* over and over. I suppose it was some priest or lay brother in a mountain village. But what we felt was — it's good to think such things still happen — to think some peasant goes off in the late evening and delights to play that carillon. I sometimes have a fear that simple-hearted people are no more. I was ashamed of that fear last night. The little bell seemed to say, but joyfully: " Be not afraid. All is not lost."

All being well as they say, Wingley should arrive this week. He'll be terrified after the journey. We shall have to get him snow boots for the winter and an airman's helmet made of mouse's skin.

J.: Ask the old boy if he has seen Charlie Chaplin in " The Kid." And tell him to let us know what he thinks of it.

K.: I will.

K. to R.: ?

R.:

To the Hon. Dorothy Brett September 1921

The Cezanne book, Miss, you won't get back until you send a policeman or an urgent request for it. It is fascinating, and you can't think how we enjoy such a book on our mountain tops. It's awfully sympathetic to me. I am absolutely uneducated about painting. I can only look at it as a writer, but it seems to me the real thing. It's what one is aiming at. One of his men gave me quite a shock. He's the *spit* of a man I've just written about, one Jonathan Trout.[1] To the life. I wish I could cut him out and put him in my book.

I've just finished my new book. Finished last night at 10.30. Laid down the pen after writing " Thanks be to God." I wish there was a God. I am longing to (1) praise him, (2) thank him. The title is *At the Bay.* That's the name of the very long story in it — a continuation of *Prelude.* It's about 60 pages. I've been at it all last night. My precious children have sat in here, playing cards. I've wandered about all sorts of places — in and out — I hope it is good. It is as good as I can do, and all my heart and soul is in it . . . every single bit. Oh God, I hope it gives pleasure to someone. . . . It is so strange to bring the dead to life again. There's my Grandmother, back in her chair with her pink knitting, there stalks my uncle over the grass; I feel as I write, " You are not dead, my darlings. All is remembered. I bow down to you. I efface myself so that you may live again through me in your richness and beauty." And one

[1] See " At the Bay."

feels *possessed*. And then the place where it all happens. I have tried to make it as familiar to " you " as it is to me. You know the marigolds? You know those pools in the rocks, you know the mouse trap on the wash-house window-sill? And too, one tries to go deep — to speak to the secret self we all have — to acknowledge that. I mustn't say any more about it.

No, we certainly shan't be back in England for years. Sometimes, in bed at night, we plan one holiday a year, but everywhere else feels nearer than England. If we can get the money we shall build here in two or three years' time. We have already chosen the way to look — the way the house shall face. And it is christened *Châlet Content*. We are both most fearful dreamers, especially when it's late and we lie staring at the ceiling. It begins with me. M. declares he won't talk. It's too late. Then I hear: " Certainly not more than two floors and a large open fire-place." A long pause. *K.:* " What about *bees?* " *M.:* " Most certainly bees, and I aspire to a goat." And it ends with us getting fearfully hungry and M. going off for two small whacks of cake while I heat two small milks on the spirit stove.

You know Wingley? The Mountain brought him over. He arrived with immense eyes after having flown through all that landscape and it was several hours before the famous purr came in to action. Now he's completely settled down and reads Shakespeare with us in the evenings. I wonder what cat-Shakespeare is like. We expect him to write his reminiscences shortly. They are to be bound in mouse skin. . . .

Goodbye. I am taking a holiday to-day after my labours last week. I wrote for nine solid hours yesterday.

Who do you think turned up at the end of this letter? Mrs. H. G. Wells and two young H. G. Wells. *Very* nice boys. We are full of gaiety.

To Richard Murry   *September 22, 1921*

Just a note to say that Wingley, our gooseberry-eyed one has arrived. Thin — terribly — with the bones sticking out of his rump like a cow's bones do. A mingy little ruff and fur that has turned brown like an actor's black overcoat. You can imagine his *look* after the journey, flashing across the world on the end of a string.

But when J. lay on the floor and rubbed noses with him he turned over and showed off his white weskit in just his old way. He is now quite settled down, reads Shakespeare with us every night and marks the place in his copy with a dead fly. It's awfully nice to have him. He's like a little anchor, here. We hope later on he may be persuaded to write his reminiscences. . . .

Sunday

We thought your criticism of " The Kid " was extremely interesting. At last we got an idea what it really was like. It's a pity Charles lets these other things creep in — a great pity. I should very much like to see him with the infant. I feel that would be fine. But most of the rest — dear me, *no!* As to the tabloid of the lady with the cross — such things make one hang one's head.

We have been squirrel-gazing this afternoon through field-glasses. They are exquisite little creatures — so intent, preoccupied, as it were, and so careless. They flop softly from branch to branch, hang upside down, just for the sake of hanging. Some here are as small as rats, with reddish coats and silver bellies. The point about looking at birds and so on through glasses is one sees them in their own world, off their guard. One spies, in fact.

I'd like to send you some *moss*. Do you like moss? There are many kinds here, and just now it is in its beauty. It's nice to sit down and ruffle it with one's hand. Flowers are gone. A few remain, but they are flat on the grass without their stalks — dandelions and purple ones. The mountain ash is *terrific* against the blue. There aren't many leaves here to turn, but the wild strawberry makes up for them. Minute leaves of every colour are scattered on the ground.

In fact, if possible, this early autumn is all the bes' — even better than summer or spring. I mustn't send you a catalogue, though. I must refrain.

To Sylvia Lynd *September 24, 1921*

I have been waiting to talk to you — to have you to myself, no less — until I could chase my new book out of the house. I thought it never would go. Its last moments lingered on and on. It got up, turned again, took off its gloves, again sat down, reached the door, came back, until finally M. marked it down, lassooed it with a stout string and hurled it at Pinker. Since when there's been an ominous silence. True, I haven't had time to hear yet, but one has a shameful feeling that it ought to have been "recognised" even at the bottom of the first mountain and a feeble cheer — a cheer left over from Charlie C. — might have been raised. . . . No, that sounds proud. It's not really pride but FEAR!

But it's gone. May I give you a small hug for your marvellous letter? It really is a heavenly gift to be able to put yourself, jasmine, summer grass, a kingfisher, a poet, the pony, an excursion and the new sponge-bag and bedroom slippers all into an envelope. How does one return thanks for a piece of somebody's life? When I am depressed by the superiority of men, I comfort myself with the thought that they can't write letters like that. You make me feel, too, that whatever star they were born under it wasn't the dancing one. Keep well! Never be ill again! . . .

I lapped up the gossip. . . . What is happening to "married pairs"? They are almost extinct. I confess, for my part, I believe in marriage. It seems to me the only possible relation that really is satisfying. And how else is one to have peace of mind to enjoy life and to do one's work? To know *one other* seems to me a far greater adventure than to be on kissing acquaintance with dear knows how many. It certainly takes a lifetime and it's far more "wonderful" as time goes on. Does this sound hopelessly old-fashioned? I suppose it does. But there it is — to make jam with M., to look for the flowers that NEVER are in the Alpine Flora book, to talk, to grow things, even to watch M. darning his socks over a *lemon,* seems to me to take up all the time one isn't working. People nowadays seem to live in such confusion. I have a horror of dark muddles. Not that life is easy, really, or that one can be "a child" all the time, but time to *live* is needed. These complications take years to settle, years to get over. I wish you'd write a novel about married happiness. It is time for one. . . . It is time for a *good* novel on any subject, though. Perhaps we don't see them here. . . .

One thing one does miss here, and that is seeing people. One doesn't ask for many, but there come moments when I long to *see* and *hear* and listen — that most of all.

Otherwise this September has been perfect. Every day is finer. There's a kind of greengage light on the trees. The flowers are gone. All except flat starry yellow and silver ones that lie tight to the turf. M. is a fierce mushroom hunter. He spares none. Little mushroom " tots " swim in the soup and make me feel a criminal. The mountain ash is brilliant — flashing bright against the blue. And the quince jam is boiling something beautiful, M'm, as I write. I love Autumn. I feel it's better than summer, even. Oh, the moss here! I've never seen such moss, and the colour of the little wild strawberry leaves that are threaded through. They are almost the only leaf that turns here, so turn they do with a vengeance.

I hardly dare mention birds. It's rather hard Harold M. should have such a very large bird in his bonnet; it makes all the rest of us go without. There are some salmon pink ones here just now passing through, which but for Harold M. I should enjoy. . . .

To Violet Schiff   *October 1921*

I am sure Switzerland is the place for health and for work — I mean especially and above all for nerves. There is an extraordinary feeling of ease here. It seems it is easy to live; one feels remote and undisturbed. I've never known anything like the feeling of peace and when one isn't working the *freshness* in the air, the smell of pines, the taste of snow in one's teeth — that's exaggeration — it's only the spiritual flavour. I think I really judge a place by how vividly I can recall the past. One lives in the Past — or I do. And here it is living.

My book is to lie in Constable's bosom until after the New Year. It's called, after all, *The Garden Party*. I hope you like the title. The *Mercury* is publishing one of the stories in a month or two. Terribly long. Too long for the *Mercury*. But that's enough and too much about me —

And now I have forgotten my health. Thank you, dearest Violet. I think my lungs are quiescent — rather the disease is. My heart is the same at present. But I feel much better — a different person altogether on the whole. No longer an invalid, even tho' I still can't walk and still cough and so on. . . .

To the Hon. Dorothy Brett October 1, 1921

I am sitting writing to you in the balcony among teacups, grapes, a brown loaf shaped like a bean, a plaited cake with almond paste inside and nuts out. M. has forsaken it to join our Cousin Elizabeth. She appeared to-day behind a bouquet — never smaller woman carried bigger bouquets. She looks like a garden walking, of asters, late sweet peas, stocks, and always petunias.

She herself wore a frock like a spider web, a hat like a berry — and gloves that reminded me of thistles in seed. Oh, how I love the appearance of people — how I delight in it, if I love them. I have gathered Elizabeth's frocks to my bosom as if they were part of her flowers. And then when she smiles a ravishing wrinkle appears on her nose — and never have I seen more exquisite hands. Oh, dear, I hope we shall manage to keep her in our life. It's terrible how one's friends disappear and how quickly one runs after to lock the door and close the shutters. . . . The point about her is that one loves her and is proud of her. Oh, that's so important! To be proud of the person one loves. It is essential. It's deep — deep. There's no wound more bitter to love than not be able to be proud of the other. It's the unpardonable offence, I think.

But no doubt Elizabeth is far more important to me than I am to her. She's surrounded, lapped in lovely friends. Read her last book, if you can get hold of it. It's called *Vera* and published by Macmillan. It's amazingly good!

Except for her we are lost in the forest. And next month the weather will change. Six weeks or two months in the clouds, with nothing to see but more cloud, before it clears and the snow falls. Other people who flee from the mountains in the between seasons seem to think it will be a very awful time. But there is so much to do. And I love to be in a place all the year round, to know it in all its changes.

I am very interested in your doll still life. I've always wondered why nobody really saw the beauty of dolls. The dollishness of them. People make them look like cricket-bats with eyes as a rule. But there is a kind of smugness and rakishness combined in dolls and heaven knows how much else that's exquisite, and the only word I can think of is *precious*. What a life one leads with them! How complete! Their hats — how perfect — and their shoes, or even minute boots. And the pose of a doll's hand — very dimpled with spreading fingers. Female dolls in their nakedness are the most female things on earth. . . .

I keep on being interrupted by the sound in the trees. It's getting late — the tree-tops look as if they had been dipped into the gold-pot and there's a kind of soft happy sighing or swinging or ruffling — all three — going on. A bird, bright salmon pink with mouse-grey wings hangs upside down pecking a fir cone. The shadows are growing long on the mountains. But it's impossible to describe this place. It has so brought back my love of nature that I shall spend all the rest of my life . . . trekking. A winter in Spitzbergen is an ambition of ours after some photographs in *The Sphere*. It looks marvellous. The only question is will our cat be able to stand it! The nearest other cat is in China. . . .

I've started and torn up two bad stories and now I am in the middle of the third. It's about a hypocrite. My flesh creeps as I write about him and my eyes pop at his iniquities. . . .

Don't get caught in the cold blasts. Wrap yourself up. Make the charlady feed you on bakin. In my infancy I used to cry myself to bed with the tragic lines:

> I bought a pound of ba—kin
> An fried it in a *pan*
> But nobody came to e—eat it
> But me—e and *my* young man!

October 5, 1921

I've got another old chill. I'm lying on the balcony in J. M. M.'s jaeger cardigan with a jaeger blanket up to my chest and fever. The *best* part of a chill is fever. Then the world has just that something added which makes it almost unbearably beautiful. It is worth it.

I am so glad you are hearing some music. I don't think music ever makes me feel as Mozart does you, for instance. It's like being gloriously dead — if you know what I mean. One *is* not any more — one is wafted away, and yet there's a feeling of rejoicing and a kind of regret — ah, such regret — mixed together that, I feel, disembodied spirits must know. But to tell the absolute truth, though Beethoven does that for me, so does Caruso on a really good gramophone. . . .

M. and I, before this chill seized me, have been taking some more driving *exercise*. Even the horse was amazed last time and stopped every three minutes and turned round and ogled us. I am going to wear riding breeches next time and M. pink coat and stock made of a dinner napkin. We leapt up into the air, bounded from side to side, shook, fell forward, were tossed back. The road was an ancient water-course with upside-down mountains in it. But the view! The beauty of everything! The gold-green pastures with herds of tiny rams and cattle and white goats. We arrived finally in a valley where the trees were turning. Cherry trees, a bright crimson, yellow maples, and apple-trees *flashing* with apples. Little herd girls and boys with switches of mountain ash ran by. There was a very old saw-mill that had turned too, a deep golden red. There can't be any place in the world more wonderful than the road to Lens. It is near there we mean to pitch our ultimate tent.

To Mrs. Charles Renshaw   *October 14, 1921*

My little Sister,

Your handkerchief is such a very gay one, it looks as though it had dropped off the hankey tree. Thank you for it, darling. I remember one birthday when you bit me! It was the same one when I got a doll's pram and in a rage let it go hurling by itself down the grassy slope outside the conservatory. Father was *awfully* angry and said no one was to speak to me. Also the white azalea bush was out. *And* Aunt Belle had brought from Sydney a new recipe for icing. It was tried on my cake and wasn't a great success because it was much too brittle. I can see and feel its smoothness now. You make me long to have a talk with you, in some place like the lily lawn. Ah, Jeanne, anyone who says to me, "Do you remember?" simply has my heart . . . I remember everything, and perhaps the great joy of Life to me is in playing just that game. Going back with someone into the past — going back to the dining-room at 75, to the proud and rather angry-looking seltzogene on the sideboard, with the little *bucket* under the spout. Do you remember that hiss it gave and sometimes a kind of groan? And the smell inside the sideboard of Worcester sauce and corks from old claret bottles?

But I must not begin such things. If we are ever together down the Pelorus Sounds come off with me for a whole day — will you? — and let's just remember. How Chummie loved it, too! Can't you hear his soft boyish laugh and the way he said, "Oh—abso-*lute*-ly!"

To the Hon. Dorothy Brett   October 15, 1921

All this week I have been most fearfully busy with a long story which was only finished late last night. Finished it is, however. Thanks be to God. It's called *The Garden Party,* and I have decided to call my new book by that title instead of the other. In the meantime the *Mercury* is bringing out that very long seaweedy story of mine *At the Bay.* I feel inclined to suggest to them to give away a spade an' bucket with each copy. . . .

Oh, how I saw that awful party! What a nightmare! I have a perfect horror of such affairs! They are always the same. One has to be encased in vanity like a beetle to escape being hurt. And the ghastly thing is they are so hard to forget; one lives them over and over. Don't go to them. But what's the use of saying that; there are times when one has to go. It's difficult to see what compensations there are in city life. I think the best plan is to live away from them and then, when one has done a good deal of work and wants a holiday, take a real holiday in a place like Paris, or Madrid or even London (but not for me London). It is nice sometimes to be with many people and to hear music and to be " overcome " by a play and to watch dancing. Walking in streets is nice, too. But one always wants to have an avenue of escape. One wants to feel a stranger, for these things to have their charm, and — most important of all — one wants to have a solid body of work behind one. The longer I live the more I realise that in work only lies one's strength and one's salvation. And such *supreme joy* that one gives thanks for life with every breath.

Midday. Oh, why can't you hear that darling little bell in the valley? It's misty to-day, and the sun shines and the mist is silver. It's still. And somewhere there rings over and over that little chime, so forgetful, so easy, so gay. It's like a gay little pattern, gold and butterflies and cherubs with trumpets in the very middle of the page — so that one pauses before one begins the afternoon chapter. We are going for a picnic. We take the jaeger rug and the bastick. And then we lie under a tree. Stir our tea with a twig, look up, look down, wonder why. But it begins to get dark earlier. At seven o'clock the moon is in full feather on my balcony. . . .

To the Countess Russell   *October 16, 1921*

We — I — miss you, lovely little neighbour. I think of you often. Especially in the evenings, when I am on the balcony and it's too dark to write or to do anything but wait for the stars. A time I love. One feels half disembodied, sitting like a shadow at the door of one's being while the dark tide rises. Then comes the moon, marvellously serene, and small stars, very merry for some reason of their own. It is so easy to forget, in a *worldly* life, to attend to these miracles. But no matter. They are there waiting, when one returns. Dawn is another. The incomparable beauty of every early morning, before human beings are awake! But it all comes back to the same thing, Elizabeth — there's no escaping the glory of Life. Let us engage to live for ever. For ever is not half long enough for me.

London feels far away from here. We thrill, we are round-eyed at the slightest piece of news. You cannot imagine how your letter was taken in — absorbed. I see you stepping into carriages, driving to the play, dining among mirrors and branched candlesticks and far away sweet sounds. Disguised in " Kepanapron," I open your door to illustrious strangers, Mighty Ones, who take off their coats in the large hall and are conducted into your special room where the books are. . . . Do not forget us.

J. has been so deep in Flaubert this week that his voice has only sounded from under the water, as it were. He has emerged at teatime and together we have examined the . . . very large, solid pearls . . . I must say I do like a man to my tea.

And here are your petunias, lovely as ever, reminding me always of your garden and the grass with those flat dark rosettes where the daisy plants had been.

But this isn't a letter. Farewell. May Good Fortune fall ever more deeply in love with thee.

To S. S. Koteliansky   *October 18, 1921*

Dear Koteliansky, my enemy,

Can you tell me anything about that Russian doctor? If there was a chance of seeing him and if he was not too expensive I would go to Paris in the Spring and ask him to treat me. . . .

Not a day passes but I think of you. It is sad that we are enemies. If only you would accept my love. It is *good* love — not the erotic bag kind.

But no. You cannot answer my letters. When my name is mentioned you cross yourself and touch wood.

                                     It is sad for me.
                                                   Katherine.

Don't return the post card. [A photograph of herself.] If you hate me too much — burn it in a candle.

To the Countess Russell   *Sunday*
                                                October 1921

I actually had the strength of mind to keep your letter unopened until J. came back from his wood-gathering. Then spying him from my balcony while he was still afar off, I cried in a loud voice. And he came up and we read it together and thanked God for you. . . . You do such divine things! Your visit to Stratford, Hamlet in the Churchyard, the snapdragons, the gate of Anne's cottage, King Lear on the river — it all sounded perfect. In fact, one felt that if the truth were known William had gathered you the snapdragon and you had leaned over the gate together.

What are you reading, Elizabeth? Is there something new which is very good? I have turned to Milton all last week. There are times when Milton seems the only food to me. He is a most blessed man.

             ". . . Yet not the more
       Cease I to wander where the Muses haunt
       Cleer Spring, or shadie Grove, or sunnie Hill,
       Smit with the love of sacred song; "

But the more poetry one reads the more one longs to read! This afternoon J., lying on my furry rug, has been reading aloud Swinburne's *Ave Atque Vale* — which did not sound fearfully good. I suspect those green buds of sin and those grey fruits of shame. And try as one may, one can't see Baudelaire. Swinburne sits so very tight on the tomb. Then we read Hardy's poem to Swinburne, which J. adored. I, being an inferior being, was a little troubled by the picture of Sappho and Algernon meeting en plein mer (if one can say such a thing) and he begging her to tell him where her manuscript was. It seemed such a watery rendezvous. But we went on reading Hardy. How exquisite, how marvellous some of those poems are! They are almost intolerably near to one. I mean I always long to weep . . . that love and regret touched so lightly — that autumn tone, that feeling that "Beauty passes though rare, rare it be . . ."

But speaking of autumn, it is here. Yesterday, soft, silky, sweet-smelling summer kissed the geraniums, and waving the loveliest hand, *went*. Oh, Elizabeth, how I longed for you this morning on my balcony! The sun came through, a silver star. In the folds of the mountains little clouds glittered like Dorothy Wordsworth's sheep. And all that paysage across the valley was a new land. The colour is changed since you were here. The green is gold, a very deep gold like *amber*. On the high peaks snow was falling. And the Wind walking among the trees had a new voice. It was like land seen from a ship. It was like arriving in the harbour, and wondering, half frightened and yet longing, whether we would go ashore. But no, I can't describe it. Soon after all was grey and down came the white bees. The feeling in the house changed immediately. Ernestine became mysterious and blithe. The Faithful One ran up and down as though with cans of hot water. One felt the whisper had gone round that the pains had begun and the doctor had been sent for.

I am just at the beginning of a new story, which I may turn into a serial. Clement Shorter wants one. But he stipulates for 13 "curtains" and an adventure note! Thirteen curtains! And my stories haven't even a wisp of blind cord as a rule. I have never been able to manage curtains. I don't think I shall be able to see such a wholesale *hanging* through.

The knitting becomes almost frenzied at times. We may be sober in our lives, but we shall be garish in our shrouds and flamboyant in our coffins if this goes on. J. now *mixes* his wools thereby gaining what *he* calls a " superb astrachan effect." Chi lo sa! I softly murmur over my needles. I find knitting turns me into an imbecile. It is the female tradition, I suppose.

To John Galsworthy　　　　　　　　　　*October 25, 1921*

By an unfortunate mischance your letter only reached me to-day. My silence must have seemed very ungracious. . . . Though, even now, I scarcely know how to thank you. Your noble generous praise is such precious encouragement that all I can do is try to deserve it. I want to promise you that I will never do less than my best, that I will try not to fail you. But this sounds superficial and far from my *feeling*. There the letters are, tied up in the silk handkerchief with my treasures. I shall never forget them. I wish, some day, I might press your hand for them. Thank you " for ever."

I ought to tell you — for after all, you have the key — I have been haunting the little house in Bayswater Road last week — looking at the place where the humming birds stood — and standing where Soames stood in the hall by the hat stand. How I can hear Smithers' word " Bobbish " — But one must not begin. One could go on for ever. All the life of that house flickers up, trembles, glows again, is rich again, in these last moments. And then there is Soames with Fleur running out of his bosom, so swift, so careless — leaving him bare. . . . Thank you for these wonderful books. . . .

You asked me about my work. I have just finished a new book which is to be published at the New Year. And now I am " thinking out " a long story about a woman which has been in my mind for years. But it is difficult. I want her whole life to be in it — a sense of time — and the feeling of " farewell." For by the time the story is told her life is over. One tells it in taking leave of her. . . . Not one of these modern women but one of those old-fashioned kind who seemed to have such a rich being, to live in such a living world. Is it fancy? Is it just that the harvest of the past is gathered? Who shall say?

In November or December the *London Mercury* is publishing a day in the life of the little family in *Prelude*. If I may, I should very much like to send you a copy.

The mountains here are good to live with, but it doesn't do to look lower. The Swiss are a *poor lot*. Honesty and Sparsamkeit — in themselves — don't warm one's heart.

To S. S. Koteliansky   *November 4, 1921*

Thank you for your letter, dear Koteliansky. As I cannot go to Paris until the Spring I shall not write to the doctor until then. But I am very glad to have his address.

I am glad that you criticised me. It is right that you should have hated much in me. I was false in many things and *careless* — untrue in many ways. But I would like you to know that I recognise this and for a long time I have been trying " to squeeze the slave out of my soul." You will understand that I do not tell you this to prove I am an angel now! No. But I need not go into the reasons; you know them.

It's marvellous here just now. The first snow has fallen on the lower peaks, and everything is crystal clear. The sky is that marvellous transparent blue one only sees in early Spring and Autumn. It looks so high and even joyful — tender. . . . And an exciting thing has happened to-day. My ancient geranium which is called Sarah has been visited by the angel at last. This geranium has *real personality*. It is so fearfully proud of this new bud that every leaf is curling.

To the Countess Russell   *November 1921*

It is J.'s turn but I can't refrain from slipping a Bon Jour into the envelope. It's such a marvellously Bon Jour, too; I wish I could send it you, intact. Blazing hot, with a light wind swinging in the trees and an exquisite transparent sky with just two little silver clouds lying on their backs like cherubs basking.

We don't only read Shakespeare and the poets. I have re-read *Queechy* lately, " fresh bursts of tears " and all. I loved it. " ' Mr. Carleton, who made *that*? ' said the child, pointing to the slowly sinking orb on the horizon with streaming eyes. The young English peer had no answer ready. His own eyes filled. ' Will you lend me your little Bible,' he said gently. ' *Oh*, Mr. C.! ' Sobs were her only answer, but happy sobs, grateful sobs. She could not see to hand it to him, nor he to see it offered." I have also been reading modern novels for the *Daily News*. They are a vulgar, dreary lot. Why all this pretence when we have not said a quarter of what there is to say. Why can't writers be warm, living, simple, merry or sad as it pleases them? All this falsity is so *boring*.

To the Hon. Dorothy Brett *November 11, 1921*

I must begin a Service of Thanks. First for your letter and then for the little photograph which is the spit of you, and then for t'other photograph in the cape and cap. How well I remember those caps, especially pinned down at the back on to one's wad of hair. I had a pale blue one for one of my journeys to New Zealand and, draped with a pale blue gossamer veil, I felt fearfully chic and dashing. Human flesh and blood doesn't dare to think what it really looked like. . . . My sister has an immense book full of photographs from the age of six months. It is the most chastening book I know. Really, one's hats, one's *waists,* and a small black round cap with wings I used to affect, which I called always my Wooza. It was rather a good name for it. But worn in conjunction with a linen collar and large tie. . . . I shall *never* let M. see that book. It is too shattering.

Thanks again for the *Mercury* which arrived gummed to its eyebrows. I tore my way into it, at last. But a harder roll has never entered Switzerland. That blue paper of yours for one thing is a kind of very superior rag-book paper. If you drew a crocodile on a piece and gave it to an infant the crocodile would live for ever. I have preserved a small portion to be used as a patch when M. starts learning to ski. . . . I wish people would not write that kind of article for another five years at least. Though I was very glad the man liked my *Daughters of the Late Colonel.* For I put my all into that story and hardly anyone saw what I was getting at. Even dear old Hardy told me to write more about those sisters. As if there was any more to say! But, speaking dead seriously, I could do with a great deal less praise than I get. It's . . . frightening, and I feel with all my heart I want to have another two years' work done at least before I am worth *talking about.* However, I am certain my new book will be a failure. There will be reactions against it. I count on that, so I mean to make the *next* one really as good as I can. . . .

The attitude to Art — all Art — of the rich and great in London is odious — isn't it? It always reminds me of the story of Tchekhov where the man wants to say, longs to say, "Paws off!" to the plebeian. I'd like to say it to not only Lady —— et Cie. . . .

Words cannot describe the cold here. We have central heating which never goes out, but even then on my balcony I freeze absolutely hard. The Mountain sends up all the food buttoned into tight little suet jackets and we both wear red Indian boots, fur lined. They are so nice. One's feet feel like small animals, you discover them playing together all on their own. But what shall we do if it gets colder? At present the BIG Snow hasn't fallen. All is frozen hard, and each tree has a little mat of white before it. Oh dear, it is so beautiful. The mountains are so noble and this snowy cover makes one see their shapes — every hollow, every peak is modelled. But all agree the snow is not serious yet. It falls, small and light like confetti, or it swarms like white bees — M. comes back from his walks hung with real icicles . . .

I had to break off there, for I was absolutely pursued by birds. They were flying right inside the balcony, the lovely creatures, a bright salmon pink with silver heads and beaks. I am afraid they must have been left behind. So now I have begged a great slice of bread from Ernestine and my balcony rail is a very nice restaurant. If only they'd come and eat. Precious little creatures — how I love them. Have I told you about my balcony? It is as big as a small room, the sides are enclosed and big double doors lead from it to my workroom. Three superb geraniums still stand on the ledge when it's fine, and their rosy masses of flowers against *blue space* are wonderful. It is so high up here that one only sees the tops and half way down of the enormous mountains opposite, and there's a great sweep of sky as one only gets at sea — on a ship — anchored before a new, undiscovered country. At sunset, when all the clouds are really too much to bear alone I call out, "Mountains on your right a deep blue," and M. shouts from below, "Right!" and I hear him go out on *his* balcony to observe. But it's most beautiful at night. Last night, for instance, at about 10 o'clock, I wound myself up in wool and I came out here and sat watching. The world was like a huge ball of ice. There wasn't a sound. It might have been ages before man. . . .

Tchekhov *said* over and over again, he protested, he begged, that he had no problem. In fact, you know, he thought it was his weakness as an artist. It worried him, but he always said the same. No problem. And when you come to think of it, what was Chaucer's problem or Shakespeare's? The " problem " is the invention of the 19th Century. The artist takes a *long look* at life. He says softly, " So this is what life it, is it? " And he proceeds to express that. All the rest he leaves. Tolstoy even had no problem. What he had was a propaganda and he is a great artist in spite of it.

November 12, 1921

It's very late at night and I ate such a stupid man with my tea — I can't digest him. He is bringing out an anthology of short stories and he said the more " plotty " a story I could give him the better. What about that for a word! It made my hair stand up in prongs. A nice " plotty " story, please. People *are* funny.

The Fat Cat sits on my Feet.

Fat is not the word to describe him by now. He must weigh pounds and pounds. And his lovely black coat is turning white. I suppose it's to prevent the mountains from seeing him. He sleeps here and occasionally creeps up to my chest and pads softly with his paws, singing the while I suppose he wants to see if I have the same face all night. I long to surprise him with terrific disguises.

M. calls him " My *Breakfast* Cat " because they share that meal, M. *at* the table and Wingley *on*. It's awful the love one can lavish on an animal. In his memoirs which he dictates to me M.'s name is always Masteranman — one word — my name is Grandma Jaegar — the Mountain is always called " Fostermonger " and for some reason our servant he refers to as The Swede. He has rather a contempt for her.

Letters 1921

To William Gerhardi   *November 12, 1921*

First of all, immediately, I think your novel [1] is awfully good. I congratulate you. It is a living book. What I mean by that is, it is warm; one can put it down and it goes on breathing. I think it has defects. But before we speak of them I'd like to tell you the things I chiefly admire. I think, perhaps, the best *moment* is at the end; the scene of your hero's return and his walk with Nina. There you really are discovered — a *real* writer. There is such feeling, such warmth, in these chapters. Nina's " whimsical " voice, those kittens, the sofa with broken springs, the " speck of soot on your nose " — and then at the very end the steamer that would not go. I am not quoting these things at random, for their charm. But because, taken altogether, they seem to convey to the reader just the " mood " you wished to convey. I think at the very beginning the tone is just a trifle tragic as it ought not to be. But once you are launched it's remarkable how quickly and easily you take the reader into that family; and how *real* you make the life, the ways, the surroundings. Fanny Ivanovna is *very* good. I *see* her. But if you were here I could go into details in a way I can't in a letter. And another thing that is good is the play of humour over it all. That makes it flexible, warm, easy, as it should be. Only in Chapter XI, in your description of the " sisters," I think you falsify the tone; it seems to me, you begin to tell us what we must feel about them, what the sight of them perched on the chairs and sofas really meant, and that's not necessary. One feels they are being " shown off," rather than seen. And you seem in that chapter to be hinting at something, even a state of mind of your hero's, which puts the reader off the scent a little. But that's just my feeling, of course.

Now we come to your second " plot," as it were, the Admiral, Sir Hugh and the Russian General. What opportunities you must have had, what excellent use you made of those opportunities! This part of your book is interesting for several reasons. I mean the " situation " *quâ* situation is immensely attractive, and your principal characters are painted to the Life — They are almost too good to be true. Your Russian General is a *rare* find. I have

---

[1] *Futility*, which was sent to K. M. in manuscript. " After this letter," says Mr. Gerhardi, " *Futility* was overhauled thanks to K. M.'s helpful advice."

known just such another, though he wasn't a general. But the beating in the face, in my friend's case was "beaten to death, simply" — and the reason was, "to use the English formula, the man was a blighter . . ."

I think the only thing that does not convince me is Nina's novel. That feels "strained." It seems to stand out too clearly, to be out of focus, even. It's such a remarkable thing to have done, that instead of wondering *why* she did it, one stops short at *how*. It gives the reader the wrong *kind* of shock.

Two things more I want to say. One is there are so many unexpected awfully good things that one comes upon as one reads, with a small shock of delight. It's as though, being taken by the author through his garden you suddenly discover, half tucked away, another flowery tree. "So you have these in your garden, too . . ." That's the feeling. It makes one want to see more of your work.

The other is, I don't think this book really holds together enough, even allowing for the title. It ought to be more squeezed and pressed and moulded into shape and wrung out, if you know what I mean. And sometimes the writing is careless. All the same, if I were you, I would publish it more or less as it stands. I would let it go. You will have to take out a good many of the Russian expressions and single words. I expect you hear them so distinctly in your brain that you feel they must be there. But they will put people off.

. . . At that moment I lit a cigarette and re-read what I have written, with dismay. . . . In trying to be honest I sound carping and cold. Not a bit what I feel. Let me end where I began by warmly, sincerely congratulating you. That's the most important thing of all. And when I say I don't think your novel "holds together enough" please remember I'm speaking "ideally" . . .

I hope you will write to me. If you feel offended please tell me. It's not easy to talk man to man at a distance.

And here's your book back again. The Swiss who can let nothing in or out of their country without taking a share, have, I am afraid, nibbled the edges of the cover.

P.S. — The rain *thumped*. Don't you mean the rain *drummed?*

Monday
November 14, 1921

The wools came to-day. They are quite lovely and I feel inclined to carry them about, just as they are, like fat dolls. M. was deeply moved by their beauty, he is an expert with the needles. . . . But we found by piercing the postage signs that you had paid vast sums to have them sent over. So here is another cheque, and I hope you hear our grateful, thankful thanks all standing in a row and singing your praises.

Isn't leming yellow a *fascinating* colour? There is a very pink pink here too — aster pink, which is heavenly fair. I could get a wool complex very easily. . . . These are *simply perfect* in every way.

This is not a letter. Now you owe me one, pleasant thought. The day is simply divine — so hot that my pink perishall won't keep out the sun enough. Blazing! With air that one's very soul comes up to breathe, rising like a fish out of the dark water.

You were not serious about the sweater, were you? But can you make *sleeves*? I can't turn corners for nuts.

P.S. — No, I don't like mousy colours. We began to wind after lunch to-day. The cat almost had delirium tremens. We thought we should have to chloroform him finally. He sat up and began to wind his own tail.

P.P.S. — 1 purl 1 plain wool in front of needle knit two together *slip* one cross stitch for 94 lines *purl* again decrease to form spiral effect up leg *now* use needle as for purl casting on first and so continue until length can be divided by *three*. Care should be taken to keep *all flat*. Press with warm iron and serve. . . .

Just a little home recipe, ma chère, for a *wet* evening.

November 21, 1921

Your fearfully nice letter makes me wish that instead of upsetting your table you would sit down at mine and drink tea and talk. But I hasten to answer it for this reason. Have you found a publisher for your novel? I know Cobden-Sanderson very well. I should be delighted to write to him about it if you would care for me to do so. He is a publisher who has only been going for a couple of years or so but he has a very good name already. . . . If you care to send him yours I shall ask Middleton Murry to write as well. For I confess, I let him see your novel. Was that a bad breach of confidence? I hope not. He agreed enthusiastically that it ought to be published. . . .

You know, if I may speak in confidence, I shall not be "fashionable" long. They will find me out; they will be disgusted; they will shiver in dismay. I like such awfully unfashionable things — and people. I like sitting on doorsteps, and talking to the old woman who brings quinces, and going for picnics in a jolting little wagon, and listening to the kind of music they play in public gardens on warm evenings, and talking to captains of shabby little steamers, and in fact, to all kinds of people in all kinds of places. But what a fatal sentence to begin. It goes on for ever. In fact, one could spend a whole life finishing it.

But you see I am not a high-brow. Sunday lunches and very intricate conversations on Sex and that "fatigue" which is so essential and that awful "brightness" which is even more essential — these things I flee from.

I'm in love with life, terribly. Such a confession is enough to waft *Bliss* out of the Union [1] . . .

I am sending you a post card of myself and the two knobs of the electric light. The photographer insisted they should be there as well. Yes, I live in Switzerland because I have consumption. But I am not an invalid. Consumption doesn't belong to me. It's only a horrid stray dog who has persisted in following me for four years, so I am trying to lose him among these mountains. But "permanently compelled" Oh — no!

To Lady Ottoline Morrell December 1921

I have just found the letter I wrote you on the first of November. I would send it you as a proof of good faith but I re-read it. Grim thing to do — isn't it? There is a kind of fixed smile on old letters which reminds one of the bridling look of old photographs. So it's torn up and I begin again.

I don't know what happens to Time here. It seems to become shorter and shorter; to whisk round the corners; to become all

[1] The library of the Oxford Union.

tail, all Saturday to Monday. This must sound absurd coming from so remote a spot as our mountain peaks. But there it is. We write, we read, M. goes off with his skates, I go for a walk through my fieldglasses and another day is over. This place makes one work. Perhaps it's the result of living among mountains; one must bring forth a mouse or be overwhelmed.

If climate were everything, then Montana must be very near Heaven. The sun shines and shines. It's cold in the shade, but out of it it is hot enough for a hat and a parasol — far and away hotter than the S. of France, and windless. All the streams are solid little streams of ice, there are thin patches of snow, like linen drying, on the fields. The sky is high, transparent, with marvellous sunsets. And when the moon rises and I look out of my window down into the valley full of clouds it's like looking out of the ark while it bobbed above the flood.

But all the same I shall never get over my first hatred of the *Swiss*. They are the same everywhere. Ugly, dull, solid lumps, with a passion divided between pigs and foreigners.

Foreigners are what they prefer to gorge themselves with but pigs will serve. As to their ankles — they fill me with a kind of anguish. I should have an ankle complex if I lived in Switzerland long. But one never lives anywhere *long*. . . .

M. and I are reading Jane Austen in the evenings. With delight. *Emma* is really a perfect book — don't you feel? I enjoy every page. I can't have enough of Miss Bates or Mr. Woodhouse's gruel or that charming Mr. Knightley. It's such an exquisite comfort to escape from the modern novels I have been forcibly reading. Wretched affairs! This fascinated pursuit of the sex adventure is beyond words boring! I am so bored by sex *quâ* sex, by the gay dog sniffing round the prostitute's bedroom or by the ultra modern snigger — worse still — that I could die — at least.

It has turned me to Proust however at last. I have been pretending to have read Proust for years but this autumn M. and I both took the plunge. I certainly think he is by far the most interesting living writer. He is fascinating! It is a comfort to have someone whom one can so immensely admire. It is horrible to feel so out of touch with one's time as I do nowadays — almost frightening.

To S. S. Koteliansky *November 29, 1921*

If I trouble you with this request please simply tell me so.

Do you know where I can obtain any information about Dr. Manoukhin's treatment? I mean — has it appeared in any possible papers or journals that I can get hold of? I ask for this reason. I cannot possibly go to Paris at present. I have no one to send. In fact, I have not mentioned this idea to *anyone* except my doctor here. Such things I prefer to do alone. It is not just a whim. My doctor here says he will very gladly consider any information I can get him about this treatment and as he has a very good X-ray apparatus, it could, if it is not the "professional patent" of Doctor Manoukhin, be tried here, immediately.

What should you advise me to do?

My difficulty about writing direct is the language. It is one thing to explain one's case by speech, it is another to write it in a foreign tongue. I should simply antagonise him. . . . But the doctor here is quite intelligent and very honest. He is interested sincerely. And I have such faith in this "unknown" treatment. I feel it is the right thing.

And I want to stop this illness, as soon as possible.

It is a beautiful, still winter day. There is the sound of a saw mill. The sun shines like a big star through the dark fir trees.

How are you?

To Sydney Schiff *December 3, 1921*

I am still here to all appearance. But the "essential moi," as Daudet would say, is in Paris sitting in a small darkish room opposite a man called Manoukhin. Whether I shall follow this one I don't know yet. When does one *really begin* a journey — or a friendship — or a love affair? It is those beginnings which are so fascinating and so misunderstood. There comes a moment when we realise we are already well on our way — déjà.

Let us drink champagne when we meet again. Where will that be and when? That glimpse of London in your letter — just that lift of the curtain showing lights, big gay rooms, ——'s mouth, the Ballet — a strain, heard from afar — and people round the table and the sound of the bell . . . you took me there for the moment and I passed away from my mountains.

To the Hon. Dorothy Brett   *December 5, 1921*

These last few days have been rather bad ones — tired ones. I haven't been able to do anything but read. It's on these occasions that one begins to wish for queer things like gramophones. It wouldn't matter if one could just walk away. But that's out of the question at present. But no more of it.

Wasn't that Van Gogh shown at the Goupil ten years ago? Yellow flowers, brimming with sun, in a pot? I wonder if it is the same. That picture seemed to reveal something that I hadn't realised before I saw it. It lived with me afterwards. It still does. That and another of a sea-captain in a flat cap. They taught me something about writing, which was queer, a kind of freedom — or rather, a shaking free. When one has been working for a long stretch one begins to narrow one's vision a bit, to fine things down too much. And it's only when something else breaks through, a picture or something seen out of doors, that one realises it. It is — literally — years since I have been to a picture show. I can *smell* them as I write.

I am writing to you before breakfast. It's just sunrise and the sky is a hedge-sparrow-egg blue, the fir trees are quivering with light. This is simply a marvellous climate for sun. We have far more sun than in the South of France, and while it shines it is warmer. On the other hand — out of it — one might be in the Arctic Zone, and it freezes so hard at night that we dare not let the chauffage down, even. It is queer to be in the sun and to look *down* on the clouds. We are above them here. But yesterday for instance it was like the old original flood. Just Montana bobbed above the huge lakes of pale water. There wasn't a thing to be seen but cloud below.

Oh dear! I am sure by now you are gasping at the dullness of this letter. To tell you the truth — I am horribly unsettled for the moment. It will pass. But while it is here I seem to have no mind except for what is worrying me. I am making another effort to throw off my chains — *i.e.,* to be well. And I am waiting for the answer to a letter. I'm half here — half away — it's a bad business. But you see I have made up my mind to try the Russian doctor's treatment. I have played my card. Will he answer? Will anything come of it? One dares not speak of these things.

It is so boring, for it is all speculation, and yet one *cannot* stop thinking . . . thinking . . . imagining what it would be like to run again or take a little jump.

To S. S. Koteliansky   December 5, 1921

I have written to M. to-day. Whatever he advises that will I do. It is strange I have faith in him. I am sure he will not have the kind of face one walks away from. Besides — Think of being "*well.*" Health is as precious as life — no less. Do you know I have not walked since November 1920? Not more than to a carriage and back. Both my lungs are affected; there is a cavity in one and the other is affected through. My heart is weak, too. Can all this be cured. Ah, Koteliansky — wish for me!

To Stephen Hudson   December 8, 1921

I have read your *Elinor Colhouse* more than twice, and I shall read it again. I do congratulate you sincerely from my heart. It's amazingly good! So good one simply can't imagine it better. One pushes into deep water easily, beautifully, from the first sentence, and there's that feeling — so rare — of ease, of safety, of wishing only to be borne along wherever the author chooses to take one.

But how you have *conveyed* the contrast between Elinor and Richard! Am I fantastic in dating it from the moment when Richard leaves her after their first meeting, when he opens the door on to the brilliant light one feels the appeal of his *fairness* and her *darkness* in an astonishing way. That moment remains with me throughout the book. Let me dare to say it's almost a mystical interpretation of their relations.

Why aren't you here — that we might talk it over and over. I'd like to recall so much — scene after scene rises in my mind. But although it is Elinor's book and a triumph for Elinor it's your presentation of Richard which I admire so tremendously. I don't mean only his boyish charm — though Heaven knows that is potent enough — or even his naturalness — which at times takes my breath away. But it's Richard's innocence of the wiles and arts of Life! It's the sight of him, in the midst of all that scheming and plotting and his horror, finally, that this should happen to him. . . .

Of course, all the detail, so fastidious, so satisfying, is beyond praise.

Elinor *lives*. I see her, hear her, recognise those fingers with the long pointed brilliant nails, look into that little brain.

Yes, I honour you for it. It's an achievement. I rejoice in your success.

To the Countess Russell   *December 1921*

So awful is the weather that I have retired under the édredon until it changes. There is no snow. But there is a cold sheet of icy mist, like a slate, pressing against the windows, and we feel like slate pencils inside. Nothing warms one. The chauffage goes night and day, but one shivers night and day as well. If this is the between season people are wise to avoid it. The worst of it is our brains are frozen, too. We live for the postman, and he brings us bills. We long for letters — the kind of letters exiles are supposed to receive, and a copy of *The Nation* comes instead. In fact, all is very devilish, and if it weren't for Jane Austen in the evenings we should be in despair. We are reading her through. She is one of those writers who seem to not only improve by keeping but to develop entirely new adorable qualities. *Emma* was our first. John sighed over Jane Fairfax. I felt that Mr. Knightley in the Shrubbery would be happiness. But her management of her plot — the way — just for the exquisite fun of the thing — she adds a new complication — *that* one can't admire too greatly. She makes modern episodic people like me, as far as I go, look very incompetent ninnies. In fact, she is altogether a chastening influence. But ah, what a rare creature!

To the Hon. Dorothy Brett   *December 13, 1921*

Why do all my fountain pens die? I care for them as if they were babies and they absolutely refuse to live. Is there such a thing as a real pen?

What a pity it is you can't get a house in St. John's Wood. I think it is the *one* darling part of London. And I always am seeing such houses advertised on the back pages of *The Sunday*

Times and *The Observer*. They sound ideal. Don't you prefer it to Hampstead? It has a *charm*. But perhaps that is because I lived there in Carlton Hill for a long time when I was young and very very happy. I used to walk about there at night — late — walking and talking on nights in Spring with two brothers. Our house had a real garden, too, with trees and all the rooms were good — the top rooms lovely. But it's all the musical people who make St. John's Wood so delightful. Those grunting 'cellos, those flying fiddles and the wonderful pianos. It's like a certain part of Brussels. And then the house at 5 Acacia Road. It has memories — but it's not only precious because of them. It was a charming house.

Oh, this cold! I feel like an explorer sending you these lines before the snow kills him. It's fearful! One can't work; the brain is frozen hard, and I can't breathe better than a fish in an empty tank. There is no air, it's a kind of frozen ice. I would leave here to-morrow but where can one go? One begins the wandering of a consumptive — fatal! Everybody does it and dies. However, I have decided to leave this particular house in June, for another more remote. I passed it one day lately when I was driving. It's in the most superb spot. The forests are on both sides but in front there are huge meadows — with clumps of fir trees dotted over them — a kind of 18th century landscape. Beyond the meadows tower the gaunt snow mountains, and behind them is a big lake. It is to let in June. We shall take it for a year. My chief reason is for the haymaking. One will be in the very midst of it all through August. To watch — to hear — mowing — to see the carts — to take part in the harvest is to share the summer in a way I *love*. You will really swoon at the view or at least I shall expect you to!! And we shall eat out of doors — eat the hay with trimmings and get a little boat and float on the lake and put up a hammock and swing in the pines and paddle in the little stream. Don't you love to paddle?

I must end this letter. It's so dull. Forgive it. Now a pale sun like a half-sucked peppermint is melting in the sky. The cat has come in. Even his poor little paws are cold, they feel like rubber. He is sitting on my feet singing his song. Wingley does not only purr; there is a light soprano note in his voice as well. He is very nearly human because of the love that is lavished on him. And now that his new coat is grown he is like a cat in a bastick tied with ribbon — He has an immense ruff and long curly new fur. Cats are far nicer than dogs. I shall write a cat story one day. But I shall give the cat to C.'s dressmakers, the Misses R. What appalling dressmakers they were! They seemed to fit all their patterns on to cottage loaves — life-size ones — or on to ham sandwiches with heads and feet. But it was worth it to have gone in to their house and heard them as one did.

Goodbye for now.

P.S. — *Dearest* Brett.

Your letter has just come.

Stop!

You are not to send a gramophone.

Please stop *at once*.

None of us can possibly afford such a thing. You will be bankrupt after it. Don't do anything of the kind! Only millionaires can buy them, I know. I scan the papers! But for the really frightfully dear thought a thousand thanks. Yes, I will go to Paris if Manoukhin answers. But I can get no reply. Which is disappointing.

December 19, 1921

Since I wrote to you I have been in my familiar land of counterpane. The cold got through as I knew it would and one wing only wags. As to Doctor Manoukhin I got the Mountain to 'phone Paris yesterday and found he was absent and only there from time to time, très rarement. It was impossible for the secretary to say when. So that doesn't sound very hopeful. I am disappointed. I had made him my " miracle." One must have a miracle. Now I'm without one and looking round for another. . . . Have you any suggestions?

It has been a fine day. The sun came into this room all the afternoon but at dusk an old ancient wind sprang up and it is shaking and complaining. A terrible wind — a wind that one always mercifully forgets until it comes again. Do you know the kind of wind I mean! It brings nothing but memories — and by memories I mean those that one cannot without pain remember. It always carries my brother to me. Ah, Brett, I hope with all my heart you have not known anyone who has died young — long before their time. It is bitterness. But what am I thinking of? I wanted to write you a Christmas letter. I wanted to wish you joy. I *can* in spite of everything in life. I *can,* and by that I don't mean that it's any desperate difficulty. No, let us rejoice — that we are alive and know each other and walk the earth at the same time. Let us make plans, and fulfil them, and be happy when we meet, and laugh a great deal this year and never cry. Above all, let us be friends. There was that in your last letter which made you dearer to me than ever before. I don't know what it was. It was as though you came out of the letter and touched me and smiled and I understood your *goodness.*

To Thomas and Bessie Moult   December 20, 1921

I cannot let Christmas come without sending you both my love and greetings. I love Christmas. . . . In that other world where wishes are laws, there would be a great shining wreath of holly on the door knocker, lights at all the windows, and a real party going on inside. We meet in the hall and warmly re-clasp hands. Good Heavens! *I'm* not above a tree, coloured candles and crackers — are you? Wait. We shall have it all — or something better! I will never despair of a real gay meeting, one of these days, for us all. It's always only an accident that the day is not fine, that one happens for the moment to be under an umbrella. It will all flash and sparkle, I truly *believe* that, sooner than we expect. — The very fact that we rebel at our little terms of imprisonment is proof that freedom is our real element.

To the Hon. Dorothy Brett   December 22, 1921

I'm very interested by what you say about *Vera.* Isn't the end extraordinarily good. It would have been so easy to miss it. She carried it right through. I admired the end most, I think. Have you never known a Wemyss? Oh, my dear, they are *very* plentiful! Few men are without a touch. And I certainly believe that husbands and wives talk like that. Lord, yes!

You are so very superior, Miss, in saying half an hour would be sufficient. But how is one to escape? And also, though it may be "drivel" in cold blood, it *is* incredible the follies and foolishness we can bear if we think we are in love. Not that I can stand the Wemyss "brand." No. But I can perfectly comprehend Lucy standing it. I don't think I agree about Lucy either. She could not understand her father's "*intellect*" but she had a sense of humour (except where her beloved was concerned). She certainly had her own opinions and the Aunt was very sodden at the funeral because of the *ghastly* effect of funerals! They make the hardest of us melt and gush. But all the same I think your criticism is awfully good of the Aunt, of the whole book in fact. Only one thing, my hand on my heart, I could swear to. Never *could* Elizabeth be influenced by me. If you knew how she would scorn the notion, how impossible it would be for her. There is a kind of turn in our sentences which is alike but that is because we are worms of the same family. But that is all.

About Paris. I have now received the doctor's address from a secretary of the Institute and have written him again to-day. If I hear I will let you know. It seems more hopeful now that I send direct. I am still in bed and dear knows when I shall be out. A reply from Manoukhin would be the only thing, I think. (I am a bit disheartened to be *back here* again with all the old paraphernalia of trays and hot-water bottles. Accursèd disease!)

To S. S. Koteliansky   *December 24, 1921*

I have heard from M. to-day. A good letter — *very*. As soon as I am well enough to get up I shall go to Paris. He says the treatment takes 15 weeks if one is not much advanced. But no matter. It is fearfully exciting to have heard!

To Anne Estelle Rice   *Christmas Eve, 1921*

Suddenly this afternoon as I was thinking of you there flashed across my inward eye a beautiful poppy that we stood looking at in the garden of the Hotel at Looe. Do you remember that marvellous black sheen at the base of the petal and the big purplish centre? Then that took me back to our improvised café — just the same table with a bottle on it, and ourselves, out of space and time . . . for the moment! And from that I began to think of your très blue eyes that I love so and your neck, and the comb you wore in your hair the last time you dined with us and a pink pinny you had on the first time I saw you in the studio in Paris. These things are not the whole of my Anne, but they are signs and tokens of her and for the want of a thousand others what wouldn't I give at this moment to put my arms round her and give her a small squeeze.

I shall be in Paris, I hope, from May on this year. Will you by any chance be there? I am going on a preliminary visit almost at once to see a specialist there — a *Russian* — and to have some teeth pulled out and pulled in again. Then I come back here to save pennies for my flight in May. I believe this Russian cures people with my complaint. He sounds wonderful.

It's so long since I have heard of any of the *old set*. Where are they? New friends are not — never can be — the same, and all mine seem to be people I know as a writer, not as a common garden human being. Whether they care personally for the smell of tangerines or not I haven't the least idea. I can't really care for people who are cut off at the head. I like them to exist as far as their hearts *au moins*. Don't ever come to Switzerland, Anne. It's all *scenery*. One gets the same on a Mountain Railway at 6d. a go and get off after the last bumping. But the Swiss!! They are always cutting down trees and as the tree falls the hausfrau rushes out of the kitchen to see, waving a pig-knife and shouting a joyful *voilà!* I believe they are full of virtue but virtue is a bad boisson to be *full* of.

To Lady Ottoline Morrell   *December 27, 1921*

How lovely the handkerchiefs are with the little swans sailing round them. They arrived on Christmas Day its very self, too. You know how one watches for that Christmas post at this distance — I was in bed too, which made my longing even more fearful. I had to wait until someone crept up the stairs instead of lurking at the door. I really feel that I could write an entire book with each chapter beginning, "The post did not come that day" *or* "That morning the post was late." And I at least would thrill and shiver with the horror of it. It's awful to spend *such* emotions on postmen! But there it is.

We had a "proper" Christmas — even to a Tree, thanks to the Mountain, who revels in such things and would like all the year to be December. The house whispered with tissue paper for days, a pudding appeared out of the bosom of the air and the sight of *that* fired even my gentle Ernestine who began, from the sounds, to gambol on the ground floor and toss the iron rings of the stove on to the floor. The crackers, however, would not pull, which cast a little gloom over M., who relishes crackers, and the mottoes which were German were very depressing: "Mädchen, möcht ich Frau dir sehen."

I am glad it is all over — but the traces, the signs remain for a long time. . . .

To O. Raymond Drey December 27, 1921

My dear Drey, what a shockingly proud man you must be! I should do no more work. I should just look at him, puff out my chest and say to the passers-by, "Il est à nous."

The butler impressed me terribly. At this height and among these mountains we scarcely dare think of butlers. My one domestic, the gentle Ernestine, who weighs about 14 stone, bounds up and down the stairs like a playful heifer and bursts into a strange, terrible singing whenever she hears a pig being killed, is civilizations away from butlers. When I come to see you I expect the second footman to take my umbrella and I shall curtsey to Anne and present a bouquet. You are very grand *but* not so grand as Willy. His party must have been a very powerful affair, Drey. Talk about numbered cloakroom tickets. Willy will have to have them for his wives, next time. He will be a terribly busy man in Heaven. I am sure the restitution of conjugal rights is a specialité de la maison, there.

My cat has just leapt on my bed and begun to clean his face and his two little chimneys. It's a queer thing. He started life in a humble way, like One greater than he — he was born in a stable and was just an ordinary little black and white kitten. But since he came here he has turned into a real Persian with an enormous ruff and feathers on his legs. I suppose it is the cold. The Swiss, of course, don't keep cats. They are frightened a cat might eat the old cabbage stalk they are saving up for the baby to cut its teeth on. They are a thrifty race.

By the way, I suppose you do not know the address of a first-class dentist in Paris? I have to go to Paris very soon and while I am there I want to put my head into the jaws of a really good painless modern man. Is there such an one? If you would send me a card with his name and address I would be awfully grateful. Are you wondering why I ask you? I have a feeling you know all these things. I am going as soon as my feet are on the earth again, for my teeth are falling like autumn leaves. They have very large wooden buns here for tea with nails in them and powdered glass on the top, exprès pour les anglais. I defy anyone to grind them to powder without an accident!

To Sydney Schiff   *December 28, 1921*

I have chosen to-day to write because Manoukhin has come a great deal nearer. He has told me that if I go to Paris he will treat me by his new method and there is the word *guérison* shining in his letter. I believe every word of it; I believe in him implicitly. As soon as I am out of bed (the cold has been *too* cold) Jones will pack the boxes and I shall go to see him and arrange to return to town in May. I want to spend the winter here. But in May I shall go to Paris for the course of treatment which takes 15 weeks. (Manoukhin is not only a doctor. He is a whole new stage on the journey. I hardly know why.) His treatment consists of applications of the rayons X.

One word I must say about Joyce. Having re-read *The Portrait* it seems to me on the whole awfully *good*. We are going to buy *Ulysses*. But Joyce is (if only P. didn't think so, too) immensely important. Some time ago I found something so repellent in his work that it was difficult to read it. It shocks me to come upon words, expressions and so on that I'd shrink from in life. But now it seems to me the seeking after Truth is so by far and away the most important thing that one must conquer all minor aversions. They are unworthy.

To the Hon. Dorothy Brett   *January 9, 1922*

You are right. I think of Manoukhin more than anyone can imagine. I have as much faith in him as Koteliansky has. I hardly dare think of him fully. No, I *dare* not. It is too much. But about money. I have £100 saved for this *Last Chance* and as soon as I know he can help me I shall make more. Work is ease, joy, light to me if I am happy. I shall not borrow from anyone if I can possibly help it.

I am not frightened of money, for some blessed reason. I know I can make it. Once I am well I can make all I want. I don't want much. In fact, my plans go on and on, and when I go to sleep I dream the treatment is over and I am running, or walking swiftly and carelessly by and no one knows I have been ill, no one hands me a chair in a shop. Ah, it is too much!

This awful writing is frozen writing, Brett. I am writing with two icicles for fingers. We have 6 feet of snow here, all is frozen over and over, even the bird's tails. Is not that hideous cruelty? I have a large table for these precious atoms daily, and the first cocoanut in Switzerland is the Big Joint. They can't yet believe in the cocoanut. It overwhelms them. A special issue of the *Bird Times* is being issued, the bird who discovered it is to be photographed, interviewed and received at Pluckingham Palace and personally conducted tours are being arranged. What with them and my poor dear pussy-wee, who got out to-day and began to scratch, scratched away, kept at it, sat up, took a deep breath, scratched his ear, wiped his whiskers, scratched on, SCRATCHED, until finally only the tip of a quivering tail was to be seen and he was rescued by the gentle Ernestine. He wrung his little paws in despair. Poor lamb! to think he will not be able to scratch *through* until April. I suppose snow is beautiful. I hate it. It always seems to me a kind of humbug — a justification of mystery, and I hate mystery. And then there is no movement. All is still, white, cold, deathly, eternal. Every time I look out I feel inclined to say I *refuse* it. But perhaps if one goes about and skims over, all is different.

I'm working at such a big story that I still can only just see the end in my imagination ... the longest by far I've ever written. It's called *The Doves' Nest*. But winter is a bad black time for work, I think. One's brain gets congealed. It is very hard.

Letters 1922

To S. S. Koteliansky   January 13, 1922

What a supremely good piece of translation is this story by Bunin in *The Dial*.[1] One simply cannot imagine it better done and I am, with everybody else, deeply grateful for the opportunity of reading it.

Bunin has an immense talent. That is certain. All the same — there's a limitation in this story, so it seems to me. There is something hard, inflexible, separate in him which he exults in. But he ought not to exult in it. It is a pity it is there. He just stops short of being a great writer because of it. Tenderness is a dangerous word to use, but I dare use it to you. He lacks tenderness — and *in spite of everything,* tenderness there must be. . . .

I have been in a horrible black mood lately, with feelings of something like hatred towards "everybody." I think one reason was I wrote a story — I projected my little people against the bright screen of Time — and not only nobody saw, nobody cared. But it was as if the story was refused. It is bitter to be refused. Heaven knows one does not desire praise. But *silence* is hard to bear. I know one ought not to care. One should go on quietly. But there it is.

I am leaving for Paris in a fortnight. A chill and the weather and money have kept me back. But I shall go then. Shall I write to you from there?

Koteliansky — I HATE snow and icicles, and blizzards. It is all such mock mystery and a wrestling with the enemy. I love the fertile earth — Spring. Wouldn't you like to be now this instant, in a beech forest with the new leaves just out?

To Sydney Schiff   January 15, 1922

About Joyce, and my endeavour to be doubly fair to him because I have been perhaps unfair and captious. Oh, I can't get over a great great deal. I can't get over the feeling of wet linoleum and unemptied pails and far worse horrors in the house of his mind — He's so terribly *unfein;* that's what it amounts to. There is a tremendously strong impulse in me to beg him not to shock me! Well, it's not very rare. I've had it before with men and

---
[1] *The Gentleman from San Francisco,* translated by S. S. Koteliansky and D. H. Lawrence.

women many times in my life. One can stand much, but that kind of shock which is the result of vulgarity and commonness, one is frightened of receiving. It's as though one's mind goes on quivering afterwards. . . . It's just exactly the reverse of the exquisite rapture one feels in for instance that passage which ends a chapter where Proust describes the flowering apple trees in the spring rain.

Elizabeth has returned to the Châlet. In minute black breeches and gaiters she looks like an infant bishop. When she has talked about London and the literary " successes " I am thankful to be out of it. But Elizabeth " fascinates " me; and I admire her for working as she is working now, all alone in her big châlet. She is courageous, very. And for some reason the mechanism of Life hardly seems to touch her. She refuses to be ruffled and she is not ruffled. This is incomprehensible to me. I find it devilish, devilish, devilish. Doors that bang, voices raised, smells of cooking, even steps on the stairs are nothing short of anguish to me at times. There is an inner calm necessary to writing, a sense of equilibrium which is impossible to reach if it hasn't outward semblance. But I don't know. Perhaps I am asking for what cannot be.

I must end this letter. The sun has been out to-day and yesterday, and although there is about seven foot of snow and great icicles hang from the window frames it is warm, still, *delicious*. I got up to-day and I feel I never want to go to bed again . . . this air, this radiance gives one a faint idea of what spring must be here — early spring. They say that by April the snows have melted and even before all is quite gone the flowers begin. . . .

January 1922

I should like to have friends, I confess. I do not suppose I ever shall. But there have been moments when I have realised what friendship might be. Rare moments — but never forgotten. I remember once talking it over with Lawrence and he said " We must swear a solemn pact of friendship. Friendship is as binding, as solemn as marriage. We take each other for life, through everything — for ever. But it's not enough to say we will do it. We must *swear*." At the time I was impatient with him. I thought it extravagant — fanatic. But when one considers what this world is like I understand perfectly why L. (especially being L.) made such claims. . . . I think, myself, it is pride which makes friendship most difficult. To submit, to bow down to the other is not easy, but it must be done if one is to really understand the being of the other. Friendship isn't *merging*. One doesn't thereupon become a shadow and one remain a substance. Yes, it is terribly solemn — frightening, even.

Please do not think I am all for Joyce. I am *not*. In the past I was unfair to him and to atone for my stupidity I want to be fairer now than I really feel. . . . I agree that it is not all art. I would go further. Little, to me, is art at all. It's a kind of stage on the way to being Art. But the act of projection has not been made. Joyce remains entangled in it, in a bad sense, except at rare moments. There is, to me the great distinction between him and Proust. . . .

To Anne Estelle Rice　　　　　　　　　　*January 16, 1922*

Can you tell me the name of a Hotel in Paris, that has an ascenseur that really does go up and down and isn't too terribly unsympathetic? I simply don't know one nowadays and shall have to sit on my luggage while someone looks. Last time I stayed at one that Cook's recommended with one of those glass-topped beds and strong tea coming out of the hot water tap. They plucked me to my last pinfeather for these luxuries. I don't mind where it is as long as the lift will go up as well as down — so important, that. In Switzerland the lifts only go down, never up. It's a mystery to me. I'd like Fergusson's views on it or Blum's.

K.: " How does it happen that this lift never goes up? "
Swiss (smiling): " It always goes down, Madame."
K.: ? ? ? ? ? ? ?
Swiss: ! ! ! ! ! ! !

To the Hon. Dorothy Brett　　　　　　　　*January 20, 1922*

I can't get off to Paris just yet, for I am still in bed! Six weeks to-day with one day's interval. I can't shake off this congestion and ALL the machinery is out of order. Food is a horror. But I won't give in to it. If I can get well enough to go to Paris, it's all I ask. I am fighting for that now. . . . I wish I had got there before this last bout. I was so much stronger than I am now. But this is a bad black month, darling. There is a new moon on the 27th. Look at it and wish. I will look at it and wish for you. I feel so in your mood — listless, tired, my energy flares up and won't last. I'm a wood fire. However, I swear to finish my big story by the end of this month. It's queer when I am in this mood I always write as though I am laughing. I feel it running along the pages. If only the reader could see the snail in its shell with the black pen!

I have just heard from de la Mare about my little family in the *Mercury* and from America where another story of the same people is coming out in *The Dial*. I feel like Lottie's and Kezia's mother after the letters I have got this month. It is surprising and very lovely to know how people love little children — the most unexpected people.

Here's the doctor stumping up the stairs.

To Lady Ottoline Morrell   January 1922

I tremble to think of the time we spend in bed *un*happily. It is out of all proportion. I am fleeing to Paris on Monday next to see if that Russian can bake me or boil me or serve me up in some more satisfying way — I suppose the snow is very good for one. But it's horrid stuff to take and there's far too much of it. Immense fringes of icicles hang at our windows. Awful looking things like teeth — and every Sunday the Swiss fly into the forest on little sledges shrieking *Ho-jé! Ho-jé* positively makes my blood curdle. So off I go on Monday with the Mountain very breathless carrying two large suitcases and begging the suitcases' pardon when she bumps them into things. I shall only go to spy out the land and buy some flowers and wallow in a hot bath. But if the Russian says he can cure me, M. and I shall go to Paris in the Spring and live there for a time. One writes the word " cure " — but — but I don't know.

I must ask you if you have read Congreve lately. I have just finished *The Way of the World. Do* read it! for the sake of the character Mrs. Millamant. I think she is so exquisitely done when she first appears " full sail " and tells the others how she curls her hair. The maid is marvellous in that little scene, too, and the other scene is where she decides finally to have Mirabel. That little conversation between the two seems to me really ravishing in its own way — It's so delicate — so gay — But it's much best read aloud. What a brilliant strange creature Congreve was — so anxious *not* to be considered a writer, but only a plain gentleman. And Voltaire's shrewd reply, " If you had been only a gentleman I would not have come to see you ". . . I love reading good plays; and so does M. We have such fun talking them over afterwards. In fact, the pleasure of all reading is doubled when one lives with another who shares the same books. It is one of the many pleasures of our solitary life. Pleasures we have — ever increasing. I would not change this *kind* of life for any other. There are moods of course when we long for people. But they pass, leaving no regret, no disillusionment, no horrid remembrance — And one does have time to work. But I wish my new book were a better one. I am *terrified* of it. But it can't be helped now. M. is writing hard, and I am in the middle of what looks like a short novel.

I am so glad you liked *The Veil*.[1] There is one poem:

> Why has the rose faded and fallen
> And these eyes have not seen. . . .

It haunts me. But it is a state of mind I know so terribly well — That regret for what one has not seen and felt — for what has passed by — unheeded. Life is only given once and then I *waste* it. Do you feel that?

To the Hon. Dorothy Brett *January 26, 1922*

I'm deadly tired to-night! I wrote and finished a story yesterday for *The Sketch*.[2] The day after that happens is always a day when one feels like a leaf on the ground — one can't even flutter. At the same time there is a feeling of joy that another story is finished. I put it in such a lovely place, too. The grounds of a convent in Spring with pigeons flying up in the blue and big bees climbing in and out of the freezias below. If I lived in the snow long I should become very *opulent*. Pineapples would grow on every page, and

---

[1] *The Veil and Other Poems*, by Walter de la Mare.
[2] *Taking the Veil* — see *The Doves' Nest*.

giant bouquets would be presented to each character on his appearance. Elizabeth was here yesterday and we lay in my room talking about flowers until we were really quite drunk, or I was. She — describing "a certain very exquisite *Rose,* single, pale yellow with coral tipped petals" and so on. I kept thinking of little curly blue hyacinths and *white* violets and the bird-cherry. My trouble is I had so many flowers when I was little, I got to know them so well that they are simply the breath of life to me. It's no ordinary love; it's a passion. Wait — one day I shall have a garden and you shall hold out your pinny. In the meantime our cat has got his nose scratched beyond words and he's in such a condition that he looks as though he has been taking part in a boxing match up a chimney. He is to have lessons on the fiddle this Spring. All the BEST cats can play at least Hey-diddle-diddle. He *must* learn. The strings of his fiddle will be of wool, of course, and the bow will have a long tassel on it. I believe he can play the piano. He sits up and plays with his two front paws:

> Nellie Bly
> Caught a fly
> Put it in her tea!

This exquisite morceau was in *my* Pianoforte Tutor, words and all. Who can have composed it? However, it suits Wingley. It's a subject he can feel sympathy about. He comes down with such a terrific whack on the FLY! He is the most unthinkable lamb, really, and I am sorry if I am silly about him.

But I meant to write about the Flu. You are nervous of it, aren't you? But you can ward it off with food. MILK, my dear. That's not hard to take.

I'm tired of telling you to eat. I now command you to drink. Get the milk habit, and become a secret tippler. Take to drink, I implore you. What the devil does it matter how fat one gets, we shall go to Persia where fatness alone is beauty.

To John Galsworthy *Paris*
January 31, 1922

Your letter came just as I was on the point of leaving home. How happy I am that you liked *At the Bay* and that Madame likes my little children and the dog! But it is not your praise that

I value most, although I am honoured and proud to have that. It is the fact you are watching my work, which is the most *precious* encouragement.

Yes, I have been working a great deal, but in my horrid bed where I've been for the past two months. I hope there are no beds in Heaven. But I managed to finish a long story there and several short ones.

Now I have come to Paris to see a Russian doctor who promises to give me new wings for old. I have not seen him yet — so — though it's still a miracle — one believes. When I have seen him I shall go back to Montana again. After these long months in the mountains it's the flower shops I long to see. I shall gaze into *them* as little boys are supposed to gaze into pastry-cook's. . . .

I hope you are well. It would be very delightful to think we might meet one day. But please remember how grateful I am.

To S. S. Koteliansky
Victoria Palace Hotel
6 Rue Blaise Desgoffe
Rue de Rennes
February 1, 1922

I have seen Manoukhine. Yes, one has every confidence in such a man. He wishes me to begin the treatment at once. I am taking steps to try to do so, but it is not quite easy to arrange. It will cost me *much* money. I have £100 saved but I must make not only another £100 but enough to live on here and for special food and so on. Also I have L. M. to keep as well until I am strong enough to walk about and so on. It is all difficult, and for some reason I find it hard to accept all its difficulties, as one must. Perhaps for one thing it is not nice in a city. I had forgotten how women parade about, idle and unworthy, and how ignoble are the faces of men. It shocks me to see these faces. I want more than anything to cry! Does that sound absurd? But the lack of *life* in all these faces is terribly sad.

Forgive me. Let me speak of something else for a moment. While I was waiting at the clinic to-night the doors were all open and in the doctor's cabinet people were talking Russian. They talked all together. Doctor M.'s voice was above the other voices, but there was a continual *chorus* — all speaking. I cannot tell you how I love Russian. When I hear it spoken it makes me think of course always of Tchekhov. I love this speech. I thought also of you; and I wished you were with me.

Now a bell is striking as though it turned over in its sleep to strike. It's very late. Good night.

February 3, 1922

There is no answer to this letter. But I wanted to tell you something very good that happened to-day. Yesterday I decided that I must take this treatment and I telephoned M. I was sitting alone in the waiting-room of the clinique reading Goethe's conversations with Eckermann when M. came in. He came quickly over to me, took my hand and said simply, " Vous avez décidé de commencer avec le traitement. C'est très bien. Bonne santé! " And then he went as quickly out of the room saying, " Tout de suite " (pronounced "*toot sweet*" for he speaks very little French). But this coming in so quickly and so gently was a beautiful act, never to be forgotten, the act of someone *very good*.

Oh, how I love gentleness. All these people everywhere are like creatures at a railway station — shouting, calling, rushing, with ugly looks and ways. And the women's eyes — like false stones — hard, stupid — there is only one word, corrupt. I look at them and I think of the words of Christ, " Be ye therefore perfect even as your Father in Heaven is perfect " — But what do they care? How shall they listen? It is terribly sad. Of course, I don't want them to be all solemn or Sundayfied. God forbid. But it seems there is so little of the spirit of love and gaiety and *warmth* in the world just now. Why all this pretence? But it is true — it is not easy to be simple, it is not just (as A. T.'s friend used to say) a sheep sneezing.

It is raining. There is a little hyacinth on my table — a very naïve one.

To Anne Estelle Rice   *February 4, 1922*

Just a mot to say how grateful I am for the address of this hotel. It's just what I wanted, and it simply flows with hot baths. I have a heaven-kissing room au 6me with a piece of sky outside and a view into the windows opposite — which I love. It's so nice to watch la belle dame opposite bring her canary *in* when it rains and put the hyacinth *out*. I have decided to stay in Paris and not go back to that Switzerland. There is a man here — did I tell you about him? (It sounds rather an ambiguous beginning, by the way). But enfin, there *is* a man here who treats my maladie with the X-rays and I am going to him for this treatment. I had the first yesterday and feel at this moment full of the rayons bleus — rather like a deep sea fish. But he promises to cure me by the summer. It's hard to believe it. But if it is true, I shall take a Puffi to your very door an' come an' have tea with David out of a very little small teapot. The only fly in the ointment is the terrific expense. It's 300 francs a time. However, I have been fortunate with my work lately and I'll just have to do a double dose of it until this is paid off. Money is a bore, but I never take it *dead* seriously, and I don't care if I haven't a sou as long as I can leap and fly alone.

You know I really do expect you in the SPRING. I feel the winter is over already and I read in the *Daily Mail* yesterday that the Dog's Mercury is out. But what *is* the Dog's Mercury? And does the Dog know? I hope he's very pleased but I expect he just looks at it and bolts it and goes on with a kind of " So that's that " air. Sad for the Dog's Mercury, don't you think?

Well, dearest, I feel a bit weak in the pen this morning, and inclined to laugh at rien — you know the feeling. It's a fool of a day here, sunny and wintry. Fat old men lose their hats and cry houp-là as they stagger after them.

To J. M. Murry   *February 7, 1922*

I have had no news from you to-day yet (3 P.M.). I expect it is the snow. Arctic conditions prevail in Switzerland, so the papers say. I hope that you manage to keep warm and that Wingley's tail is not frozen.

Advise me — will you? I am looking for a tiny flat — very small — a mouse's hole just big enough to nibble a pen in. If I find anything suitable I shall take it until the end of May and L. M. will look after it to save money on servants and so on. But (this is where I want your advice) to whom can I apply for a reference? They are sure to ask me for at least two. Can you think of anybody? I wish you could answer this as soon as possible. A card will suffice, as they say. It's rather urgent. Flats are so scarce here and I want to be settled as soon as possible once something is found. Of course, it may be all a wild goose chase. L. M. has gone off to an agent this afternoon. But there it is!

I have started a new Shakespeare note book. I hope you will let me see yours one day. I expect they will be legion by that time. And, reading with the point of view of taking notes, I begin to see those marvellous short stories asleep in an image as it were. For instance,

> . . . " Like to a vagabond flag upon the stream,
>   Goes to and back, lackeying the varying tide,
>   To rot itself with motion."

That is terrible, and it contains such a terribly deep psychological truth. " That *rots* itself " . . . and the idea of it returning and returning, never swept out to sea finally. You may think you have done with it for ever, but comes a change of tide and there is that dark streak reappeared, more sickeningly rotten still. I understand that better than I care to. I mean — alas! — I have proof of it in my own being.

There are awful good oranges to be had in Paris. But there's nothing else good that I know — nothing *fresh, sound,* or *sweet.* But mine's a partial view, of course. I have done with cities for ever. I want flowers, rather sandy soil, green fields, and a river not too deep to paddle in, also a large number of ancient books and a small but *very* pretty cow. In fact, I should like the cow to be strikingly pretty. I shall put it in the advertisement. " No plain cows may apply." No, I can't do that. It's too cruel. But it's an airy-fairy herd for a long time, I'm afraid. How is your work going? If I am very dull for five weeks, you must remember that for 5 weeks this treatment makes one rather worse. After that you will have to snatch my letters (like snapdragons) all blaging out of the postman's bag.

To William Gerhardi *February 8, 1922*

I can't tell you how honoured I am by your asking me to be Godmother. I have the warmest feelings towards your little nouveau-né and shall watch its first steps with all the eagerness a parent could desire. I cast about in my mind as to what to send it. Not a silver mug. No, not a mug. They only tilt them over their noses and breathe into them. Besides, the handle of mine, being silver, was always red hot, so that I had to lap up what was inside, like a kitten. . . . The matter I see demands time for consideration. But very seriously, I am most happy Cobden-Sanderson liked your book. I am sure it will be a success. And I look forward to reading it again and making other people read it. All success to you and many many thanks.

Please do not praise me too much. It is awfully nice to be praised, but at the same time it makes me hang my head. I have done so little. I should have done so much more. There are these rows of stories, all waiting. All the same, I can't deny that praise is like a most lovely present, a bright bouquet coming to me (but gently! I hope) out of the air.

Don't imagine for one moment though, that I think myself wonderful! That is far, far from the truth. I take writing too seriously to be able to flatter myself. I've only begun. The only story that satisfies me to any extent is the one you understand so well, *The Daughters of the Late Col.,* and parts of *Je ne parle pas*. But Heavens, what a journey there is before one!

By the way, for proof of *your* being a writer you had only to mention a bath chair and it crept into your handwriting. It was a queer coincidence. I had just been writing about a bath chair myself and poor old Aunt Aggie, who had lived in one and died in one — *glided* off, so that one saw her in her purple velvet steering carefully among the stars and whimpering faintly as was her terrestial wont when the wheel jolted over a particularly large one. But these conveyances are not to be taken lightly or wantonly. They are terrible things. No less.

I hope if you do come to Paris at Easter you will come and see me. By then I expect I shall have a little flat. I am on the track of a minute appartment with a wax-bright salon where I shall sit like a bee writing short stories in a honeycomb. But these retreats are hard to find.

I am here undergoing treatment by a Russian doctor, who claims to have discovered a cure for tuberculosis by the application of X-rays. The only real trouble is it's terribly expensive. So much so that when I read the price I felt like Tchekhov wanted Anna Ivanova to feel when she read his story in a hot bath — as though someone had stung her in the water and she wanted to run sobbing out of the bath-room. But *if* it all comes true it means one will be invisible once more — no more being offered chairs and given arms at sight. A close season for ever for hot-water bottles and glasses of milk. Well, people don't realise the joy of being invisible — it's almost the greatest joy of all. But I'll have to write at least a story a week until next May, which is a little bit frightening.

Oxford, from the papers, sounds very sinister. And why when people receive anonymous boxes of chocolate do they always wait to hand them round until friends come to tea? What ghouls they are, to be sure! Professor X., who saved the lives of Doctor and Mrs. R. sounds *profoundly* moved. I should feel very tempted were I in Oxford — to — hm — hm — better not. No doubt the secret police has steamed this letter over a cup of warm tea. . . .

To the Hon. Dorothy Brett　　　　*St. Valentine's Day*
　　　　　　　　　　　　　　　　　　February 14, 1922

I do hope your tooth is better. Why have we got teeth? Or why haven't we brass ones. I cling to mine but I feel they will all go one day and the dentist is such a terrifying animal. I hate to think of dear Tchekhov in Nice, with toothache, where he says, " I was in such pain I crawled up the wall." That just describes it. It is maddening and exhausting to have toothache; I do hope yours is over.

Where *is* your little house! It is somewhere — but where? Sometimes I think it must be in the branches of a tree. Do let me know. I think you are very wise not to take a big one. Little houses are always best. A house is like an ark — one rides the flood in it. Little ones bob over the waves and can rest on the extreme tops of mountains much better than great big ones. Can I be official Godmother to the garden? I should like to STARTLE you with the most superb things and to send you seeds from the far corners of the earth and have a boronia plant below the studio window. Do you know the scent of boronia? My grandma and I were very fond of going to a place called McNab's

Tea Gardens and there we used to follow our noses and track down the boronia bushes. Oh, how I must have tired the darling out! It doesn't bear thinking about.

I hope G.'s show goes off well. It's not a very good moment for selling pictures, or so I should think. There is an unrest in every one. It's between light and dark, between winter and spring. People are neither open or closed. The moment to catch them is just a little bit later. I think the time for a picture show or to publish a book is in the first days of real spring or just at the beginning of Autumn. We are more alive then than at any other time. We are in the mood to receive. It seems to me one ought to link up all one's projects as much as possible with the earth's progress. The more I know of life the more I realise it is profoundly influenced by certain laws, no matter how many people ignore them. If we obey them our work goes well; we get our desire. It's like studying the tides before we put out to sea in our fishing boat. We are all sailors, bending over a great map. We ought to choose the weather for our journey.

M. is here. Two days were enough to disgust him with Switzerland. He will stay here now, and at the end of March we are going into a flat which we have found. Awfully nice — high up — but absurdly furnished, like the Arabian Nights by Poiret. Very sumptuous and exotic. When you come to see me a little black boy with a pineapple on his head will open the door.

This is an excellent hotel. We have two rooms at the end of a passage, cut off from the rest of the hotel, with a bath-room and masses of hot water. Rooms cost from 13 francs a day. There is a lift, of course, and we can eat on the premises. If I were you I'd come here at Easter. All rooms have hot and cold water. After 7 months in that cleanliness I feel water and soap are the great necessities. M. and I have settled down according to programme, as we always do. We work, play chess, read, make our tea and drink it out of our small bowls. I can do nothing but get up and lie down, of course, and Manoukhin says in three weeks I shall have a real reaction and then be able to do even less than that for the next three weeks. It's rather like waiting to have an infant — new born health. My horrid time ought to be just over by Easter.

I must begin work. Seven stories sit on the doorstep. One has its foot inside. It is called *The Fly*. I must finish it to-day. This is a hard moment for work — don't you feel? It's hard to get *life* into it. The sun is not up yet. Oh Spring, hurry, hurry! Every year I long more for Spring.

It's a pig of a day — a London fog outside the windows and I have to pull my stockings on. Think of pulling one's stockings on like winking — without noticing even. Can that happen to me again?

February 26, 1922

What is it doing in London to-day? Here it is Spring. For days past it has been warm, blue and gold, sunny, faint, languishing, soft, lovely weather. Isn't it the same over there? The reckless lift boy says "dans un mois il serait pleine été!" That's the kind of large remark I love the French for. They have very nearly hung out their sun-blinds; they have quite turned the puddings into little ices in frills. But why can't I send some of this weather over to you? Can't it be done? Look in the glass. If there is a very bright gay sunbeam flittering on your hair — I sent it from Paris — *exprès*. At any rate, you *are* putting out new leaves, crêpe de chine ones and baby ribbon ones. The craving for a new hat is fearful in the Spring. A light, crisp, fresh new-curled hat after these winter dowdies. I suffer from it now. If I had one I should wear it in bed! But the barber is cheaper. He came yesterday and gave me a coup de fer to my wool. Now it's all waves on top. (I have a *great* tendre for barbers.)

About painting. I agree. Good as he is I shall never forget seeing a ballet-dancer of his — it was the last thing I saw of his — at his studio. A *ballet*-dancer. A big, big meaty female dressed in a cauliflower! I don't mean to be horrid; but I do not and cannot understand how one can paint such pictures. They are so dull they make me groan. Hang it all, Brett — a picture must have *charm* — or why look at it? It's the quality I call *tenderness* in writing, it's the tone one gets in a really first-chop musician. Without it you can be as solid as a bull and I don't see what's the good.

Talking about feeling. I had a shock yesterday. I thought my new book would enrage people because it had too much feeling — and there comes a long review talking of the " merciless analysis of the man of science." It's a mystery. If you do see my book read a story called *The Voyage* — will you? Keep it if you like it. . . .

Now I have arrived at the word " primroses " and I see them. Delicate pinkish stems, and the earthy feeling as one picks them so close to the damp soil. I love their leaves too, and I like to kiss buds of primroses. One could kiss them away. They feel so marvellous. But what about blue-bells? Oh dear! Blue-bells are just as good. White ones, faint blue ones that grow in shady hollows, very dark blue ones, pale ones. I had a whole spring full of blue-bells one year with Lawrence. I shall never forget it. And it was warm, not very sunny, the shadows raced over the silky grass and the cuckoos sang.

Later. I then got up, had a big blue bath and a rather horrid lunch. Then played chess, wrote for a couple of hours, had tea and foie gras sandwiches and a long discussion with M. on " literature." Now the light is lighted. Outside there's a marvellous deep lilac sky and I shall work again until dinner. It's strange how nice it is here. One could scarcely be more free. The hotel servants are just a little bit impudent and that's nice, too. There is no servility. I want to tell you that the barber was in raptures with your still life. I think that's a great compliment, don't you? It grows before one's eyes, said he. " Il y a de la vie — un mouvement dans les feuilles." Excellent criticism! He, good man, was small and fair and like all barbers smelt of a violet cachou and a hot iron. He begged, he implored me to go to the cinema near here. Downstairs it was a little mixed but upstairs, on the balcon, there were armchairs of such size and beauty that one could sleep in them. . . . Oh Brett, how I like *simple* people — not all simple people, some are simple pigs — but on the whole — how much more sympathetic than the ——'s this world! Whatever else they have, they are alive. What I cannot bear is this half-existence. This life is the head alone. It's deadly boring.

I think my story for you will be called *Canaries.* The large cage opposite has fascinated me completely. I think and think about them — their feelings, their *dreams,* the life they led before they were caught, the difference between the two little pale fluffy ones who were born in captivity and their grandfather and grandmother who knew the South American forests and have seen the immense perfumed sea. . . . Words cannot express the beauty of that high shrill little song rising out of the very stones. . . . It seems one cannot escape Beauty . . . It is everywhere.

I must end this letter. I have just finished a queer story called *The Fly*. About a fly that falls into an inkpot and a Bank Manager. I think it will come out in the *Nation*. The trouble with writing is that one seethes with stories. One ought to write one a day at least, but it is so tiring. *When* I am well I shall still live always far away in distant spots where I can work and look undisturbed. No more literary society for me *ever*. As for London, the idea is too awful. I shall sneak up to Pond Street every now and again — very rarely indeed and I'll beg you not to let a soul know. It's no joke, my dear, to get the letters I do from people who want to meet one. It's frightening!

To William Gerhardi   March 3, 1922

I meant, only the first chapter, not the " confession." [1] No, I don't think that's a bit too " tragic." I can assure you I never stick pins into my cat; he's far more likely to stick pins into me.

And the reason why I used the " florid " image [2] was that I was writing about a garden party. It seemed natural, then, that the day should close like a flower. People had been looking at flowers all the afternoon, you see.

Thank you for your delightful letter. I shall write en quelques jours. Just for the moment I'm having rather a fight with the rayons X.

To Lady Ottoline Morrell   March 4, 1922

It's a joy to know that *The Garden Party* has given you pleasure and especially that you like my poor old girls, the " Daughters." I shall never forget lying on that wretched little sofa in Mentone writing that story. I couldn't stop. I wrote it all day and on my way back to bed sat down on the stairs and began scribbling the bit about the meringues.

But your beautiful letter is too generous. I can't pretend praise isn't awfully nice! And especially as I have not heard one word

[1] *Futility*, in the original version.
[2] " I had written jokingly to K. M. of a criticism [of *The Garden Party*] overheard on that score." W. G.

from anyone whom I know personally since the book appeared. Reviews there have been and a few notes from strangers. But that's not at all the same. I didn't expect to hear and yet my "subconscious mind" has been intensely interested in whether there are any letters or not! I don't think it's bad pride that makes one feel like that. It's the "You feel that too? You know what I was trying to say," feeling which will be with me while life lasts. Or so I feel. I treasure your letter, even though my *Garden Party* doesn't deserve it.

Brett sent me a couple of pages from *Vogue* with reproductions of Gertler's paintings.

I cannot say what is happening. I believe — just blindly believe. After all illness is so utterly mysterious that I don't see why one shouldn't recover as mysteriously. I have a sneaking feeling all the time that Coué is really the man and Coué would only charge 3d. where this man squeezes three hundred francs a *time* out of me. Happily I have saved £100 so I can pay. But if it is all my eye at the end I shall look awfully silly and dear knows what will happen. But anything, anything to be out of the trap — to escape, to be free. Nobody understands that "depression" who has not known it. And one cannot ever explain it. It's one's own secret. And one goes on rebelling. Yes, I do, too. But don't you think we do feel it more than other people because of our love of life? Other people really don't care so much. They have long periods of indifference, when they almost might as well be ill. But this poignant, almost unbearable feeling that all is pasisng. People who are well do not and cannot understand what it is. . . .

We have not seen one French person to talk to. We live here like hermits in our two caves at the end of a long dark passage. We work, play chess, read, M. goes out and does the shopping; we make tea and drink it out of dove-blue bowls. For some reason, it's all very nice. I should hate to live in a city — in fact I could not, but this is only to last till May. And out of my window I look on other windows and see the funny things people put on the window sills, a hyacinth, a canary, a bottle of milk, and there's a large piece of light, pale sky, and a feeling of Spring. Real Spring. Yesterday on my way to the clinic I saw new leaves on one little tree. It's quite warm too and sunny. We have planned to go to Germany or to Austria this summer if — if — IF. . . .

Letters 1922

To the Hon. Dorothy Brett March 9, 1922

As to my being humble. Oh dear! That's between me and my God. I should retire behind 500 fans if anyone *told* me to be humble! You don't imagine that reviews and letters and requests for photographs and so on make me proud, do you? It's a deep joy to know one gives pleasure to others, but to be told that increases one's store of *love* not *pride*. Also what has it got to do with one's work? I know what I have done and what I must do; nothing and nobody can change that.

A whiff of London came from the last pages of your letter, a whiff of years and years ago, a kind of ashy feeling. Oh, I shall never go back to England again except en passant. Anywhere, anywhere but England! As I write there's a sound of sweet scolding from the pigeons outside. Now it rains, now it's sunny. The March lion is chasing the March lamb, but not very seriously. The lamb does not mind much. They have an understanding. I was reading La Fontaine's Fables in bed early. Do you know them? They are *fearfully* nice — too nice for words. What a character the ant is, a little drop of bitterness and fury and slamming her door in everybody's face; and the frog. I am so sorry for him. He had a sister, too. She should have warned him. Instead she stood by and gloated. La Fontaine must have been an adorable man — a kind of Fabre. Very distrait, very amorous. He didn't even know his own children. He *forgot* their faces and passed them by in the street. I don't expect they cared.

France is a remarkable country. It is I suppose the most civilised country in the world. Bookshops swarm in Paris and the newspapers are written in a way that English people would not stand for one moment. There's practically *no* police news. True, they did write about Landru's execution, but so well it might have been de Maupassant! They are corrupt and rotten politically, that's true. But oh, how they know how to live! And there is always the feeling that Art has its place . . . is accepted by everybody, by the servants, by the rubbish man as well as by all others as something important, necessary, to be proud of. That's what makes living in France such a rest. If you stop your taxi to look at a tree the driver says, " En effet c't' arbre est bien jolie," and ten to one moves his arms like branches. I learnt more about France from my servant at Mentone than anywhere. She was *pure* French, highly highly civilized, nervous, eager, and she would have understood anything on earth you wished to explain to her, in the artistic sense. The fact is they are always *alive,* never indifferent as the English are. England has political freedom (a terrific great thing) and poetry and lovely careless lavish green country. But I'd much rather admire it from afar. English people are I think superior Germans. (10 years hard labour for that remark.) But it's true. They are the German ideal. I was reading Goethe on the subject the other day. He had a tremendous admiration for them. But all through it one feels " so might we Germans be if we only knocked the heads of our police off."

It's fascinating to think about nations and their " significance " in the history of the world. I mean in the spiritual history. Which reminds me I've read lately 2 amazing books about present-day Russia. One by Merejkovski and Zinaida Hippius and the other by Bunin. It is a very extraordinary thing that Russia can be there at our back door at furthest, and we know nothing, pay no attention, hear nothing in English. These books were in French. Both were full of *threats.* "You may think you have escaped. But you have not escaped. What has happened to us will happen to you. And worse. Because you have not heard our prayers." The ghastly horror and terror of that life in Petrograd is impossible to imagine. One must read it to know about it. But English people, people like us, would never survive as some of these Russian intellectuals have survived. We would die of so many things, vermin, fright, cold, hunger, even if we were not assassinated. At this present moment life in Russia is rather like it was four centuries ago. It has simply gone back four centuries. And anyone who sympathizes with Bolshevism has much to answer for. Don't you think that the head of Lenin is terrifying? Whenever I see his picture it comes over me it is the head of something between an awful serpent and a gigantic bug. Russia is at present like an enormous hole in the wall letting in Asia. I wonder what *will* happen, even in our little time.

But do you really feel all beauty is marred by ugliness and the lovely woman has bad teeth? I don't feel quite that. For it seems to me if Beauty were Absolute it would no longer be the kind of Beauty it is. Beauty triumphs over ugliness in Life. That's what

I feel. And that marvellous triumph is what I long to express. The poor man lives and the tears glitter in his beard and that is so beautiful one could bow down. Why? Nobody can say. I sit in a waiting-room where all is ugly, where it's dirty, dull, dreadful, where sick people waiting with me to see the doctor are all marked by suffering and sorrow. And a very poor workman comes in, takes off his cap humbly, beautifully, walks on tiptoe, has a look as though he were in Church, has a look as though he believed that behind that doctor's door there shone the miracle of *healing*. And all is changed, all is marvellous. It's only then that one sees for the first time what is happening. No, I don't believe in your frowsty housemaids, really. Life is, all at one and the same time, far more mysterious and far simpler than we know. It's like religion in that. If we want to have faith, and without faith we die, we must *learn to accept*. That's how it seems to me.

To William Gerhardi — *March 13, 1922*

Please do not think of me as a kind of boa-constrictor who sits here gorged and silent after having devoured your two delightful letters, without so much as a " thank you." If gratitude were the size and shape to go into a pillar box the postman would have staggered to your door days ago. But I've not been able to send anything tangible. I have been — I am ill. In two weeks I shall begin to get better. But for the moment I am down below in the cabin, as it were, and the deck, where all the wise and happy people are walking up and down and Mr. Gerhardi drinks a hundred cups of tea with a hundred schoolgirls, is far away. . . . But I only tell you this to explain my silence. I'm always very much ashamed of being ill; I hate to plead illness. It's taking an unfair advantage. So please let us forget about it. . . .

I've been wanting to say — how strange, how delightful it is you should feel as you do about *The Voyage*. No one has mentioned it to me but Middleton Murry. But when I wrote that little story I felt that I was on that very boat, going down those stairs, smelling the smell of the saloon. And when the stewardess came in and said, " We're rather empty, we may pitch a little," I can't believe that my sofa did not pitch. And one moment I had a little bun of silk-white hair and a bonnet and the next I was Fenella hugging the swan neck umbrella. It was so vivid — terribly vivid — especially as they drove away and heard the sea as slowly it turned on the beach. Why — I don't know. It wasn't a memory of a real experience. It was a kind of *possession*. I might have remained the grandma for ever after if the wind had changed that moment. And that would have been a little bit embarrassing for Middleton Murry. . . . But don't you feel that when you write? I think one always feels it, only sometimes it is a great deal more definite.

Yes, I agree with you the insulting references to Miss Brill would have been better in French. Also there is a printer's error, " chère " for " chérie." " Ma petite chère " sounds ridiculous. . . .

And yes, that is what I tried to convey in *The Garden Party*. The diversity of life and how we try to fit in everything, Death included. That is bewildering for a person of Laura's age. She feels things ought to happen differently. First one and then another. But life isn't like that. We haven't the ordering of it. Laura says, " But all these things must not happen at once." And Life answers, " Why not? How are they divided from each other? " And they *do* all happen, it is inevitable. And it seems to me there is beauty in that inevitability.

I wonder if you happened to see a review of my book in *Time and Tide*. It was written by a very fierce lady indeed. Beating in the face was nothing to it. It frightened me when I read it. I shall never dare to come to England. I am sure she would have my blood like the fish in Cock Robin. But why is she so dreadfully violent? One would think I was a wife beater, at least, or that I wrote all my stories with a carving knife. It is a great mystery.

To the Hon. Dorothy Brett *March 15, 1922*

If you were here, as it happens you wouldn't have listened to a word of what I've been saying. Your eyes, green with envy would have been fixed on, hypnotised by two very old apothecary's jars on my dressing table. Murry, who is a *very* good nose-flattener has been gazing at them for days and yesterday he bought them. They are tall milk-white jars painted with a device in apple green, faint yellow and a kind of astery pink. They have gold tops. On one in exquisite lettering is the word *Absinthii,* on the other

Theriaca. We intend to keep pot-pourri in them during our lives and after our deaths we intend to put our ashes in them. I'm to be *Absinthii* and M. *Theriaca.* So there they stand, our two little coffins, on the dressing table and I've just sent M. out for some fresh flowers to deck them with as I've not pot-pourri. But if I am well enough to nose-flatten at Easter, you and I must go off with our little purses in our little hands and glare!

Are you aware that there is an extremely fine Punch and Judy in the Luxembourg? In a theatre of its own. Stalls 2d., Pit 2d. too. The audience screams frightfully and some are overcome and have to be led out. But there it is. We had better buy some comfits from the stall under the chestnut tree and go there, too. I believe there is a one-eyed thief who comes in, rather, looks round a corner, who really *is* awful. M. said " he let out a yell himself " and the little boy next to him roared. You know the kind of eye. [A drawing of it.]

The weather is glorious here. Warming, sunny. So mild one hears the voices of people in the open air, a sound I love in Spring, and all the windows opposite mine stand wide open, so that I see at one the daughter sewing with her mother, at another the Japanese gentleman, at another two young people who have a way of shutting their bedroom window very quickly and drawing the curtain at most unexpected moments. . . . I can't go out, though, not even for a drive. I am and shall be for the next ten days rather badly ill. In fact, I can only just get about at all. But Manoukhin says the worse one is at this time the better later on. So there's nothing to be done but to be rather dismally thankful.

Later. M. has just come in with 2 bunches of anemones, two small tea plates and a cake of *rose thé* soap. We have had *our* tea and I'm going back to bed. What is a nuisance is I can*not* work for the moment and Shorter has ordered 13 stories, all at one go, to be ready in July. So they are in addition to my ordinary work. I shall have to spend a furious May and June.

The chestnuts are in big bud. Don't you love chestnut buds? I shall have a look at them on Friday. I think they are almost the loveliest buds of all.

Oh, your cinerarias. I wish I could see them. Do you know the blue ones, too! And the faint, faint pink kind? Mother loved them. We used to grow masses in a raised flower bed. I love the shape of the petals. It is so delicate. We used to have blue ones in pots in a rather white and gold drawing room that had green wooden sunblinds. Faint light, big cushions, tables with "photographs of the children" in silver frames, some little yellow and black cups and saucers that belonged to Napoleon in a high cupboard and someone playing Chopin — beyond words playing Chopin. . . . Oh how beautiful Life is. How beautiful! A knock at my door. The maid has come in to close the shutters. That's such a lovely gesture. She leans forward, she looks up and the shutters fold like wings.

To Sir Harold Beauchamp *March 18, 1922*

I have found it almost impossible to do any work so far, as the treatment is exceedingly tiring. But my new book has been a success and that is a comfort. It is extraordinary the letters I receive from strangers — all kinds of people. I have certainly been most fortunate as a writer. It is strange to remember buying a copy of *The Native Companion* on Lambton Quay and standing under a lamppost with darling Leslie to see if my story had been printed.

The more I see of life the more certain I feel that it's the people who live remote from cities who inherit the earth. London, for instance, is an awful place to live in. Not only is the climate abominable but it's a continual chase after distraction. There's no peace of mind — no harvest to be reaped out of it. And another thing is the longer I live the more I turn to New Zealand. I thank God I was born in New Zealand. A young country is a real heritage, though it takes one time to recognise it. But New Zealand is in my very bones. What wouldn't I give to have a look at it!

To the Hon. Dorothy Brett *March 19, 1922*

Oh, I am so longing to get over this last crisis and begin to climb the hill so that by the time you come I shall not be such a Job-in-the-ashes. Manoukhin says in eight days now the worst will be over. It's such a queer feeling. One burns with heat in one's hands and feet and bones. Then suddenly you are racked with neuritis, but such neuritis that you can't lift your arm. Then one's head begins to pound. It's the moment when if I were a proper martyr I should begin to have that awful smile that martyrs in the flames put on when they begin to sizzle!

But no matter, it will pass. . . .

It is real spring here, really come. Little leaves are out. The air is like silk. But above all, beyond all there is a kind of fleeting beauty on the faces of everybody, a timid look, the look of someone who bends over a new baby. This is so beautiful, that it fills one with awe. The fat old taximan has it and the fisherman on the Pont d' Alma that I passed yesterday and the young lady at the office with her scent and her violet cachou and her shoes like beetles — all — all are the same. For this alone one is thankful to have lived on the earth. My canaries opposite are, of course, in a perfect fever. They sing, flutter, sing and make love. Even the old clock that strikes over the roofs says *one* — *two* no longer, but drowsily, gently says Spring — Spring. . . .

Yes, paint the Luxembourg Gardens! Do paint a new tree, a just-come-out chestnut — wouldn't that be good to paint? When the leaves are still stiff they look as though they had sprung out of the buds. Chestnut trees are marvellous. But so are limes and acacias and umbrella pines. I can't say I like firs awfully, though. If you had lived among them as we did in Switzerland you would have found them *stodgy*.

To Mrs. Oliver Onions   *March 24, 1922*

What a letter you have sent me! If I could hope one of my stories had given you one moment of the happiness you have given me I would feel less at a loss how to thank you. I have sat here, looking at the pages, and thinking " So she felt like that about *The Stranger,* she notices Florrie the cat, she understood my poor old Ma Parker and Miss Brill. . . ."

For it's not your praise I value most (though, of course, one does like praise) it's the fact that you have so beautifully, so generously seen what I was trying to express. It is a joy to write stories but nothing like the joy of knowing one has not written in vain. I have lived too remote from people for the last four years seeing nobody except my husband for months on end — And that makes one a little bit frightened sometimes lest one has lost touch with life. But a letter like yours is such encouragement that the only way I can thank you is by trying to write better. . . . You say scarcely anything about the big black holes in my book (like the servant's afternoon out). But I know they are there. I must mend them next time.

How glad I am that you did not listen to the person who said you had "much better not." One does not *expect* such letters — how could one — few people are rich enough to be able to afford to give such presents.

To the Countess Russell   *March 24, 1922*

I have been on the point of writing to you for days. And now — merciful Powers! — it's winter again with real live snow and I've not been out of this hotel once since I arrived in Paris eight weeks ago except to go to the clinic and back. Oh to be on grass-feed again after all this hay and dry food. I've read Michelet, Madame d'Epinay and Remy de Gourmont (exasperating old stupid as often as not) and I cling to Shakespeare. But even Shakespeare . . . It's awful. However, the Russian promises that after this week I really begin to mend, so I have no right to make moan.

But cities are the very devil, Elizabeth, if one is embalmed in them. And here's this post card of the Châlet Soleil in summer in all its ravishing loveliness, with two perfect guardian angels, large, benign, frilly ones, in full leaf, behind it. I think they are oaks. I cherish, embedded in *Twelfth Night,* a sprig of mignonette from the bush that ran wild in its second generation by the front door. And do you remember smelling the geraniums in the late afternoon in the hall? It seemed just the time and the place to smell those geraniums. I can't even imagine what going back there would be like; it would be too great happiness. But I shall remember that day for ever.

To Richard Murry   *March 29, 1922*

Yes, I too was very interested in S.'s review, though I didn't agree with it all. For instance his quotation from Tolstoy, "There are no heroes, only people." I believe there *are* heroes. And after all it was Tolstoy who made the remark who was — surely — a large part of a hero himself. And I don't believe in the limitations of man; I believe in "the heights." I can't help it; I'm *forced* to. It seems to me that very feeling of inevitability that there is in a great work of art — is a proof — a profession of faith on the part of the artist that this life is not *all*. (Of course, I'm not talking of personal immortality as we were taught to imagine it.) If I were to agree with S. I'd have to believe that the *mind* is supreme. But I don't — not by a long long chalk. The mind is only the fine instrument, it's only the slave of the soul. I do agree that with a great many artists one never sees the *master,* we only know the slave. And the slave is so brilliant that he can almost make you forget the absence of the other. But one is only really *living* when one acknowledges both — or so it seems to me — and great art is achieved when the relation between these two is perfected. But it's all very difficult.

About religion. Did you mean the "study of life" or Christ's religion, "Come unto Me all ye that labour and are heavy laden and I will give you rest"? The queer thing is one does not seem to contradict the other — one follows on the other to me. If I lose myself in the study of life and give up *self* then I am at rest. But the more I study the religion of Christ the more I marvel at it. It seems almost impertinent to say that. But you understand. . . .

I wish you read German. Goethe's *Conversations with Eckermann* is one of those books which become part of one's life and what's more, enrich one's life for ever. Our edition is in two volumes. We lie in bed each reading one — it would make a funny drawing.

To the Hon. Dorothy Brett   *Tuesday*
April 4, 1922

I'm interested in what you say of Wyndham L. I've heard so very much about him from Anne Rice and Violet Schiff. Yes, I admire his line tremendously. It's beautifully obedient to his wishes. But it's queer I feel that as an artist in spite of his passions and his views and all that he lacks a real *centre*. I'll tell you what I mean. It sounds personal but we can't help that, we can only speak of what we have learnt. It seems to me that what one aims at is to work with one's mind and one's soul *together*. By soul I mean that "thing" that makes the mind really important. I always picture it like this. My mind is a very complicated, capable instrument. But the interior is dark. It *can* work in the dark and throw off all kinds of things. But behind that instrument like a very steady gentle light is the soul. And it's only when the soul *irradiates* the mind that what one does matters. . . . What I *aim* at is that state of mind when I feel my soul and my mind are one. It's awfully, terribly difficult to get at. Only solitude will do it for me. But I feel Wyndham Lewis would be inclined to call the soul tiddley-om-pom. It's a mystery, anyway. One aims at perfection — knows one will never achieve it and goes on aiming as though one knew the exact contrary.

By the way, do you know Marquet's work well? I have a book of reproductions I will show you. He's not a very great painter but he's most awfully good sometimes. What a bore! As I write about him he suddenly seems very small beer. And the reproduction of a picture by le Nain (in the Louvre), *Repas de Paysans*, which is four-pinned on my wall is miles better than all Marquet's kind of thing.

*Saturday
April 9, 1922*

Are you coming on the 18th? I went out to-day, Miss, and bought myself a sweet-pretty-hat-it-was-indeed, and walked away in it carrying my dead one in a paper bag. Which is to say:

That this reaction seems to be nearly over. I do feel much better. Manoukhin is very pleased — was yesterday.

Oh, Brett, I can't say what it's like! I still don't dare to give myself up to believing all is going to be quite well. But all the same. . . .

The following letter needs a note of explanation. The part in italics was written by J. M. Murry. It was, in fact, the beginning of an ordinary polite social letter to the wife of a French friend. He left it unfinished on his writing table and went out. When he returned he found it completed for him.

> Victoria-Palace Hotel
> rue Blaise-Desgoffe,
> Paris 6ème
> le 11 avril 1922

Chère Madame,
   Je vous remercie de votre lettre. Je regrette beaucoup de ne pas avoir eu le plaisir de voir V. ; mais j'espère que je serai encore à Paris quand il revient du Midi, et qu'il sera tout à fait rétabli par le beau soleil. J'ai un si bon souvenir de ma soirée chez vous, Madame, que l'idée même d'une autre me donne un rouge vif aux genoux. Vous souvenez-vous du moment quand vous avez versé sur mon pantalon gris-perle la petite tasse de chocolat et ma reponse en vous frappant (façon anglais) avec ma porte-plume ? " Helas mon passé ! Où est-il passé ? " comme disait votre soidisant mari.
   Aver un de mes fameux baisers sur la joue,
      Croyez-moi chère Madame,
         Votre Boule-Dogue le plus fidèle,
            John Middleton Murry.

To the Hon. Dorothy Brett   *Easter*
                              April 17, 1922

Brett, how ever dare you breathe the idea of *scrubbing*. If you ever take a scrub brush in your hand I hope it will sting you and run after you like a beetle. Don't work any more than you can possibly help! It's cheaper for you to employ slaves for those jobs. I hope your servant is a good creature and will really look after you. I wish I knew more about your house and its fixings but it's tiring to write such things. You'll tell me when you come over. I'm sure we shall be in Paris until the middle of June, for once Manoukhin is over, I must get my teeth seen to before we go off again. Then we think of making for Austria or Bavaria and perhaps our old love, Bandol for the winter. That's what we *want* to do. I foresee I shall have to pick up a young maid in Bavaria. I can't do without somebody, not a Mountain, but a maid. Who takes one's gloves to be cleaned. Looks after one's clothes, keeps them brushed and so on. And then there's one's hair and all that.

It takes such a terrific time to keep everything going. There is an endless succession of small jobs. And then one wants little things bought, new sachets and toothpaste. All those things to keep renewed. I can't keep up with it, not if I was as strong as ever. There's too much to write and too much to read and to talk about. I can't for the life of me understand how women manage. It's easier for men because of the way they dress and so on. Also they aren't dependent on small things like we are. No, a little nice Bertha or Augusta is my ambition.

By the way, I have discovered something interesting about the Russian colony in Paris. I mean Manoukhin and his friends. They are intensely religious. Before the revolution they were all sceptics, as far from religion as the English intelligentsia. But now that is changed. They go to Church perpetually, kneel on the cold stones, *believe* really in religion. This is very strange. Last Good Friday at the clinic Manoukhin was late and his partner, Donat, a handsome white-bearded man with a stiff leg, talked to us about it. They have become mystics, said he. Mystic! that strange word is always touching the fringes of and running away from . . .

Forgive this letter. All is scraps and pieces. I am shamefully tired and only fit for business communications. I try to whip myself up but it's no good. I've a new story coming out in the *Nation* called *Honeymoon*. Read it if you have the time, will you? I'd like to feel you had seen it.

To the Countess Russell   *April 26, 1922*

I feel I have spent years and years at this hotel. I have eaten hundreds of wings of hotel chickens, and only God knows how many little gritty trays with half cold coffee pots on them have whisked into my room and out again. It doesn't matter. Really, one arrives at a rather blissful state of defiance after a time, when nothing matters and one almost seems to glory in everything. It rains every day. The hotel window sills have sprouted into very fat self-satisfied daisies and pitiful pansies. Extraordinary Chinamen flit past one on the stairs followed by porters bearing their boxes, which are like large corks; the lift groans for ever. But it's all wonderful — all works of the Lord — and marvellous in His sight. John and I went for a drive in the Bois the other day. Elizabeth, it was *divine*. That new green, that grass; and there were cherry trees in flower — masses of adorable things.

Are you working? I won't ask you what you are reading. Do you sometimes get tired of books — but terribly tired of them? Away with them all! It being a cold night, lately, John and I lay in one bed each with an immense Tomb of Eckermann's *Conversations with Goethe* perched on our several chests. And when my side of the bed began to shake up and down

J.: " What in God's name are you laughing at? "
K.: " Goethe is so very, very *funny!* "
But it hadn't " struck " John.

To Anne Estelle Rice   May 1, 1922

I have just been through that déchirante experience, two lovely young creatures from the chemisier with little frocks " pour essayer seule-ment, Madame." I'm sitting, fringe straight again at last, writing to you in the one they forced on me — a kind of plum grey — tout droit, with buttings on the hips and no trimmings at all except a large embroidered lobster bien posé sur la ventre!!! Shall I ever wear it again? It's beginning to look extraordinary every moment. The little creatures twittering *Chic-chic-chic!* would have made me buy a casserole for a chapeau with two poireaux in the front. That is the worst of living as I do far from the female kind. These moments come and I'm lost.

Yes, I'll be here first week in June for sure. Do come then. Otherwise I don't know where I shall be off to. I've got a wandering fit on. Anywhere, anywhere but England. The idea would be to have a small permanent nid in Paris and another in the South and then a small car and so on, ma chère. Very nice — only one thing missing to make it complete. However, I never care much about money. I always feel sooner or later it will turn up — one will find it somewhere, in the crown of one's hat or in the jampot.

If only it would stop raining — large spots of rain as big as mushrooms fall every day — Paris would be perfect just now. I don't see much of it for I have still two weeks of my X-ray " cure " to go. But after that I shall really begin to prowl. I can't say much about the cure till it's over. I dare not. But I feel very different already. I'm so sorry to hear of your servant débâcle. If I go to

Germany this summer (we've almost settled to go) I mean to find a good sober German and keep her attached to me for ever. Shall I look out one for you? Germans are the ideal servants, I think, and they are so lasting. They don't ladder at once like the English kind. I want to get a very nice one with a pincushion in the shape of a strawberry pinned on her buste and she will catch my ribbons when they run out of my chemises and run them in again and be a comfort. That's what one really wants. A Comfort. They ought to be bred specially.

To the Hon. Dorothy Brett *Saturday*
May 1, 1922

About Joyce — Don't read it unless you are going to really worry about it. It's no joke. It's fearfully difficult and obscure and one needs to have a really vivid memory of the Odyssey and of English Literature to make it out at all. It is wheels within wheels within wheels. Joyce certainly had not one grain of a desire that one should read it for the sake of the coarseness, though I confess I find many "a ripple of laughter" in it. But that's because (although I don't *approve* of what he's done) I do think Marian Bloom and Bloom are superbly seen at times. Marian is the complete complete female. There's no denying it. But one has to remember she's also Penelope, she is also the night and the day, she is also an image of the teeming earth, full of seed, rolling round and round. And so on and so on. I am very surprised to hear a Russian has written a book like this. It's most queer that it's never been heard of. But has Kot *read* Ulysses? It's not the faintest use considering the coarseness except purely critically.

I am very interested that Koteliansky thinks the German-Russian treaty really good. Manoukhin and all the Russians here say it means war in the *near* future. For certain, for certain! It is the beginning of Bolshevism all over Europe. The Bolsheviks at Genoa are complete cynics. They say anything. They are absolutely laughing in their beards at the whole affair, and treating us as fools even greater than the French. The French at least have a sniff of what may happen but we go on saying "Let us all be good," and the Russians and Germans burst with malicious glee. I was staggered when I heard this. Manoukhin's partner here, a very exceptional Frenchman, started the subject yesterday, said, Why did not we English immediately join the French and take all vestige of power from Germany? This so disgusted me I turned to Manoukhin and felt sure he would agree that it simply could not be done. But he agreed absolutely. And they declare, the Russians here, we are in for another war and for Bolshevism *partout*. It's a nice prospect, isn't it?

I must say I never in my life felt so entangled in politics as I do at this moment. I hang on the newspapers. I feel I dare not miss a speech. One begins to feel, like Gorky feels, that it's one's duty to what remains of civilisation to care for those things and that writers who do not are traitors. But it's horrible. It's like jumping into a treacle pot. However, perhaps to-morrow one will stop reading the papers or caring a fig.

>A B C
>Tumble down D
>The cat's in the cupboard
>And can't see me.

I must end this letter. Don't take it for a real letter. It's written from bed where I lie with influenza for tumpany. I am sure I'm over the worst of it to-day. But I still feel very boiled and put through the wringer. You see the weather here is simply beyond words. It rains and rains and it's cold and it hails and the wind whistles down the corridors. Only frogs and mushrooms, being noseless, could refrain from catching things. Influenza puts the fear of God into me. The very word has a black plume on its head and a tail of coffin sawdust. But I hope to get up and go out next week. Don't think I'm discouraged. Not a bit of it. On the contrary, if a pudding head could sing, I would.

M. comes in every afternoon with a fresh victim to tell me of. Everybody has got it, woman at milkshop, woman at library, bread woman. Where does all the rain come from? And the Channel is rough every day. When you come in May if I were you I'd fly. So simple, no horrid old changing from boats to trains and diving into cabins and along gritty station platforms. Flying seems so clean, like cutting out one's way with a pair of sharp scissors.

To the Hon. Dorothy Brett — May 3, 1922

It's rather an important day for me. I am beginning my long serial ... half of which has to be finished in a month from now. And I have also signed away all the rest of my book to be ready sans faute by the end of the summer. The serial is very exciting. It is 24,000 words, a short novel in fact. I want it to end with a simply scrumptious wedding, rose pink tulle frocks for the bridesmaids, favours on the horses' heads, that marvellous moment at the church when everyone is waiting, the servants in a pew to themselves. *The Cook's hat!* But all, all divinely beautiful if I can do it ... gay, but with that feeling that "beauty vanishes beauty passes, Though rare, rare it be. ..."

To Hugh Jones — May 5, 1922

My dear little Hugh,

First I must beg your pardon for not having thanked you for that lovely post card you painted for me. But I wanted to run out and buy you a little present to pop in the letter and I have not been able to yet, for I have been ill, too. But I won't forget. The very first time I go out I will drive to a shop that sells presents.

How very nicely you painted that bee-hive. I have always wanted to live in a bee-hive, so long as the bees were not there. With a little window and a chimney it would make a dear little house. I once read a story about a little girl who lived in one with her Grandma, and her Grandma's name was old Mrs. Gooseberry. What a funny name!

Mr. Murry thinks you write very well. He liked the "R" best. He said it looked as if it was going for a walk. Which letter do you like making best? "Q" is nice because of its curly tail.

I have pinned the post card on the wall so that everybody can see it. I hope you are nearly well again.

With much love from
"Mrs. Murry."

To Richard Murry *Sunday. Paree.*
May 23, 1922

But seriously — isn't it almost frightening the difference fine weather can make? I wish Einstein could find some way of shooting a giant safety-pin at the sun and keeping it there. It has been tremendously hot in Paris. Like an oven. Jack and I gave up writing altogether. We were overcome and could do nothing but fan ourselves, he with a volume of Anthony Trollope (very cool) and me with my black penny paper one. The strawberries and cherries came out in swarms — very big cherries and little wild strawbugs. Finally we found a spot in the Louvre among the sculpture which was cool as a grotto. Jack had an idea of making himself a neat toga, taking the *Nation* for a parchment roll and standing becalmed upon a Roman pedestal until the weather changed. There are glorious things in that first room in the Louvre. Greek statues — portions of the Parthenon Frieze, a head of Alexander, wonderful draped female figures. Greek drapery is very strange. One looks at it — the lines seem to be dead straight and yet there is movement — a kind of suppleness and though there is no suggestion of the body beneath one is conscious of it as a living, breathing thing. How on earth is that done? And they seemed to have been able to draw a line with a chisel as if it were a pencil. One line and there is an arm or a nose — perfect. The Romans are deaders compared to them. We had a long stare at the Venus de Milo, too. One can't get away from the fact — she is marvellously beautiful. All the little people in straw hats buzz softly round her. Such a comfort to see something they know. "Our Maud has ever such a fine photograph of her over the piano." But "she doesn't care."

About Rubens. I never can forget his paintings in Antwerp. They seemed to me far more brilliant than the London ones — I mean impressive. He must have enjoyed himself no end a doing of them. But I confess I like his small paintings best. One gets really too much for one's money in the big ones — There's rather a fat woman wading in a stream in the National Gallery — Quite a small one. It's very good — isn't it?

I shall have no time to look at pictures here till we get back from Switzerland. It's terrible how Jack and I seem to get engaged. We are pursued by dinners and lunches and telephone bells and dentists. Oh, Richard, do you FEAR the dentist? He reduces me to a real worm. Once I am established in that green plush chair with my heels higher almost than my head all else fades. What a fiendish business it is! One day I shall write a story that you will have to tie up your face to read. I shall call it *Killing the Nerve*.

Since I last wrote to you a great deal seems to have happened. But that is the effect of living in a city. I long to get away and to work. We are spending June and July at a hotel about 750 feet below Montana. It is a very simple place and isolated, standing in one of those forest clearings. There are big grassy slopes almost like lawns between the clumps of trees and by the time we get there the flowers will all be out as they were last year. Paris is a fine city but one can't get hold of any big piece of work here; the day splits up into pieces and people play the piano below one's window or sing even if one sits with the door locked and the outside world put away.

To the Hon. Dorothy Brett

*Hotel d'Angleterre
Montana-sur-Sierre
Valais, Suisse
June 5, 1922*

We had an awful journey. The station was crammed with a seething mob. No porters — people carrying their luggage. No couchettes after all — only a packed 1st-class carriage, coated in grime. It was Whitsun, of course. . . . I've never taken Whitsun seriously before, but now I know better. Poor dear M. left things in the rack, gave a 500 note instead of a 50, lost the registered luggage tickets. . . . When we reached Sierre, and that lovely clean hotel, smelling of roses and lime blossom, we both fell fast asleep on a garden bench while waiting for lunch. Then at Randogne, after shinning up a hill to reach the little cart, a big black cloud saw us far off, *tore* across and we'd scarcely started when down came the cold mountain rain. Big drops that clashed on one like pennies. It poured in sheets and torrents. We hadn't even a rug. The road, which has only just been dug out and is like a river-bed, became a river, and for the most of the time we seemed to drive on two wheels. But it was heavenly, it didn't matter. It was so marvellously fresh and cool after Paris. A huge dog plunged after our cart and leapt into all the streams — a dog as big as a big sofa. Its name was Lulu. When we arrived, sleek as cats with the wet, a little old grey woman ran out to meet us. There wasn't another soul to be seen. All was empty, chill and strange. She took us into two very plain bare rooms, smelling of pitch pine, with big bunches of wild flowers on the tables, with no mirrors, little washbasins like tea basins, no armchairs, no nuffin. And she explained she had no servant even. There was only herself and her old sister who would look after us. I had such fever, by this time, that it all seemed like a dream. When the old 'un had gone J. looked very *sad*. Oh, how I pitied him! I saw he had the awful foreboding that we must move on again. But I had the feeling that perhaps we had been living too softly lately. It was perhaps time to shed all those hot-water taps and horrid false luxuries. So I said it reminded me of the kind of place Tchekhov would stay at in the country in Russia! This comforted M. so much that the very walls seemed to expand. And after we had *un*packed and eaten eggs from the hen, not the shop, M. got into a pair of old canvas shoes and a cricket-shirt.

The air is so wonderful. It's not really hot here except in the sun: There just a breeze — a freshet that blows from across the valley. It's all silky and springlike. The grasshoppers ring their little tambourines all day and all night, too. The view is so marvellous that you must see it to believe it. And behind this hotel that are immense lawns dotted with trees; it's like a huge, natural park. We sat there yesterday watching the herds — a few bright sheep, an old woman with her goat, a young girl, far away with some black ones. When the beasts were being driven home at milking time they began to *play*. I have never seen a more beautiful sight. They are so joyful to be out again and in the green field that great cows lowed softly for delight and skipped and jumped and tilted at each other and little sheep flew along like rocking horses and danced and gambolled. The slender girls with mushroom white handkerchiefs on their heads ran after them. But they caught the infection and began to laugh and sing, too. It was like the beginning of the world again.

Cities are cursed places. When I have my little house in the South. I'll never go near them and I shall *lure* you away. I long for you to be here next month. The hotel will still be empty. But that's nice. It is so still. As one crosses the hall it echoes. The old woman has very kind eyes. She is simple and gentle. She keeps promising me that I will get better here, and she is determined to make me drink all kinds of teas made of fresh strawberry leaves and hay and pine needles. I suppose I shall drink them — Bless her heart!

*Sunday
June 9, 1922*

Summer has deserted us, too. It's cool and we are up in the clouds all day. Huge white woolly fellows lie in the valley. There is nothing to be seen from the windows but a thick, soft whiteness. It's beautiful in its way. The sound of water is beautiful flowing through it and the shake of the cows' bells.

Yes, I know Utrillo's work from reproductions; M. has seen it. It's very sensitive and delicate. I'd like to see some originals. What a horrible fate he should be mad. Tragedy treads on the heels of those young French painters. Look at young Modigliani — he had only just begun to find himself when he committed suicide. I think it's partly that café life; it's a curse as well as a blessing. I sat opposite a youthful poet in the filthy atmosphere of the L'Univers and he was hawking and spitting the whole evening. Finally after a glance at his mouchoir he said, " Encore du sang. Il me faut 24 mouchoirs par jour. C'est le désespoir de ma femme! " Another young poet, Jean Pellerin, (awfully good) died, (but not during the evening!) making much the same joke.

Talking about "illness," my dear. I feel rather grim when I read of your wish to hustle me and make me run! Did it really seem to you people were always telling me to sit down? To me that was the fiercest running and the most tremendous hustling and I couldn't keep it up for any length of time. In fact, as soon as I got here I wrote to L. M. and asked her to come back and look after things as otherwise I'd never be able to get any work done. All my energy went in "hustling." So she's coming back to me in a strictly professional capacity to look after us both. M. needs someone very badly, too, and I can't face the thought of a stranger. No, I'm afraid it's not only a question of weak muscles; I wish it were! You ask Manouhkin! Don't let's discuss my health.

I must get up and start work. There's a huge beetle creeping over my floor — so cautiously, so intently. He has thought it all out. One gets fond of insects here; they seem to be in their place and it's a pleasure to know they are there. M. was saying the other night how necessary *snakes* are in creation. Without snakes there would be a tremendous gap, a poverty. Snakes complete the picture. Why? I wonder. I feel it, too. I read an account of unpacking large deadly poisonous vipers at the Zoo the other day. They were lifted out of the boxes with large wooden tongs. Can't you see those tongs! like giant asparagus tongs. And think of one's feelings if they suddenly crossed like sugar tongs too — Brrrr!

*Sunday
June 9, 1922*

The weather is *im*perfect — to be very polite to it. It's warm, and then it's chill. Not so much windy as draughty. But where is perfect weather? Palm Beach, California, they say. But if I arrived, there'd be a snow-storm. L. M. arrived yesterday. The relief to have her is *so* great that I'll never never say another word of impatience. I don't deserve such a wife. All is in order already. M. and I sigh and turn up our eyes. M., in fact, to pay her a little compliment, has wrenched the ligaments of his foot and can't walk. *He* is tied to a chaise longue! Isn't it awful bad luck? But what marvellously *good* luck that L. M. was here and produced bandages and vinegar and all that was needful. The Ancient Sisters, of course, hovered over him, too, and made him cover his foot in a poultice of *parsley* last night. He went to bed looking like a young leg of lamb.

I wish you had been here this afternoon. They brought us in branches of cherries, all dark and glistening among the long slender leaves.

To William Gerhardi   *June 14, 1922*

Your handwriting on the envelope made me feel a guilty thing; I hardly dared open the letter. And when I did there wasn't a single reproach in it. That was very kind of you — very generous.

The truth is I have been on the pen point of writing to you for weeks and weeks but always Paris — horrid Paris — snatched my pen away. And during the latter part of the time I spent nearly every afternoon in a tight, bony dentist's chair while a dreadfully callous American gentleman with an electric light on his forehead explored the root canals or angled with devilish patience for the lurking nerves. Sometimes, at black moments, I think that when I die I shall go to the DENTIST's.

I am glad you did not come to Paris after all; we should not have been able to talk. It's too distracting. It is like your "twelve complete teas, ices and all" — all the time. One is either eating them or watching other people eat them, or seeing them swept away or hearing the jingle of their approach, or waiting for them, or paying for them, or trying to get out of them (hardest of all). Here it is ever so much better. If, on your walk to-day, you pass one of those signs with a blameless hand pointing to the Hotel d'Angleterre, please follow. The cherries are just ripe; they are cutting the hay. But these are English delights, too. Our *speciality* is the forest à deux pas, threaded with little green paths and hoarse quick little streams. If it happens to be sunset, too, I could shew you something very strange. Behind this Hotel there is a big natural lawn, a wide stretch of green turf. When the herds that are being driven home in the evening come to it they go wild with delight. Staid, black cows begin to dance, to leap, to cut capers. Quiet, refined little sheep who look as though buttercups would not melt in their mouths suddenly begin to jump, to spin round, to bound off like rocking-horses. The goats are complete Russian Ballet Dancers; they are almost too brilliant. But the cows are the most surprising and the most naïve. You will admit that cows don't look like born dancers, do they? And yet my cows are light as feathers, bubbling over with fun. Please tell dear little Miss Helsingfors that it's quite true they *do* jump over the moon. I have seen them do it — or very nearly. Ah, Mr. Gerhardi, I love the country! To lie on the grass again and smell the clover! Even to feel a little ant creep up one's sleeve was a kind of comfort . . . after one had shaken it down again. . . .

I am in the middle of a very long story [1] written in the same style — horrible expression! — as *The Daughters of the Late Colonel*. I enjoy writing it so much that even after I am asleep, I go on. The scene is the South of France in early spring. There is a real

[1] *The Doves' Nest*.

love story in it, too, and rain, buds, frogs, a thunderstorm, pink spotted Chinese dragons. There is no happiness greater than this leading a *double life*. But it's mysterious, too. How is it possible to be here in this remote, deserted hotel and at the same time to be leaning out of the window of the Villa Martin listening to the rain thrumming so gently on the leaves and smelling the night-scented stocks with Milly? (I shall be awfully disappointed if you don't like Milly.)

Have you read Bunin's stories? They are published in English by the Hogarth Press. *The Gentleman from San Francisco* is good, but I don't care much for the others. He tries too hard. He's too determined you shall not miss the cucumbers and the dyed whiskers. And the last story called *Son* I can't for the life of me understand. I met Bunin in Paris and because he had known Tchekhov I wanted to talk of him. But alas! Bunin said " Tchekhov? Ah — Ah — Oui, j'ai connu Tchekhov. Mais il y a longtemps, longtemps." And then a pause. And then, graciously, " Il a ecrit des belles choses." And that was the end of Tchekhov. " Vous avez lu mon dernier. . . . ? "

I shall be here until the end of August. After that I go back to Paris for two months and then I want to go to Italy to a little place called Arco near the Lake of Garda for the winter.

When you are in the mood please write to me and tell me what you are writing. I am sorry you did not like *The Fly* and glad you told me. I *hated* writing it. Yes, I remember the story about the little boy and the buzzing insects. His father comes home from the town and finds him sitting up to the table cutting Kings and Queens out of a pack of playing cards. I can always see him.

Here comes my ancient landlady with a cup of tea made from Iceland moss and hay flowers. She is determined to make a new man of me — good old soul — and equally convinced that nothing but herb tea will do it. My insides must be in a state of the most profound astonishment.

Goodbye for now. All success — every good wish for your book. And don't be grateful to me, please; I've done nothing.

Letters 1922

To the Hon. Dorothy Brett
June 22, 1922
In the Forest

I'm sitting writing to you in a glade under a pine tree. There are quantities of little squat yellow bushes of a kind of broom everywhere that give a sweet scent and are the humming houses of bees. M. and I have been here all day. Now he is climbing up to Montana to buy a large bottle of castor oil! It's sad to feel so completely a creature of air as one does in this forest and yet to find one's insides have ordered a general strike. Such is our awful condition. It's divinely lovely out here, and warm again — with just a light breeze singing in the trees. A little blue sky with puffs of white cloud over the mountains.

Last evening as I sat on a stump watching the herds pass I felt you may take furiously to cows and paint nothing but cows on green lawns with long shadows like triangles from this-shaped tree [a drawing] and end with a very grave cow-complex. I have one. Up till now I have always more than resisted the charm of cows but now it's swep' over me all of a heap, Miss. Insects, too, even though my legs are both bitten off at the knees by large and solemn flies. Do you mind turning brown, too? Or peeling? I had better warn you. These things are bound to happen. And I am *hatefully* unsociable. Don't forget that. It's on the cards you may turn frightfully against me here and brain me with your Toby.[1] You see, every day I work till 12.30 and again from 4.30 until supper — every blessed day, Sunday included. Can you bear that? In the mornings we may meet as I go abroad and sit under the trees. But I shall regard you as invisible and you will haughtily cut me. In this way, when we *are* free, we feel free and not guilty. We can play and look at beetles in peace. I must get the ancient sisters to simplify their ideas of picnics though. To-day they brought M. boiled beef and trimmings in a saucepan. It's awful to open such a vessel under the very Eye of our Maker. I like eggs, butter-bread and milk at picnics. But M. disagrees. He regards such tastes as female flippancy.

Oh, my story won't go fast enough. It's got stuck. I must have it finished and done with in 10 days' time. Never shall I commit myself again to a stated time. It's hellish.

[1] The name of an ear-trumpet.

Letters 1922

To Arnold Gibbons *June 24, 1922*

Very many thanks for your letter and for letting me see the five stories. I'd like immensely to talk about them a little. But you'll take what I say as workshop talk — will you? — as from one writer to another. Otherwise one feels embarrassed.

I think the idea in all the five stories is awfully good. And you start each story at just the right moment and finish it at the right moment, too. Each is a whole, complete in itself. But I don't feel any of them quite come off. Why? It's as though you used more words than were necessary. There's a kind of diffuseness of expression which isn't natural to the English way of thinking. I imagine your great admiration for Tchekhov has liberated you, but you have absorbed more of him than you are aware of and he's got in the way of your individual expression for the time being. It's very queer; passages real like a translation! It's as though you were in his shadow and the result is you are a little bit blurred, a bit vague. Your real inmost self (forgive the big words but one does mean them) doesn't seem to be speaking except occasionally. It's almost as though you were hiding and hadn't the — shall I call it — courage? — of your own fine sensitiveness. When you do get free of Tchekhov *plus* all you have learnt of him you ought to write awfully good stories. *Pleasure* gives one an idea of how good. There you seem to me nearly in your own stride. It is convincing. One believes in that little cat and its meat for breakfast; one sees your old chap wiping the glass case with his handkerchief; and one sees his audience turn and then turn back to him. I think this story is much the best of the five.

To return to your Russianization for a moment. It seems to me that when Russians think they go through a different process from what we do. As far as we can gather they arrive at feeling by a process of . . . spiritual recapitulation. I don't think we do. What I imagine is we have less words but they are more vital; we *need* less. So though one can accept this recapitulating process from Russian writers it sounds strange to me coming from your pen. For instance, in *Going Home* you get in five lines: "enthusiasm, doubtful, mistrust, acute terror, anxious joy, sadness, pain, final dissolution, filth and degradation." *Or* (p. 2) "the unhappiness, the misery and cruelty, all the squalor and abnormal spiritual anguish." Again, last page but one of *The Sister*, " futility, monotony, suffocated, pettiness, sordidness, vulgar minuteness."

When one writes like that in English it's as though the *nerve* of the feeling were gone. Do you know what I mean?

I realise it's all very well to say these things — but how are we going to convey these overtones, half tones, quarter tones, these hesitations, doubts, beginnings, if we go at them *directly*? It is most devilishly difficult, but I do believe that there is a way of doing it and that's by trying to get as near to the *exact truth* as possible. It's the truth we are after, no less (which, by the way, makes it so exciting).

To Sir Harold Beauchamp   *June 26, 1922*

I hope you are enjoying a different hand of weather from our mountain variety. It is as cold as late autumn, very, very damp, with heavy mists. We are wearing full winter outfit and going to bed under our travelling rugs, with large size Swiss hot water tins. Summer seems to have spent its fortune at one fell swoop. You know that type of wind, like a draught, which plays on the back of one's neck and seems to come from all quarters equally; it is in its element at present. However, being the month of June, we can still hope that any day may see a complete change.

I envy you your voyage in the " Aquitania." It must be a most interesting experience to travel in one of those huge liners — very different to the good old " Star of New Zealand." Still, I have a very soft corner in my heart for the " Niwaru," for example. Do you remember how Mother used to enjoy the triangular shaped pieces of toast for tea? Awfully good they were, too, on a cold afternoon in the vicinity of The Horn. How I should love to make a long sea voyage again one of these days. But I always connect such experiences with a vision of Mother in her little seal skin jacket with the collar turned up. I can see her as I write.

It is a great pity J. is so wicked about her food. If she lived abroad for a time, she would realise that it is only in England that very thin ladies are the fashion (as Grandma B. would have said). I have grown foreign enough to confess that I infinitely prefer the French taste in such matters. One sees beautiful women in

Paris and all their beauty is crowned by their look of radiant health; lovely arms and throats and shoulders — not bony ones. When I burst out of all my skirts in Paris the little dressmaker who had to make 'em bigger rolled up her eyes and said, " Dieu soit loué." That's a much better spirit than the English one.

To S. S. Koteliansky *Tuesday*
Hotel Chateau Belle Vue
Sierre (Valais)
July 4, 1922

I want to write to you before I begin work. I have been thinking of you ever since I woke up, thinking how much I should like to talk to you. To-day for instance, is such an opportunity. Brett is staying here for a week or so but she has gone up the mountains for the day. And I am the only guest left in this big, empty, dim hotel. It is awfully nice here, my dearest friend. It is full summer. The grasshoppers ring their tiny tambourines, and down below the gardener is raking the paths. Swallows are flying; two men with scythes over their shoulders are wading through the field opposite, lifting their knees as though they waded through a river. But above all it is *solitary*.

I have been feeling lately a horrible feeling of indifference; a very bad feeling. Neither hot nor cold; *lukewarm,* as the psalmist says. It is better to be dead than to feel like that; in fact it is a kind of death. And one is ashamed as a corpse would be ashamed, to be unburied. I thought I would never write again. But now that I have come here and am living alone all seems so full of meaning again, and one longs only to be allowed to understand.

Have you read Lawrence's new book? I should like to very much. He is the only writer living whom I really profoundly care for. It seems to me whatever he writes, no matter how much one may " disagree," is important. And after all even what one objects to is a *sign of life* in him. He is a living man. There has been published lately an extremely bad collection of short stories — Georgian Short Stories. And *The Shadow in the Rose Garden* by Lawrence is among them. This story is perhaps one of the weakest he ever wrote. But it is so utterly different from all the rest that one reads it with joy. When he mentions gooseberries these are real red, ripe gooseberries that the gardener is rolling on a tray. When he bites into an apple it is a sharp, sweet, fresh apple from the growing tree. Why has one this longing that people shall be rooted in life? Nearly all people swing in with the tide and out with the tide again like a heavy seaweed. And they seem to take a kind of pride in denying life. But why? I cannot understand.

But writing letters is unsatisfactory. If you were here we would talk or be silent, it would not matter which. We shall meet one day, perhaps soon, perhaps some years must pass first. Who shall say? To know you are there is enough. (This is not really contradictory.)

To Sir Harold Beauchamp   *July 9, 1922*

I found mountain conditions plus cold, mist and rain too much for me once more. And shifted to this small town, which is in the valley. Here I shall stay until I return to Paris. J. has, however, remained up aloft and only comes down for week-ends. This is an excellent really first-rate hotel — the pleasantest I have ever known. It is simple but extremely comfortable and the food is almost too good to be true. Sierre is only 1,700 feet high, which makes a great difference to my heart, too. If one had no work to do it would be a dull little place, for apart from the hotel there is nothing much to be said for it. But another great point in its favour is there is a farm attached, where the faithful old Swiss gardeners allow me to explore. This is all complete with cows, turkeys, poultry and a big rambling orchard that smells already of apples. The damson trees are the first I remember seeing since those at Karori. After all, a country life is hard to beat. It has more solid joys than any other that I can imagine. I thank heaven and my papa that I was not born a town child.

Yes, indeed, I too wish that I were taking a trip home with you. It would be a marvellous experience. The very look of a " steamer trunk " rouses the old war horse in me. I feel inclined to paw the ground and smell the briny. But perhaps in ten year's time, if I manage to keep above ground, I may be able to think seriously of such a treat.

I have just finished a story with a canary for the hero, and almost feel I have lived in a cage and pecked a piece of chickweed myself. What a bother!

To William Gerhardi   *July 10, 1922*

Many many thanks for your book. I am delighted to have it, and I think it looks awfully nice. I've read it again from beginning to end. How good it is! (Here, as you don't believe in such a thing as modesty, you will say, " Yes, isn't it? ") But I can only agree. Don't change, Mr. Gerhardi. Go on writing like that. I mean with that freshness and warmth and suppleness, with that warm emotional tone and not that dreadful glaze of " intellectuality " which is like a curse upon so many English writers. . . . And there's another thing. You sound so free in your writing. Perhaps that is as important as anything. I don't know why so many of our poor authors should be in chains, but there it is — a dreadful clanking sounds through their books, and they never can run away, never take a leap, never risk anything. . . In fact, it's high time we took up our pens and struck a blow for freedom. To begin with — What about *** ? He is a ripe, fat victim. I agree with every word you say about him, his smugness is unbearable, his " Oh my friends, let us have Adventures! " is simply the worst possible pretence. You see the truth is he hasn't a word to say. It *is* a tremendous adventure to him if the dog gets into the kitchen and licks a saucepan. Perhaps it is the biggest adventure of all to breathe " Good Night, dear Lady " as the daughter of the County hands him his solid silver bedroom candlestick. All is sham, all is made up, all is rooted in vanity. I am ashamed of going to the same school with him — but there you are. And he's Top Boy, with over £7,000 a year and America bowing to the earth to him. . . . It's very painful.

But after this long parenthesis let me come back to *Futility* one moment. Shall I tell you what I think you may have to guard against? You have a very keen, very delightful sense of humour. Just on one or two occasions — (*par example* when you took Nina into a corner and slapped her hand to the amusement of the others) I think you give it too full a rein. I wonder if you feel what I mean? To me, that remark trembles towards ... a kind of smartness — a something too easy to be worth doing.

I hope one day we shall have a talk about this book. Let me once more wish it and you every possible success.

Now for your photograph. It is kind of you to have sent it to me. I am very happy to have it. When I possess a room with a mantlepiece again on the mantlepiece you will stand. Judging by it you look as though you were very musical. Are you?

I am extremely interested to hear of your book on Tchekhov. It's just the moment for a book on Tchekhov. I have read, these last weeks, *Friday Nights,* by Edward Garnett, which contains a long essay on him. Garnett seems greatly impressed by the importance of T.'s scientific training as a doctor, not the *in*direct importance (I could understand that) but the *direct*. He quotes as a proof *The Party* and T.'s letter in which he says " the ladies say I am quite right in all my symptoms when I describe the confinement." But in spite of T.'s letter, that story didn't need a doctor to write it. There's not a thing any sensitive writer could not have discovered without a medical degree. The truth of that " importance " is far more subtle. People on the whole understand Tchekhov very little. They persist in looking at him from a certain angle and he's a man that won't stand that kind of gaze. One must get round him — see him, feel him as a whole. By the way, isn't Tolstoy's little essay on *The Darling* a small masterpiece of stupidity?

... And when you say you don't think T. was really modest. Isn't it perhaps that he *always* felt, very sincerely, that he could have done so much more than he did? He was tormented by time, and by the desire to live as well as to write. " Life is given us but once.". . . Yet, when he was not working he had a feeling of guilt; he felt he ought to be. And I think he very often had that feeling a singer has who has sung once and would give almost anything for the chance to sing the same song over again — *Now* he could sing it. . . . But the chance doesn't return. I suppose all writers, little and big, feel this, but T. more than most. But I must not write about him, I could go on and on. . . .

Yes, the title of your novel is lovely, and from the practical standpoint excellent. I see so many pretty little hands stretched towards the library shelf. . . . *About Love.* I don't see how *any* body could avoid buying a copy. But très sérieusement, I am so glad you are at work on it. Do you intend to "adopt a literary career" as they say? Or do you have to make literature your mistress? I hope Bolton is not a permanent address if you dislike it so. I was there seventeen years ago. I remember eating a cake with pink icing while a dark intense lady told me of her love for Haydn Coffin and that she had thirteen photographs of him in silver frames in her bedroom. I was very impressed, but perhaps it wasn't a typical incident. I meant to tell you of the lovely place where I am staying but this letter is too long. The flowers are wonderful just now. Don't you love these real summer flowers? You should see the dahlias here, big spiky fellows, with buds like wax and round white ones and real saffron yellow. The women are working in the vines. It's hot and fine with a light valley wind. Goodbye. I am so glad we are friends.

To Arnold Gibbons   *July 13, 1922*

I am appalled that I expressed myself so clumsily as to make it possible for you to use the word "plagiarism." I beg you to forgive me; it was far from my meaning. It was *absorbed* I meant. Perhaps you will agree that we all, as writers, to a certain extent, absorb each other when we love. (I am presuming that you love Tchekhov.) Anatole France would say we eat each other, but perhaps nourish is the better word. For instance, Tchekhov's talent was nourished by Tolstoy's *Death of Ivan Ilyitch*. It is very possible he never would have written as he did if he had not read that story. There is a deep division between the work he did before he read it and after. . . . All I felt about your stories was that you had not yet made the "gift" you had received from Tchekhov your own. You had not yet, finally, made free with it and turned it to your own account. My dear colleague, I reproach myself for not having made this plainer. . . .

I'd like, if I may, to discuss the other point in your letter. Let me see if I understand you. You mean you can only "care" for such things as the little cat, the old man, the note of a bird, in the period of reaction against your belief in pain and a life of sacrifice and yourself. But as your belief is all-important to you that period of reaction means little. Am I right? Therefore the last of the five stories was the only one you really cared about for there you express your very self. . . . I mean you are writing with real conviction. Do you know what I feel? To do this successfully you will have to do it more *in*directly, you will have to leave the student out. Now there is a moment in that story where you succeed. It's where the little girl's throat works — she weeps — she wants the apple and is afraid she is not going to have it. (Always remember this is just my personal feeling.) Your student argues, explains too much. He ought perhaps to have said not a single word.

But I hope you will go on writing. The important thing is to write — to find yourself in losing yourself. (There is no truth profounder.) I do not know myself whether — this world being what it is — pain is not absolutely necessary. I do not see how we are to come by knowledge and love except through pain. That sounds too definite, expressed so baldly — if one were talking one would make reservations. . . . Believe in pain I must.

To S. S. Koteliansky   July 17, 1922

I want to talk to you for hours about — *Aaron's Rod,* for instance. Have you read it? There are certain things in this new book of L.'s that I do not like. But they are not important or really part of it. They are trivial, encrusted, they cling to it as snails to the underside of a leaf. But apart from them there is the leaf, is the tree, firmly planted, deep thrusting, outspreading, growing grandly, alive in every twig. It is a living book; it is warm, it breathes. And it is written by a living man, with *conviction.* Oh, Koteliansky, what a relief it is to turn away from these little pre-digested books written by authors who have nothing to say! It is like walking by the sea at high tide eating a crust of bread and looking over the water. I am so sick of all this modern seeking which ends in seeking. *Seek* by all means, but the text goes on " and ye shall find." And although, of course, there can be no ultimate finding, there is a kind of finding by the way which is enough, is sufficient. But these seekers in the looking glass, these half-female, frightened writers-of-to-day — You know, they remind me of the greenfly in roses — they are a kind of blight.

I do not want to be hard. I hope to God I am not unsympathetic. But it seems to me there comes a time in life when one must realise one is grown up — a man. And when it is no longer decent to go on probing and probing. Life is so short. The world is rich. There are so many adventures possible. Why do we not gather our strength together and LIVE? It all comes to much the same thing. In youth most of us are, for various reasons, slaves. And then, when we are able to throw off our chains, we prefer to keep them. Fredom is dangerous, is frightening.

If only I can be good enough writer to strike a blow for freedom! It is the one axe I want to grind. Be free — and you can afford to give yourself to life! Even to believe in life.

I do not go all the way with Lawrence. His ideas of sex mean nothing to me. But I feel nearer L. than anyone else. All these last months I have thought as he does about many things.

Does this sound nonsense to you? Laugh at me if you like or scold me. But remember what a disadvantage it is having to write such things. If we were talking one could say it all in a few words. It is so hard not to dress one's ideas up in their Sunday clothes and make them look all stiff and shining in a letter. My ideas look awful in their best dresses.

(Now I have made myself a glass of tea. Every time I drop a piece of lemon into a glass of tea I say " Koteliansky." Perhaps it is a kind of grace.)

I went for such a lovely drive to-day behind a very intelligent horse who listened to every word the driver and I said and heartily agreed. One could tell from his ears that he was extremely interested in the conversation. They are thinning the vines for the last time before harvest. One can almost smell the grapes. And in the orchards apples are reddening; it is going to be a wonderful year for pears.

But one could write about the drive for as many pages as there are in *Ulysses*.

It is late. I must go to bed. Now the train going to Italy has flashed past. Now it is silent again except for the old toad who goes *Ka*-Ka-*Ka*-Ka — laying down the law.

To Sir Harold Beauchamp *July 28, 1922*

The days seem to whisk away here so fast that I don't think the farmer's wife would be in time to chop off their tails. I spend a large part of them tapping out my new *long* story or *short* novel on my little Corona. But I have been thinking of you so much, dearest, and hoping that your climatic and physical conditions are both more settled. I heard from C. that you had been to see my good Doctor. I hope he satisfied you and that you did not think I had overpraised him. It would be very nice to know from you what you thought of him.

Since I last wrote we have had every variety of weather from Winter to Spring. To-day, for instance, began with a cold downpour, gradually changed until it was a damp, tropical morning, and now it's a sharp Autumn evening. It's very difficult to adjust one's attire to these lightning changes. The only safe recipe is to start with flannel next to the skin, and build up or cast off from that. What a frightful bother! But judging from the reports in the *Times,* England has turned over a summer leaf again. Long may it remain fair!

There is a remarkable old talker here at present — an American, aged eighty-eight — with his wife and daughter. The daughter looks about sixty-five. According to the ancient gentleman, they have been on the wing ever since he retired at the age of seventy-five, and they intend remaining on the wing for another fifteen years or so! He is full of fire still, dresses every night for dinner, plays bridge, and loves to start a gossip with, " In the year 1865." It's very interesting listening to his memories of early Noo York and of American life generally 'way back. I think he mistook me for a young person home for the holidays. For he introduced himself with the words, " Boys seem skeerce here. May be you wouldn't mind if I tried to entertain you a li'll." When he said boys, I thought at first he must be alluding to farm labourers, but then memories of American novels " put me right," as they say.

J. is still in his lofty perch among the mountains. At the weekends, whenever the weather is wet, we play billiards. There is a splendid table here and we are both very keen. It's a fascinating game. I remember learning to hold a cue at Sir Joseph Ward's, and I can see now R.'s super-refinement as if she expected each ball to be stamped with a coronet before she would deign to hit it.

To Edmund Blunden   *July 1922*

It is awfully kind of you to have sent me a copy of your lovely poem, *Old Homes*. Many, many thanks. I like especially the verse beginning:

> Thence, too, when high wind through the black clouds pouring —

One walks straight into your chill, pale, wet world as one reads. . . . I love the sound of water in poetry.

How are you, I wonder, and where are you spending the summer? It's the moment here when all the dahlias are out, every little child is eating a green apple, the vines have been cut down for the last time and the grapes are as big as marbles. In fact, this whole valley is one great ripening orchard. Heavens! how beautiful apple trees are! But you know these things a great deal better than I do.

If H. M. T. is near by — give him my love, will you?

To J. M. Murry   *August 1922*

Early Edition.

I think *Amos Barton* is awful and there's nothing to say for it.

In the first place poor George Eliot's *Hymn to the Cream Jug* makes me feel quite queasy (no wonder she harps on biliousness and begins her description of a feast: " Should one *not* be bilious there is no pleasanter sight, etc."); in the second place, the idea of lovely, gentle, fastidious, Madonna-like Mrs. Barton having 8 children in 9 years by that pock-marked poor " mongrel " (her own words) with the blackened stumps for teeth is simply disgusting! If I thought the poor little pamphlet was designed to put in a word in favour of Birth Control I could bear it. But far from it. Each chubby chubby with a red little fist and TEN black nails (how is that for charm?) rouses a kind of female cannibalism in G. E. She gloats over the fat of babies.

I have always heard *Amos Barton* was one of her best stories. You know, it's very very bad that we haven't sincerer critics. Having spread my peacock tail to that extent I had better depart.

Not before saying what a truly frightful need England hath of thee.

Later edition.
I have just got your L. review and note. . . . About your review. I think you are absolutely right in every word of it — every word. I think you occasionally use more *words* of praise than are necessary; it sounds too effusive and will raise suspicion. Shall I tone it down a bit on my typewriter, or send it as it is? I'll phone you and ask. Oh, I *long* for a paper this morning!! I have been "making up" a paper ever since I read your review. I *shall* start one, too, jolly soon. For three years only. But what years!

Don't you think it might be a good idea if this week you came on Sunday instead of Saturday? Give us a longer week. That is if you are at all pressé or inclined to the notion. Otherwise you won't mind, will you, if I do a bit of work on Saturday while you are in the garden?

H'm yes. After my Spartan suggestion has been written, I *take it back*. I say instead what I have said about working . . . and *hope* I'll be able to look out of the window and see your summer feltie below. Yes, indeed, come Saturday unless you don't want to, or think that the female will is determined to drag you here. . . .

Once *The Doves' Nest* is finished I shall leave here. But it will take a fortnight, not a week. It's too expensive. I *must* draw in my horns for the next six months, somehow. Blow!

My watch is still a li'll golden angel. And what a big brown angel that chest is! With two little windows at the sides and a chimney at the top we could almost live in it — open the lid softly for the milkman and the wild strawberry man. . . .

To S. S. Koteliansky　　　　　　　　　　　*August 2, 1922*

I hope you are better. If you need a doctor, Sorapure is a good man — intelligent and quiet. He does not discuss Lloyd George with one, either. This is a great relief. All the other English doctors that I know have just finished reading *The Daily Mail* by the time they reach me.

It is a pity that Lawrence is driven so far. I am sure that Western Australia will not help. The desire to travel is a great, real temptation. But does it do any good? It seems to me to correspond to the feelings of a sick man who thinks always " if only I can get away from here I shall be better." However — there is nothing to be done. One must go through with it. No one can stop that sick man, either, from moving on and on. His craving is stronger than he. But Lawrence, I am sure, will get well.

. . . I believe one can cure nobody, one can change nobody fundamentally. The born slave cannot become a free man. He can only become free-er. I have refused to believe that for years, and yet I am certain it is true, it is even a law of life. But it is equally true that hidden in the slave there are the makings of the free man. And these makings are very nice in ——, very sensitive and generous. I love her for them. They make me want to help her as much as I can.

I am content. I prefer to leave our meeting to chance. To know you are there is enough. If I knew I was going to die I should even ask you definitely to come and see me. For I should hate to die without one long, uninterrupted talk with *you*. But short of it — it does not greatly matter.

To Sir Harold Beauchamp *August 10, 1922*

I have delayed answering your letter — which I was most happy to receive — because I felt there was a possibility that I might be forced, for reasons of health only, to make a little change in my plans. I hoped this would not be necessary, but it is. To "come straight to the horses" — my heart has been playing up so badly this last week that I realise it is imperative for me to see Doctor Sorapure before I go on with my Paris treatment. As I am due to begin this Paris treatment on September 1st, I have decided that my best plan is to come straight to London next Tuesday, arriving Wednesday, 16th. Until I have had an opinion on the present condition of my heart I am really a thoroughly unsatisfactory companion. I could neither go about with you, nor add to your enjoyment in any way. And to sit with me in the bedroom of a foreign hotel would be extremely small beer indeed! And I could not forgive myself if my disquieting symptoms became aggravated in Paris and caused you uneasiness. You know what a heart is like! I hope this trouble is something that can be corrected easily. I feel sure it is. But until I know just what it is there is always the feeling I may be doing the very thing that will send me on my last journey before my work is anything like finished here below! That's what I have been feeling all this week.

To the Hon. Dorothy Brett August 11, 1922

I can't arrive before Thursday afternoon. No sleeper before then. Your clouds like Feather Boas are perfeck!

This — yours — is such a very nice letter that it is a good thing we shall meet so soon, I feel inclined to come by the perambulator and have done with it.

Why do things need so many nails? Why can't one use safety pins? They are so much quicker and they are deadly Secure. Once you have clasped yourself to a safety pin human flesh and blood can't separate you.

(Let us go and see Charlie Chaplin when I come. Shall we? On the Fillums, of course, I mean.)

This place is flaming with Gladioli, too. As for the dahlias they are rampant everywhere. The pears which we had for lunch are iron pears, with little copper plums and a zinc greengage or two.

L. M., smelling the luggage from afar, is in her element. She is hung round with tickets already and almost whistles and shunts when she brings me my tisane. I am moving already myself, the writing table is gliding by, and I feel inclined to wave to people in the Garden.

Elizabeth came yesterday with one of the Ladies Fair. I must say she had ravishing deep, deep grey eyes. She seemed, too, divinely happy. She is happy. She has a perfect love, a man. They have loved each other for eight years and it is still as radiant, as exquisite as ever. I must say it *is* nice to gaze on people who are in love. M. has taken up golf. I've always wondered when this would happen. . . .

To Richard Murry August 14, 1922

I did a thing to-day which it has been in my mind to do for a long time. I made a will, signed it, and got it duly witnessed. In it I left you my large pearl ring. My idea in leaving it to you was that you should give it — if you care to — to your woman whoever she may be. I hope you won't think this ghoulish. But Jack gave me the ring and I feel it would be nice to keep it in the family.

This doesn't mean, of course, that I am not as large as life and twice as natural. But just in case I was "taken sudden." I'd like you to know why the ring is yours.

To the Hon. Dorothy Brett   *August 14, 1922*

I wired you to-day. This is just to say how glad I shall be if you can put me up on Wednesday. I have been horribly ill since you left. I must see Sorapure with as little delay as possible. Please don't tell anyone I am coming, not even Koteliansky. Don't make preparations for me, will you? What would be *perfect* would be to feel you just let me in without giving me a moment's thought. You know what I mean? Everything will be nice. There's only one thing. If you can put me into a bedroom rather than the sitting room. . . . No, I take that back. That's nonsense. If you knew how those orange flowery curtains are waving in my mind at this moment! Will you *really* be at your door on Wednesday? Or is it a fairy tale!

To Sir Harold Beauchamp
6, Pond Street,
Hampstead, N.W. 3
Friday
August 18, 1922

I still feel guilty at having so disarranged your plans. My only consolation is that travelling on the Continent, at this moment, is very poor fun. Even when one has reserved seats in all the trains and so on, the immense crowds intrude. First-class carriages are full of third-class passengers, and the boat absolutely swarmed with ladies and babies all in an advanced state of mal de mer!

However, travelling never tires me as it does most people. I even enjoy it, discomforts and all. And we arrived here to find all kinds of thoughtful preparations, down to the good old fashioned

Bath Bun with sugar on the top — an old favourite of mine. It made me feel I was anchored in England again.

I saw Doctor Sorapure this morning and went over the battlefield with him. As far as one could say from a first view, it was not at all unsatisfactory. He says my heart is not diseased in any way. He believes its condition is due to my left lung, and it's tied up with the lung in some way for the present. It's all rather complicated. But the result of the interview was that there is nothing to be feared from its behaviour. I mean its tricks are more playful than fierce. And the more exercise I take in the way of walking and moving about the better. It may stretch it. Sounds rather rum, doesn't it? But the point is, darling, J. and I can meet you anywhere in London, any time. This house is rather hard to find. It's a queer nice little place, but on the Bohemian side, *i.e.,* I would trust its teas only — not its lunches or dinners.

Sorapure thought I looked amazingly better, of course. Everybody does. One feels a great fraud to have a well-built outside and such an annoying interior.

To Violet Schiff   *August 21, 1922*

It's strange to be here again. London is empty, cool, rather shadowy, extraordinarily unlike Paris. I feel sentimental about it. Only the people I've seen so far seem fatigué, fatigué beyond words! One feels that they have come to an agreement not to grow any more, to stay *just so* — all clipped and pruned and tight. As for taking risks, making mistakes, changing their opinions, being in the wrong, committing themselves, losing themselves, being *human beings* in fact — no, a thousand times! "Let us sit down and have a nice chat about minor eighteenth century poetry — " I never want to sit down and have a nice chat as long as I live.

But it doesn't matter. They can't alter the fact that life is wonderful. It's wonderful enough to sit here writing to you, dear precious friend, and to lean back and think about you. The past lets nothing be. Even our meetings in Paris are changed almost beyond recognition. One sees them, linked together now, and one realises the immense importance of the *hero*[1] of them (whom I never saw and never shall see).

[1] Marcel Proust.

But I could write to you for ever to-day — and instead I'm going out to lunch with Massingham père. Could one possibly shake him up — lean across the table and say quietly —

To Sir Harold Beauchamp *August 22, 1922*

Just a note to say how very happy I was to see you yesterday and how much I enjoyed our lunch and talk. I only hope you feel as young as you look and that your bout of ill health is a thing of the past. The girls looked so well and charming, too. Wee Jeannie, though, looks almost too young to have a real live husband. She ought to be married in a daisy chain with the wedding service read from a seed catalogue, as it used to be when we were children.

It's a sad pity that New Zealand is so far, dearest Papa. How nice it would be if we could all foregather more often.

By this same post I am sending you a copy of my book.

To Violet Schiff *August 24, 1922*

Will you forgive me if I do not accept your invitation to come and stay with you and Sydney? The truth is I am such a bad visitor (as one is a bad sailor) that I have made it a rule nowadays never to stay with anyone unless it is absolutely necessary. I hope this does not sound too extravagant and ungracious. I could give you literally hundreds of reasons for it. I look forward immensely to seeing you both in town next month. Isn't the country rather chill? The country is so terribly airy.

I have "taken" Brett's first floor for the next three miserable months and hope to be settled soon. At present all is in the air, and I can't work or even think of work. It will be very nice to have my own possessions and to be out of hotels for a time, without being en menage. I *haven't* the domestic virtues.

I see Eliot's new magazine is advertised to appear shortly. It looks very full of rich plums. I think *Prufrock* by far by far and away the most interesting and the best modern poem. It stays in the memory as a work of art — so different in that to *Ulysses*. The further I am away from it, the less I think of it. As to reading it again, or even opening that great tome — never! What I feel about *Ulysses* is that its appearance sometime was inevitable.

Things have been heading that way for years. It ought to be regarded as a portentous warning. But there is little chance of that, I fear.

Are you well? I feel so much better these last few days. My doctor, who is an angel, seems to be curing my heart with dark brown sugar!

To William Gerhardi

No, dear Mr. Gerhardi,

I don't *always* feel I have offended you. I only felt it once when the pause was so very long. But now it is hard to write to you when I know you are laughing at my poor little " y's " and " g's " and " d's." They feel so awkward; they refuse to skip any more. The little " g " especially is shy, with his tail in his mouth like an embarrassed whiting.

I am very very sorry you are ill. I hope you will soon be better. I shall send you a little packet of tea on Monday. Please have a special little pot made and drink it with un peu de citron — if you like citron. It tastes so good when one is in bed — this tea, I mean. It always makes me feel even a little bit drunk — well, perhaps drunk is not quite the word. But the idea, even, of *the short story* after a cup or two seems almost too good to be true, and I pledge it in a third cup as one pledges one's love. . . .

I have decided to stay in London for three months. Then I go to Italy to the Lago di Garda. Perhaps we shall meet before then. I have taken a minute flat at this address and by the end of next week I shall be working again. I have a book to finish and I *want* to write a play this autumn. . . . It's very nice to be in London again, rather like coming back to one's dear wife. But I wish the intelligentsia were not *quite* so solemn, *quite* so determined to sustain a serious conversation only. They make one feel like that poor foreigner arraigned before Mr. Podsnap on the hearthrug in *Our Mutual Friend*. I shall never, while Life lasts, be able to take Life for granted in the superb way they do.

Are you able to work? I am glad Middleton Murry's short notice pleased you. I hope the *Evening News* man [1] has done you proud, too. And some one wrote to me and wondered if you would come to lunch one Sunday. But who am I to say?

---

[1] This was J.M.M.

To Anne Estelle Rice   *August 28, 1922*

I can't tell you what a joy it was to see you yesterday, dear and très très belle amie. How I loved looking at you again. And hearing you. And seeing your home — everything. I so look forward to our meeting often this autumn. I do hope we may. Jack Murry sends his love. He's just had a new suit made and is standing in front of me.

J. M.: " Are the trousers full enough? "
K. M.: " Quite full enough! "
J. M.: " You're sure? "
K. M.: " Certain! "
J. M.: " They're not too full? "
K. M.: " Not in the least! "
J. M.: " You're sure? "
K. M.: " Certain! "

I must run and get a Bible and swear on it, " Those trousers are PERFECT!! " Men are funny, aren't they? But very nice, too.

To Sydney Schiff   *Monday*
    August 1922

Your letter made me feel angry with myself and very ungracious at having refused your so kind invitation. Please forgive me! I look forward more than I can say to seeing you and Violet in London. By the time you come I hope to be *settled* in my new rooms (they are at this address) I am already dreaming *no end* of a talk before my fire.

I shall never be able to say a word to the intelligentsia, Sydney. They are too lofty, too far removed. No, that is unfair. It's simply that they are not in the least interested. Nor do they appear to know what one is driving at when one groans at the present state of English writing. As I see it the whole stream of English literature is trickling out in little innumerable marsh trickles.

There is no gathering together, no force, no impetus, absolutely no passion! Why this is I don't know. But one feels a deathly cautiousness in everyone — a determination not to be caught out. Who wants to catch them out or give them away? I can't for the life of me see the need of this acute suspicion and narrowness. Perhaps the only thing to do is to ignore it all and go on with one's own job. But I confess that seems to me a poor conclusion to come to. If I, as a member of the orchestra, think I am playing right, try my utmost to play right, I don't want to go on in the teeth of so many others — not playing at all or playing as I believe falsely. It is a problem. Let us talk it all over.

About Lawrence. Yes, I agree there is much triviality, much that is neither here nor there. And a great waste of energy that ought to be well spent. But I did feel there was growth in *Aaron's Rod* — there was no desire to please or placate the public, I did feel that Lorenzo was profoundly moved. Because of this, perhaps, I forgive him too much his faults.

It's vile weather here — a real fog. I am alone in the house — 10.30 P.M. Footsteps pass and repass — that is a marvellous sound — and the low voices — talking on — dying away. It takes me back years — to the agony of *waiting* for one's love —

To Lady Ottoline Morrell Monday
August 1922

I would simply love to meet you at Taylor's whenever you ask me to come. Or if you would rather I met you anywhere else — I shall be there. I can't walk yet — absurd as it sounds — only a few puffing paces, a most humiliating and pug-like performance. But once I get my legs back or rather once my heart is stronger I shall not be dependent on taxis. I live in them since I have come to London. I have got Fat — Wyndham Lewis I hear is also fat, May Sinclair has waxed enormous, Anne Rice can't be supported by her ankles alone — I try to comfort myself with many examples. But I don't really care — it is awful how little one cares. Anything — rather than illness — rather than the sofa, and that awful dependence on others!

I rather look forward to these three months in London, once I have got out of my boxes and into a real corner of my own. I dream of brand new friends — not the dreadfully solemn " intensive " ones — not the mind-probers. But young ones who aren't ashamed to be interested. Dear little Gerhardi who wrote *Futility* is one — he *sounds* awfully nice. And there's another I met in

Switzerland — so attractive! I don't think I care *very* much for the real intelligentsia, Ottoline, dearest. And they seem to be so uneasy, so determined not to be caught out! Who wants to catch them?

I *wish* you would come to Italy for part of next winter. Do you know the Lago di Garda? They say it is so lovely. And the journey is nothing.

It will be such a real joy to see you again.

To Sylvia Lynd *September 19, 1922*

It's the most miserable news to know you are in bed again and that again such bad sorrowful things have been happening to you. . . . What can one say? I had so hoped and believed that your lean years were over. May they be over now!

I'd love to come and see you. But stairs are unclimbable by me. I am better, but I can't walk more than a few yards. I can walk about a house and give a very good imitation of a perfectly well and strong person in a restaurant or from the door across the pavement to the taxi. But that's all. My heart still won't recover. I think I shall be in England two to three months, as there is a man here who can give me the X-ray treatment I've been having in Paris. After that I shall go to Italy. But all is vague. I'm seeing the specialist to-day. I may have to go back to Paris almost immediately. What it is to be in doctors' hands!

If I stay, I do hope we shall be able to meet later on, perhaps. Let us arrange some easy place for both of us then. It would be most awfully nice to have a talk. I'm living in two crooked little rooms here in a little crooked house. It's a relief to be away from hotels after five months in Paris in a hotel bedroom overlooking a brick wall.

I'll never be able to knock any spots off this city, my dear. It frightens me. When I'm with people I feel rather like an unfortunate without a racquet standing on the tennis court while a smashing game is being played by the other three — it's a rather awful and rather silly feeling.

Don't forget how much I'd love to see you. Or how sorry I am for everything.

To J. M. Murry   September 29, 1922

... Ah, I had such a sad letter to-day from R. W. Goodbye Arno! She is afraid there will be no Arno for her. And goodbye Paris and the Manoukhin treatment! It cannot be for her. " Every day I am getting worse." Brave, noble little soul shining behind those dark, lighted eyes! She has wanted so much, she has had so little! She wants so terribly just to be allowed to warm herself — to have a place at the fire. But she's not allowed. She's shut out. She must drive on into the dark. Why? Why can't I go to Rome? I should like to start for Rome to-day, just to kiss her hands and lay my head on her pillow. It is so terrible to be alone.

Outside my window there are leaves falling. Here, in two days, it is autumn. Not late autumn, but bright gold everywhere. Are the sunflowers out at the bottom of the vegetable garden? There are quantities of small Japanese sunflowers, too, aren't there? It's a mystery, Bogey, why the earth is so lovely. ...

R. has just been in again to finish his drawing. Then we went downstairs and he played. But what am I telling you? Nothing! Yet much happened. Don't you think it's queer how we have to talk " little language " to make one word clothe, feed and start in life one small thought?

To Sylvia Lynd   September 29, 1922

How glad I should have been to have seen you next week. But I am being swep' away again to Paris next Monday, to go on with my X-ray treatment. Why do I always have to write to you about complaints! It is a horrid fate. But there it is. The bad weather here these last few days (it's fine, of course, since I bought my ticket) has brought my cough back again, stronger than ever for its small holiday. And my Paris doctor threatens me with a complete return to the sofa if I don't go through with his course. I thought I could manage to have the same thing done here. But it's not the same, and it's frightening to play with these blue rays.

So there are my steamer trunk and hat box on the carpet eyeing each other, walking round each other, ready to begin the fight all over again. And I shan't see you or talk to you or give you tea or hear about anything. I'm so very, very sorry!

Are you really better? It's good news to know you are able to come as far as Hampstead. I have been staying in a tiny little house here, behind a fan of trees, with one of those green convolvulus London gardens behind it. It's been beyond words a rest to be in a *private* house again with a private staircase and no restaurant, nobody in buttons, no strange, foreign gentleman staring at your letters in the letter rack. Oh, how I hate hotels! They are like permanent railway stations without trains.

There's the dinner bell. I must go down into the hold and eat. I have been doing the housekeeping here. It was very homelike to hear the sole domestic say, "I know a party, m'm, as is a nice 'and with mouse 'oles, 'aving them in the kitchen somethink dreadful!" So unlike pert Suzanne and jolie Yvonne.

To *Anne Estelle Rice* September 30, 1922

Here are the books; so many thanks for them. I think some of the stories in *A Hasty Bunch* are quite extraordinarily good. All of them have interested me immensely. There is something so fresh and unspoilt about the writer, even when he is a little bit self-conscious — in the youthful way, you know. But he has got real original talent and I think he'll do awfully good work. He's much more interesting than these sham young super-cultured creatures. I hope he gets on with his job. I feel I'd like to help him if I could, in some way. But I expect he'd scorn that idea.

Do you know, chérie, I'm off to France on Monday. I want to go on with that treatment there rather than here and for many many reasons I — enfin — well, there's something in England that just pushes me off the nest. It's no good. I shall never "settle" here. But Brett is keeping my two little rooms here for flying visits. It's nice to have them.

I am going to try your Hôtel Jacob. I hope they will have rooms. Of course, ever since I took my ticket, the sun has come out and there's a kind of blue tinge in the sky, quite a piece of it. But if I tore my ticket up it would be snowing at tea-time. I shall never forget my LUNCH with you.

To the Hon. Dorothy Brett   Select Hotel
Place de la Sorbonne
Paris
October 3, 1922

I can see your eyes laughing at the name of my hotel. What a name. One can only breathe it. Never mind. If only you knew how glad I am to be in it after our chase round Paris last night.

We had a divine crossing, very still silvery sea with gulls moving on the waves like the lights in a pearl. It was fiery hot in Calais — Whoof! It was blazing. And there were old women with pears to sell wherever you looked or didn't look —

Voici mes jolies poires!

Yellowy green with leaves among them. Old hands holding up the satiny baskets. So beautiful. English ladies buying them and trying to eat them *through* their veils. So awful. The way to Paris was lovely too. All the country just brushed over with light gold, and white oxen ploughing and a man riding a horse into a big dark pond. Paris, too, very warm and shadowy with wide spaces and lamps a kind of glow-worm red — not yellow at all.

Then began the chase. It ended in a perfectly FEARFUL room that looked like the scene of a long line of murders. The water in the pipes sobbed and gurgled and sighed all night and in the morning it sounded as though people broke open the shutters with hatchets.

Then I remembered this hotel where I stayed during the bombardment. Still here. Still the same. I have a funny room on the 6th floor that looks over the roofs of the Sorbonne. Large grave gentlemen in marble bath gowns are dotted on the roof. Some hold up a finger; some are only wise. A coy rather silly-looking eagle is just opposite perched on a plaque, called Géologie. I like this view *fearfully*. And every hour a small, rather subdued, regretful little bell chimes. This is not at all a chic large hotel like the Victoria Palace. It's quiet. One goes out for food, which is much the best arrangement. It's very cheap, too. Gone are my sumptuous days of suites and salles de bain. I always hated them and now I don't need them, thank God.

To William Gerhardi   October 1922

I am very shaken to-day after a small minor revolution in the night. I put a vacuum flask full of boiling tea on the table by my bed last night and at about two o'clock in the morning there was a most TERRIFIC explosion. It blew up everything. People ran from far and near. Gendarmes broke through the shutters with hatchets, firemen dropped through trap doors. Or very nearly. At any rate the noise was deafening and when I switched on the light there was my fiaschino outwardly calm still but tinkling internally in a terribly ominous way and a thin sad trickle oozed along the table.

I have nobody to tell this to to-day. So I hope your eyes roll. I hope you appreciate how fearful it might have been had it burst *out*wardly and not *in*wardly.

Bon jour, Mr. Gerhardi. I am so sorry we have not met in England. But after all I had to come abroad again and I shall spend the next three months in Paris instead of London. Perhaps we shall not meet until you are very old. Perhaps your favourite grandson will wheel you to my hotel then (I'm doomed to hotels) and instead of laughing, as we should now, a faint, light, airy chuckle will pass from bath chair to bath chair —

I don't awfully like the name of your new book,[1] but I am *sure* the booksellers will. But then I don't very much like the idea of so-called somersaults in the first person. But I am *certain* the public will.

I wonder for how long you have put aside your novel *About Love*. Please tell me when you take it up again.

No, I didn't see the *English Review*. It's raining. I must rescue my dear little John Milton from the window sill.

Rescued. . . .

People went on asking me about Mr. Gerhardi. His past, his present, his future, his favourite jam, did he prefer brown bread for a change sometimes. I answered everything.

I hope to have rather a better book out in the spring.

Goodbye. Are you quite well again? The weather is simply heavenly here.

[1] The book was abandoned. (W.G.)

To J. M. Murry   October 4, 1922

. . . I don't *feel* influenced by Y. or D. I merely feel I've heard ideas like my ideas, but bigger ones, far more definite ones. And that there really is Hope — real Hope, not half-Hope. . . . As for Tchekhov being damned — why should he be? Can't you rope Tchekhov in? I can. He's much nearer to me than he used to be.

It's nice to hear of Richard sawing off table-legs and being moved by the greengrocer. Why is it greengrocers have such a passion for bedding people out? . . . In my high little room for 10 francs a day with flowers in a glass and a quilted sateen bed-cover, I don't feel far from R. either. Oh, it's awfully nice to have passed private suites and marble-tops and private bathrooms by! Gone! Gone for ever! I found a little restaurant last night where one dines ever so sumptuous for 6–7 francs, and the grapes are tied with red satin bows, and someone gives the cat a stewed prune and someone else cries: "Le chat a mangé un compôte de pruneaux!"

True, one is no longer *of* people. But was one ever? This looking on, understanding what one can, is better.

October 6, 1922

. . . How very strange about your soldier! I wish I had seen him. Petone! The Gear Company! And fancy your remembering about those rugs. The way you told me the story reminded me of D. H. L. somehow. It was quite different. I saw the soldier so plainly, heard his voice, saw the deserted street on early closing day, saw his clothes, the sack. "Old boy . . ." It was strangely complete.

By the way, I wonder why things that happen in the rain seem always more wonderful? Do you feel that? There's such a freshness about them, something so unexpected and vivid. I could go on thinking of that for hours. . . .

It's the most lovely morning. There's just a light sailing breeze and the sun is really hot. Thinking of London is like thinking of living in a chimney. Are there really masses and masses of books? I do hope you won't forget to send me that Tchekhov. I look forward to it *very* much. Can one get hold of Tolstoy's diaries? Is there a cheap English edition that is not too cut and trimmed? I wish you'd let me know. . . .

I was wondering if next time you went to the D.'s you would take a bottle of barley-sugar to those young heroes. I feel things like barley-sugar are apt to be a little scarce in that household, and, however wonderful your Da may be, to have a pull, take it out and look at it and put it back again — does mean something. I am sure Michael especially would agree. And then you'll be for ever after the barley-sugar man — which is a nice name.

October 8, 1922

. . . Yes, this is where I stayed *pendant la guerre*. It's the quietest hotel I ever was in. I don't think tourists come at all. There are funny rules about not doing one's washing or fetching in one's cuisine from *dehors* which suggest a not rich an' grand clientèle. What is nice too is one can get a tray in the evening if one doesn't want to go out. Fearfully good what I imagine is provincial cooking — all in big bowls, piping hot, brought up by the garçon who is a v. nice fellow in a red veskit and white apron and a little grey cloth *cap!* I think some English traveller left it in a cupboard about 1879. The salt and pepper stand, by the way, is a little glass motor car. Salt is driver and Pepper Esquire is master in the back seat — the dark fiery one of the two, so different to plain old Salt. . . . What a good fellow he is, though!

Yesterday the wind was nor' north by north by east by due east by due east-north-east. If you know a colder one, it was there, too. I had to thaw a one-franc piece to get the change out of it. (That is a joke for your Sunday paper only!)

I've just read you on Bozzy. You awe me very much by your familiarity with simply all those people. You've always such a vast choice of sticks in the hall-stand for when you want to go walking and even a vaster choice of umbrellas — while I go all unprotected and exposed with only a fearful sense of the heavens lowering.

Mary! There's a most beautiful magpie on *my* roof. Are magpies still wild? Ah me, how little one knows!

To S. S. Koteliansky   October 9, 1922

I have finished the letters [1]; here they are. They are, the more one looks into them, a remarkable revelation of what goes on *behind the scenes*. Except for " Kiss the foal " and " buy the children sweets; even doctors prescribe sweets for children," there is hardly one statement that isn't pure matter-of-fact. The whole affair is like the plot of a short story or small novel by himself; he reacts to everything exactly as he would to a *written* thing. There's no explanation, no evidence of a LIVING man, a REAL man. The glimpse one has of his relationship with Anya is somehow petty and stuffy, essentially a double bed relationship. And then " Turgenev read so badly "; they say *he* (D.) read so superbly — Oh dear, Oh dear, it would take an Anna Grigorevna to be proud of such letters.

Yet this was a noble, suffering, striving soul, a real hero among men — wasn't he? I mean from his books. . . . The one who writes the letters is the house porter of the other. I suppose one ought not to expect to find the master at his own front door as well as in his study. But I find it hard to reconcile myself to that. I do not think these deep divisions in people are necessary or vital. Perhaps it is cowardice in me.

To the Hon. Dorothy Brett   October 9, 1922

Don't be cross with me if I am dull just now. My cough is so much worse that I *am* a cough — a living, walking or lying down cough. Why I am allowed to stay in this hotel I can't imagine. But there it is. I must have terribly kind neighbours. As soon as it gets better I shall present a bouquet to the left door and to the right. " From a grateful Patient." It's only the X-rays doing their worst before they do their better. But it's a nuisance. Such a queer effect on the boulevards here: the trees are out for a second Spring — frail small leaves, like you see in April. Lyrics in middle age — love song by old chestnuts over 50. All the same one's heart aches to see them. There is something tragic in Spring.

If you knew how vivid the little house is, but vivid beyond words. Not only for itself. It exists apart from all — it is a *whole*

---
[1] Dostoevsky's letters to his wife.

in life. I think of you. . . . One has such kindly soft tender feelings —

But to work — to work. One must take just those feelings and work *with* them. Life is a mystery. We can never get over that. Is it a series of deaths and series of killings? It is that too. But who shall say where death ends and resurrection begins. That's what one must do. Give it, the idea of *resurrection,* the power that death would like to have. Be born again and born again faster than we die. . . .

Tell me, why do you "warn" me? What mustn't I be "too sure" of? You mystify me. Do you think I am too sure of Love? But if Love is there one must treat it as though one were sure of it — How else? If it is not there I'd rather be sure of that, too. Or do you mean something else?

It has turned as cold as ice — and colder. The sun shines but it is soleil glacé. It's due North and due East, all mixed up in the same frozen bag. If it wasn't for the blue up above one would cry.

Don't let our next meeting be in Paris. It's no *fun* meeting in hotels. And sitting on beds and eating in nasty old restaurants. Let's wait a little longer and meet in the south in a warm still place where I can put a cricket at your third ear so that you can hear its song.

To J. M. Murry   October 11, 1922

. . . It has got very cold here. I feel it. I am adjusting myself to it and it makes me feel rather dull — *distrait,* you know. I have had to leave my dear little *grenier au 6ème* for something less loftly, more expensive, but warmer. However, it's a very nice room. "Et vous avez un beau pendule," as the garçon said. *He* thoroughly approves of the change. All the same, you say "Tell me about yourself." I'll have a try. Here goes.

A new way of being is not an easy thing to *live.* Thinking about it, preparing to meet the difficulties and so on, is one thing, meeting those difficulties another. I have to die to so much; I have to make such *big* changes. I feel the only thing to do is to get the dying over — to court it, almost. (Fearfully hard, that.) And then all hands to the business of being born again. What do I mean exactly? Let me give you an instance. Looking back, my boat is almost swamped sometimes by seas of sentiment. "Ah, what I have missed! How sweet it was, how dear, how warm, how simple, how precious!" And I think of the garden at the Isola Bella and the furry bees and the house-wall so warm. But then I remember what we really felt there — the blanks, the silences, the anguish of continual misunderstanding. Were we positive, eager, real, alive? No, we were not. We were a nothingness shot with gleams of what might be. But no more. Well, I have to face everything as far as I can and see where I stand — what *remains*.

For with all my soul I do long for a real life, for truth, and for real strength. It's simply incredible, watching K. M., to see how little causes a panic. She's a perfect corker at toppling over. . . .

October 13, 1922

. . . It's a divinely beautiful day — so was yesterday. The sky is as blue as the sky can be. I shall go to the Luxembourg Gardens this afternoon and count dahlia and baby heads. The Paris gardens are simply a glorious sight with flowers — masses of beloved Japonica, enough Japonica at last. I *shall* have a garden one day, and work in it, too. Plant, weed, tie up, throw over the wall. And the peony border really will be staggering. Oh, how I love flowers! I think of them with such longing. I go through them, one after another, remembering them from their first moments with love — oh, with rapture, as if they were babies! No, it's what other women feel for babies — perhaps. Oh, Earth! Lovely, unforgettable Earth. Yesterday, I saw the leaves falling, so gently, so softly, raining down from little slender trees, golden against the blue. Perhaps Autumn is loveliest. Lo! it is Autumn. What is the magic of that? It is magic to me.

October 14, 1922

. . . About "doing operations on yourself." I know just what you mean. It is as though one were the sport of circumstance — one *is,* indeed. Now happy, now unhappy, now fearful, now confident, just as the pendulum swings. You see one can control nothing if one isn't conscious of a purpose: it's like a journey without a goal. There is nothing that makes you ignore some things, accept others, order others, submit to others. For there is no reason why A. should be more important than B. So there one is — involved beyond words, feeling the next minute I may be bowled over or struck all of a heap. I *know* nothing.

This is to me a very terrible state of affairs. Because it's the cause of all the unhappiness (the secret, profound, unhappiness) in my life. But I mean to escape and to try to live differently. It isn't easy. But is the other state easy? And I do believe with all my being that if one *can* break through the circle, one finds " my burden is light."

I've had such a queer birthday. L. M. brought me a *brin* of mimosa. And I had my poem and the telegrams. Wasn't it awfully nice of L. E. and W. J. to send one? It's been sunny, too. But all the same I'd rather not think about my birthday.

Oh, the little Tchekhov book has come. Do you think I might have the *Lit. Sup.* with your article in it? I see no papers here at all. That's not a complaint, though. For Paris flaps with papers, as you know. I haven't seen a single newspaper since leaving London. There! Does that shock you?

October 15, 1922

. . . About being like Tchekhov, and his letters. Don't forget he *died* at 43 — that he spent how much of his life? chasing about in a desperate search after health. And if one reads " intuitively " the last letters they are terrible. What is left of him? " The braid on German women's dresses — bad taste " — and all the rest is misery. Read the last! All hope is over for him. Letters are deceptive, at any rate. It's true he had occasional happy moments. But for the last eight years he knew no *security* at all. We know he felt that his stories were not half what they might be. It doesn't take much imagination to picture him on his death-bed thinking, " I have never had a real chance. Something has been all wrong."

To the Hon. Dorothy Brett   *October 15, 1922*

I never had a lovelier letter from you. And it came on my birthday, wasn't that good fortune. Wasn't that like you, the billiard champion? I did love you for it! You have a real very rare gift for writing letters. And oh how nice and long they are! Arrows. little side borders, little flower beds very tight packed with words along the edge — I follow them all and even dip into the Egyptian Maze though never to find my way in it!

Ah, my dear. Priceless exquisite treasures came floating out of your letter. I have gathered them all up. But that reminds me of the canary feathers. I am having a pair of wings made of them for delicate occasions. Did you ever feel anything so airy-fairy? I sat in the Luxembourg Gardens to-day and I thought of you. I am glad you were not with me for I felt like a chat malade, sitting in the sun and not a friend of anybody's. But all was so ravishingly fall-of-the-year lovely that I felt how you would have responded. The gardener was sweeping leaves from the bright grass. The flowers are still glorious but still, as though suspended, as though hardly daring to breathe. Down, down, soft and light floated the leaves. They fall over babies and old people and the laughing young. The fat pigeons-out-of-the-Ark are no longer quite so fat. But they swing between the trees just as they did, swooping and tumbling as if trying to scare one. Heavens! What a lovely earth it is!

I am so glad you are going to Scotland. I feel it may do you good to have a change. And it's nice to think of you fishing. Forgive me if I feel the fish show off just a tiny little bit when you come near, flash about, blow bubbles, swim on their heads. But that's only my wickedness. For I feel you are very expert and grave really and I should stand on the bank — *awed!* You see I've only fished with things like cottage loaves and a bent pin and a worm.

Tell me about Scotland. I do so hope it's going to be nice. I wonder if you will take your velours hat. It suits you marvellously. When I am rich you shall have velours hats by the dozing, and a persian lamb jacket made like your jazz velvet coat, lined with pale yellow brocade. A pinky pigeon grey very soft pleated skirt to go with it, crocodile shoes, thick grey silk stockings. And inside the coat a straight tunic of silver jersey de soie. I confess I am quite ravished away by you in the persian lamb coat. I have just been with you to a concert — you wearing it. Everybody turned round; the orchestra stopped, the flute fainted and was carried out. A dark gentleman stepped forward and presented you with the Order of the Sun and Moon; it was the Shah of Persia. But I must stop. Though I could go on for ever.

It's Sunday evening. 6.30. I am lying in bed writing to you. Just as before, I get up at midi and have to go to bed at about half past five. But I feel far more ill this time than last time. I don't know what is the matter, I am sick all the time — and cold. But as I've never imagined cold before — an entirely new kind. One feels like wet stone. Piping hot-water bottles, covers, grandma jaegers, nothing will stop it. Then it goes and one burns instead. And all this in a little band-box of a room. Never mind, it will pass. To-morrow I am going to see Gurdjieff. I feel certain he will help me. I feel equally certain that this particular horrid hour is passing, and I'll come out of it, please heaven, a much nicer creature. Not a snail. Not a creeping worm, either. I shall come and make the *whole* of your garden before you can say " Painting-brush." You just wait!

My dear little rooms. I shall be in them in the Spring, if I manage to escape and I really think I shall.

I have seen very few people since I came. Only men connected with the Institute, a very nice Doctor Young and a quite remarkable other man — rather like the chief mate on a cargo steamer. A type I like. Work I can't at all for the present. Even reading is very difficult.

The weather is marvellous. Where it is not blue it is gold. Oh, I must tell you. We took a taxi out to lunch to-day (there's no food here except supper trays) and who should be at the restaurant but (of course, you guess) Mrs. D. Très très très chic with such an extra passionate Sunday Paris mouth — and so terrifically at home! I must say I liked her for it. It was so young. She sat behind us. As we got out she saw me and I gave her a wretched cool nod. Not on purpose. But at that moment I was overcome with this confounded sickness and hardly knew what I was doing. But I hope she won't think me very horrid for it. I don't like doing such things.

But I am still not sincere with you. In my heart I am far more desperate about my illness and about *Life* than I ever show you. I long to lead a different life in every way. I have no belief whatever in any kind of medical treatment. Perhaps I am telling you this to beg you to have faith in me — to believe that whatever I do it is because I can't do otherwise. That is to say (let me say it bang out) I may go into the Institute for three months. I don't know that I shall. But if I have more faith in it than in Manoukhin I certainly must. Keep this private. I know you will. But don't speak to anybody about it.

Manoukhin isn't a magician. He has cured some people — a great many — and some he hasn't cured. He made me fatter — that is quite true. But otherwise? I'm exactly where I was before I started. I " act " all the rest, because I am ashamed to do otherwise, looking as I do. But it's all a sham. It amounts to nothing. However — this is just speculation. But as I am thinking it I felt I ought to write it to you. See? It is not a serious proposition.

To J. M. Murry   *October 17, 1922*

I don't want any more books at present of any kind. I am sick and tired of books, and that's a dreadful fact. They are to me like sandwiches out of the Hatter's bag. I'll get back to them, of course.

A queer thing. I have cramp in my thumb and can hardly hold the pen. That accounts for this writing. L. M. and I are off to Fontainebleau this morning. I am taking my toothbrush and comb. Dr. Young 'phoned me yesterday that there is a lovely room all ready. I'll see G. and come back to-morrow. It's not sunny today. What a terrible difference *sun* makes! It ought not to. One ought to have a little core of inner warmth that keeps burning and is only added to by sun. One has, I believe, if one looks for it. . . .

I must get up. The puffi train is, as usual, steaming up and down my room at the very idea of going away, even for half a day.

To S. S. Koteliansky   *October 19, 1922*

I hope this letter will not surprise you too much. It has nothing to do with our business arrangements. Since I wrote I have gone through a kind of private revolution. It has been in the air for years with me. And now it has happened very very much has changed.

When we met in England and discussed " ideas " I spoke, as nearly as one can, the deepest truth I knew to you. But even while I spoke it I felt a pretender — for my knowledge of this truth is negative, not positive, as it were cold, and not warm with life.

For instance all we have said of "individuality" and of being strong and single, and of growing — I believe it. I try to act up to it. But the reality is far far different. Circumstances still hypnotise me. I am a divided being with a bias towards what I want to be, but no more. And this it seems I cannot improve. No, I cannot. I have tried. If you knew how many note books there are of these trials, but they never succeed. So I am always conscious of this secret disruption in me — and at last (thank Heaven!) it has ended in a complete revolution and I mean to change my whole way of life entirely. I mean to learn to work in every possible way with my hands, looking after animals and doing all kinds of manual labour. I do not want to write any stories until I am a less terribly poor human being. It seems to me that in life, as it is lived to-day, the catastrophe is *imminent;* I feel this catastrophe in me. I want to be prepared for it, at least.

The world as I know it is no joy to me and I am useless in it. People are almost non-existent. This world to me is a dream and the people in it are sleepers. I have known just instances of waking but that is all. I want to find a world in which these instances are united. Shall I succeed? I do not know. I scarcely care. What is important is to try and learn to live — really live — and in relation to everything — not isolated (this isolation is death to me).

Does this sound fatuous? I cannot help it. I have to let you know for you mean much to me. I know you will never listen to whatever foolish things other people may say about me. Those other helpless people going round in their little whirlpool do not matter a straw to me.

All this sounds much too serious and dramatic. As a matter of fact there is absolutely no tragedy in it; of course.

To J. M. Murry　　　　　　　　　　　*October 21, 1922*

... I have been through a little revolution since my last letter. I suddenly made up my mind (for it was sudden, at the last) to try and learn to live by what I believed in, no less, and not as in all my life up till now to live one way and think another ... I don't mean superficially, of course, but in the deepest sense I've always been disunited. And this, which has been my "secret sorrow" for years, has become everything to me just now. I really can't go on pretending to be one person and being another any more, Boge. It is a living death. So I have decided to make a clean sweep of all that was "superficial" in my past life and start again to see if I can get into that real simple truthful *full* life I dream of. I have been through a horrible deadly time coming to this. You know the kind of time. It doesn't show much, outwardly, but one is simply chaos within!

... No treatment on earth is any good to me, really. It's all pretence. M. did make me heavier and a little stronger. But that was all if I really face the facts. The miracle never came near happening. It couldn't, Boge. And as for my spirit — well, as a result of that life at the Victoria Palace I stopped being a writer. I have only written long or short scraps since *The Fly*. If I had gone on with my old life I never would have written again, for I was dying of poverty of life.

I wish when one writes about things, one didn't dramatize them so. I feel awfully happy about all this, and it's all as simple as can be.... In any case I shan't write any stories for three months, and I'll not have a book ready before the spring. It doesn't matter.

Le Prieuré
Fontainebleau-Avon
Seine-et-Marne
October 23, 1922

... I'll tell you what this life is more like than anything; it is like *Gulliver's Travels*. One has, all the time, the feeling of having been in a wreck and by the mercy of Providence, got ashore — somewhere.... Simply everything is different. Not only languages, but food, ways, people, music, methods, hours — *all*. It's a real new life....[1]

Dr. Young, a real friend of mine, comes up and makes me a good fire. In "return" I am patching the knee of his trousers to-day. But it's all "stranger" than that. For instance, I was looking for wood the other evening. All the boxes were empty. I found a door at the end of the passage, went through and down some stone steps. Presently steps came up and a woman appeared, very

[1] A detailed account of life at the Gurdjieff Institute is contained in an essay by Dr. James Young in *The New Adelphi* for September 1928.

simply dressed, with her head bound in a white hankerchief. She had her arms full of logs. I spoke in French, but she didn't understand — English, no good. But her glance was so lovely — laughing and gentle, absolutely unlike people as I have known people. Then I patted a log and she gave it to me and we went our ways. . . .

October 26, 1922

. . . All I am doing now is trying to put into practice the " ideas " I have had for so long, of another and a *far more truthful* existence. I want to learn something that no books can teach me, and I want to try and escape from my terrible illness. That again you can't be expected to understand. You think I'm like other people — I mean, *normal*. I'm not. I don't know which is the ill me and which is the well me. I am simply one pretence after another. Only now I recognise it. . . .

As for writing stories and " being true to one's gift," I couldn't write them if I were not here, even. I am at an end of my source for the time. Life has brought me no *flaw*. I want to write, but differently — far more steadily.

October 27, 1922

. . . What are you going to do to the fruit trees? Please tell me. We have masses of quinces here. They are no joke when they fall *exprès* on your head.

I do hope you are having this glorious weather. Day after day of perfect sunshine. It's like Switzerland: an intense blue sky, a chill in the air, a wonderful clarity so that you see people far away, all sharp-cut and vivid.

I spend all the time in the garden. Visit the carpenters, the trench diggers. (We are digging for a Turkish Bath — not to discover one, but to lay the pipes.) The soil is very nice here, like sand, with small whitey-pinky pebbles in it. Then there are the sheep to inspect, and the new pigs that have long golden hair — very mystical pigs. A mass of cosmic rabbits and hens and goats are on the way. . . . It's so full of life and humour that I wouldn't be anywhere else. It's just the same all through — *ease* after *rigidity* expresses it more than anything else. And yet I realise, as I write this, that it's no use. An old personality is trying to get back to the outside and observe, and it's not true to the present facts at all. What I write seems so petty. In fact, I feel I cannot express myself in writing just now. The old mechanism isn't mine any longer, and I can't control the new. I just have to talk this baby talk. . . .

October 28, 1922

. . . There is always this danger of deceiving oneself. I feel it, too. I only begin to get rid of it by trying and trying to relax — to give way. I am sure you will understand why it is so hard to write. We don't move in our letters. We say the same things over and over.

As I tried to explain, I'm in such a state of transition. I could not, if I would, get back to the old life and I can't deal with the new. But *anxiety* I never feel. Perhaps I shall. I cannot tell.

November 4, 1922

. . . Ever since my last letter to you I have been enraged with myself. It's so like me. I am ashamed of it. But you who know me will perhaps understand. I always try to go too fast. I always think all can be changed and renewed in the twinkling of an eye. It is most fearfully hard for me, as it is for you, not to be " intense." And whenever I am intense (really, this is so) I am a little bit false. Take my last letter and the one before. The tone was all wrong. As to any new truth — oh, Boge, I am really ashamed of myself. It's so very wrong. Now I have to go back to the beginning and start again and again tell you that I have been " over-fanciful," and I seem to have tried to force the strangeness. Do you know what I mean? Let me try now to *face facts*. Of course, it is true that life here is quite different, but violent changes to one's individuality — of course, they do not occur. . . .

All my friends accepted me as a frail half-creature who migrated towards sofas. Oh, just wait and see how you and I will live one day — so happily, so splendidly. But in the meantime, please never take what I say for " absolute." I do not take what you say for " final." I try to see it as relative.

November 1922

... The stockings arrived in perfect order. What an extraordinary brain wave, to hide them in the *Times!* They are very lovely stockings, too, just the shade I like in the evening. One's legs are like legs by moonlight.

It's intensely cold here — colder and colder. I have just been brought some small fat pine-logs to mix with my *boulets*. *Boulets* are unsatisfactory; they are too passive. I simply live in my fur-coat. I gird it on like my heavenly armour and wear it ever night and day. After this winter the Arctic even will have no terrors for me. Happily the sun *does* shine as well and we are thoroughly well nourished. But I shall be glad when the year has turned.

Are you having really perfect weather (except for the cold)? It is absolutely brilliantly sunny — a deep blue sky — dry air. Really it's better than Switzerland. But I must get some wool-lined over-boots. My footgear is ridiculous when I am where I was yesterday — round about the pig-sty. It is noteworthy that the pigs have of themselves divided their sty into two: one — the clean part — they keep clean and sleep in. This makes me look at pigs with a different eye. One must be impartial, even about them, it seems. We have two more cows about to calve in three weeks' time. Very thrilling. Also the white goat is about to have a little kid. I want to see it very much. They are so charming.

November 1922

... I don't know how you feel. But I still find it fearfully hard to cope with people I do not like or who are not sympathetic. With the others all goes well. But living here with all kinds, I am simply appalled at my helplessness when I want to get rid of someone or to extricate myself from a conversation, even. But I *have* learnt how to do it. I have learnt that the only way is to court it, not to avoid it — to face it. Terribly difficult for me in practice. But until I really do master this I cannot get anywhere. There always comes the moment when I am uncovered, *so zu sagen,* and the other man gets in his knock-out blow.

December 16, 1922

... It seems to me very mysterious how so many of us nowadays refuse to be cave-dwellers any longer, but in our several ways are trying to learn to escape. The old London life, whatever it was — but even the life we have led recently wherever we have been, is no longer even possible to me. It is so far from me that it seems to exist in another world. This, of course, is a wrong feeling. For, after all, there are the seeds of what we long after in everybody, and if one remembers that, any surroundings are ... possible, at least.

I read Youspensky's *Tertium Organum* the other day. For some reason it didn't carry me away. I think it is quite interesting, but ... perhaps I was not in the mood for books. I am not at present, though I know that in the future I shall want to write them more than anything else in the world. But different books ... I confess present-day literature simply nauseates me, excepting always Hardy and the other few whose names I can't remember. But the general trend of it seems to me quite without any value whatever.

December 20, 1922

What is the weather like with you? It's so soft and spring-like here that actually pink roses are out. So are the Christmas roses under the espalier pear-trees. I *love* Christmas; I shall always feel it is a holy time. I wonder if dear old Hardy will write a poem this year.

Boxing Day, 1922

How is the old Adam revived in you, I wonder? What aspect has he? There is nothing to be done when he rages except to remember that it's bound to be; it's the swing of the pendulum. One's only hope is, when the bout is exhausted, to get back to that you think you really care for, aim for, wish to live by, as soon as possible. It's the intervals of exhaustion that seem to waste so much energy. You see, the question is always: *Who am I?* and until that is discovered I don't see how one can really direct anything in oneself. *Is there a Me?* One must be certain of that before one has a real unshakable leg to stand on. And I don't believe for one moment these questions can be settled by the head alone. It is this life of the head, this intellectual life at the expense of all the rest which has got us into this state. How can it get us out of it? I see no hope of escape except by learning to live in our emotional and instinctive being as well, and to balance all there.

You see, if I were allowed one single cry to God, that cry would be: *I want to be* REAL. Until I am that I don't see why I shouldn't be at the mercy of old Eve in her various manifestations for ever. ... At this present moment all I know really, really, is that though one thing after another has been taken from me, I am not annihilated, and that I hope — more than hope — believe. It is hard to explain.

I heard from B. yesterday. She gave a very horrid picture of the present S. and his views on life and women. I don't know how much of it is even vaguely true, but it corresponds to S. the Exhibitionist. The pity of it is life is so short, and we waste about nine-tenths of it — simply throw it away. I always feel S. refuses to face the fact of his wastefulness. And sometimes he feels he never will. All will pass like a dream, with mock comforts, mock consolations. ...

To the Countess Russell   *December 31, 1922*

I am sending this, as you see, at the last last moment while the old year is in the very act of turning up his toes. I wish I could explain why I have not written to you for so long. It is not for lack of love. But such a black fit came over me in Paris when I realised that X-ray treatment wasn't going to do any more than it had done beyond upsetting my heart still more that I gave up everything and decided to try a new life altogether. But this decision was immensely complicated with " personal " reasons, too. When I came to London from Switzerland I did (Sydney was right so far) go through that books and undergraduates call a spiritual crisis, I suppose. For the first time in my life, everything bored me. Everything, and worse, everybody seemed a compromise and so flat, so dull, so mechanical. If I had been well I should have rushed off to darkest Africa or the Indus or the Ganges or wherever it is one rushes at those times, to try for a change of heart (One can't change one's heart in public) and to gain new impressions. For it seems to me we live on new impressions — really new ones.

But such grand flights being impossible I burned what boats I had and came here where I am living with about 50-60 people, mainly Russians. It is a fantastic existence, impossible to describe. One might be anywhere, in Bokhara or in Tiflis or Afghanistan (except, alas! for the climate!). But even the climate does not seem to matter so much when one is whirled along at such a rate. For we do most decidedly whirl. But I cannot tell you what a joy it is to me to be in contact with living people who are strange and quick and not ashamed to be themselves. It's a kind of supreme airing to be among them.

But what nonsense this all sounds. That is the worst of letters; they are fumbling things.

I haven't written a word since October and I don't mean to until the spring. I want much more material; I am tired of my little stories like birds bred in cages.

Goodbye, my dearest cousin. I shall never know anyone like you; I shall remember every little thing about you for ever.

To J. M. Murry *December 31, 1922*

My fountain pen is mislaid, so as I am in a hurry to write please forgive this pencil.

Would you care to come here on January 8 or 9 to stay until 14–15? On the 13th our new theatre is to be opened. It will be a wonderful experience. But I won't say too much about it. Only on the chance that you do come I'll tell you what clothes to bring.

One sports suit with heavy shoes and stockings and a mackintosh and a hat that doesn't matter. One " neat " suit with your soft collar or whatever collar you wear and tie (you see you are my husband and I can't help wanting you to look — what shall I say?) slippers and so on. That's all. If you have a cardigan of course bring it and a pair of flannel trousers in case you get soaking wet and want a change.

I am writing to ask B. to go to Lewis and get me a pair of shoes. Will you bring them? I may ask her to get me a jacket too. But she will give you the parcel. Will you wire me your reply — just " yes " or " no " and the date, if " yes," of your arrival.

There is a London train that reaches Paris at 4 something. You could then come on to Fontainebleau the same day. Otherwise it's far better to stay the night in Paris, as no cabs meet the late train.

You get out of the train at *Avon* and take a cab here which costs 8 francs *with* tip. Ring the bell at the porter's lodge and I'll open the gate.

I hope you will decide to come, my dearest. Let me know as soon as you can, won't you? I hope Tchekhov's wife will be here. I have gone back to my big lovely room, too, so we should have plenty of space to ourselves. We can also sit and drink *kiftir* in the cowshed. I can't write of other things in this letter. I hope to hear from you soon.

Index
VOLUME TWO

Beauchamp, Sir Harold: 456, 476, 478, 483, 487, 489, 491
Blunden, Edmund: 485
Brett, Hon. Dorothy: 302, 313, 358, 368, 391 (2), 396, 400, 405, 408, 414 (2), 423, 425 (2), 428, 432, 436, 438, 445 (2), 451, 454, 456, 459 (2), 461, 464, 466, 468 (3), 474, 488, 489, 498, 502, 505
Drey, O. Raymond: 431
Fullerton, Miss: 287
Galsworthy, John: 412, 439
Gerhardi, William: 388, 417 (3), 443, 449, 453, 471, 479, 492, 499
Gibbons, Arnold: 475, 481
Hudson, Stephen: 424
Jones, Hugh: 466
Koteliansky, S. S.: 366, 410, 413, 422, 424, 429, 434, 440, 477, 482, 486, 502, 508
Lynd, Mrs. Sylvia: 292, 364, 402, 495, 496
Morrell, Lady Ottoline: 361, 367, 384 (2), 389, 420, 430, 437, 449, 494
Moult, Thomas and Bessie: 428
Murry, J. M.: 286, 288 (3), 294 (3), 299 (2), 304 (7), 311 (2), 316 (4), 323 (12), 335 (3), 339 (5), 347 (5), 354, 355 (2), 369 (2), 374 (5), 381 (4), 442, 485, 496, 500 (3), 503 (4), 508, 509 (7), 516
Murry, Richard: 285, 293, 297, 309 (2), 322, 352 (2), 359 (2), 362, 387, 394 (2), 399, 401 (2), 458, 467, 488

Index

Onions, Mrs. Oliver: 457
Renshaw, Mrs. Charles: 407
Rice, Anne Estelle: 304, 358, 372, 429, 436, 441, 463, 493, 497
Russell, The Countess: 409, 410, 413, 425, 458, 462, 515
Schiff, Sydney: 347, 355, 365, 422, 432, 434 (2), 493
Schiff, Sydney and Violet: 308, 312, 314, 334, 381
Schiff, Violet: 313, 314 (3), 404, 490
Walpole, Hugh: 337
To ——: 366

A NOTE ON THE TYPE IN WHICH THIS BOOK IS SET

This book is set on the Linotype in Granjon, a type which is neither a copy of a classic face nor an original creation. George W. Jones drew the basic design for this type from classic sources, but deviated from his model wherever four centuries of type-cutting experience indicated an improvement or where modern methods of punch-cutting made possible a refinement that was beyond the skill of the sixteenth-century originator. This new creation is based primarily upon the type used by Claude Garamond (1510–1561) in his beautiful French books and more closely resembles the work of the founder of the Old Style letter than do any of the various modern-day types that bear his name.

SET UP, ELECTROTYPED,
PRINTED AND BOUND BY
PLIMPTON PRESS, NORWOOD, MASS.
PAPER MANUFACTURED BY
W. C. HAMILTON & SONS,
MIQUON, PA.